Brute Power: The Autobiography of Buggsy McGraw

Brute Power: The Autobiography of Buggsy McGraw

By

Buggsy McGraw
with Ian Douglass

Foreword

There are only a handful of performers in the history of the wrestling business who were as entertaining, well-traveled and selfless as Buggsy McGraw. When I met Buggsy in the late 1960s, it was during the beginning of my wrestling career, and he was working in Detroit under a mask as "The Big O." He was such a huge man with a massive chest, and common sense dictated that he would be booked as a bad guy. When you weighed more than 300 pounds like Buggsy did, and you were beating on guys who only weighed 200 pounds, fans would never have accepted you as a good guy or as someone they should take pity on.

When we moved on to the San Francisco territory, I worked with Buggsy quite a bit, and in terms of personality, he was one of the best performers in our business. Roy Shire correctly booked Buggsy as a monster, and I was one of only four or five top-drawing African Americans in the wrestling business at the time. I'd originally planned to go to San Francisco for six months, and they kept me for five years because I was drawing so many of the black fans to the arenas that they didn't want to let me go! Buggsy and I had great matches which drew tremendous heat from the Northern California fans. We drew a lot of money together, because people always turned out to watch me try to *kill* him every night!

Our matches were not without controversy. Buggsy got a little too racial during a television interview while he was hyping one of our confrontations. This occurred when the Black Panther Party was a prominent fixture in Northern California, so they really weren't too happy about it. Obviously, Buggsy wasn't doing it to be a racist; he's certainly *not* a racist. He was trying to get the fans worked up to the point where they would say, "Boy... when Rocky gets done with him, he's going to regret saying *those* things!" To that end, Buggsy was willing to do whatever it took to captivate fans and get them emotionally involved in what they were seeing.

In our business, everyone is constantly trying to outdo each other. Nowadays, they're all performing high-risk moves from 25 feet in the air, but they're forgetting about *psychology*. Unlike many modern wrestlers, Buggsy had great psychology. He would wait for just the right moment to tell me, "*Now*! Make your comeback!" When he gave me the cue, I would hit him with my big jabs and dropkicks to drive the fans into a frenzy.

You're only as good as the guy you're working with is willing to *make* you look, and ideally it should be a 50-50 proposition. Nowadays, too many wrestlers try to tilt things too far in their own favor, and that's because they believe their own publicity. Instead of believing his own publicity, Buggsy did everything he could to make his opponents look credible, and his story is the tale of someone who did whatever he could to make his opponents look good, make the fans happy, and leave people with lasting memories from the nights they saw him perform.

If more wrestlers these days were as selfless as Buggsy McGraw was throughout his career, the wrestling business would be *much* better off than it is today.

Rocky Johnson
WWE Hall of Fame Inductee
October 22nd, 2018

Brute Power: The Autobiography of Buggsy McGraw

"I saw a werewolf with a Chinese menu in his hands walking down the street in the rain. Don't you know... he was looking for a big dish of chow mein! Awooooooo! Draw blood!"

ONE – "It hurts; let's do it again"

Although many people know me popularly as Herman E. "Buggsy" McGraw, I was born as Michael Davis in Indianapolis, Indiana on November 1st, 1944, and my parents brought me home to a tiny apartment on Fletcher Avenue. When I was born, World War II was still in progress. My parents, Hubert M. Davis and Remine H. Lincks, met four years before the outbreak of the war, and they got married shortly after the United States was drawn into the conflict.

My parents were both hardworking individuals who provided me with a safe, secure home environment to grow up in. I don't know if the fact that I was an only child had anything to do with it, but I was treated extremely well by both of my parents.

Even though I was raised during a time period when it was relatively rare for women to work outside of the home, my mother worked in a factory for the United States Rubber Company, and she held that job for 43 years. She came from a line of German immigrants who arrived in the U.S. in the mid 1800s, and who'd worked their way up through Kentucky to Indiana.

Mom's great-grandfather was Fred Lincks, an immigrant who ran away from home and joined the army of Napoleon Bonaparte at the age of 16. After the war, Fred made his way over to the United States in indentured servitude and worked off his indebtedness over a period of seven years. After settling in Kentucky, he went on to become a prolific businessman and an equally prolific sirer of children, having 16 children with four women. When he married his final bride, he was 80 years old and she was only 20. He passed away in 1887 at the age of 92.

Fred Lincks, 1795-1887

My father began working at a young age. In his very early 20s, he was a manager of a Kroger store during the Prohibition era, during which all alcohol consumption was banned in the U.S. Dad's Kroger store sold more potatoes than any other Kroger store in the country during that time period, but there was a catch to it. When his customers purchased their weekly sack of potatoes, there was always a pint of whiskey hidden inside of it. Dad told me stories about his connection to the infamous gangster, John Dillinger, who himself

5

was a native of Mooresville, Indiana. Apparently, Dillinger's brother would deliver goods from his bakery to my father's store.

Later, Dad heard stories from close relatives who swore to have seen Dillinger alive after his reported death. Even though Dillinger's body was viewed by more than 15,000 people after he was killed, there were plenty of people around who insisted Dillinger's death was faked.

At the time I was born, my father was actively working as a wartime radioman with the U.S. Army Air Forces. He had the good fortune not to be shipped overseas during the war, so he was thoroughly blessed in that regard. He was drafted, served and never complained, unlike many of the conscientious objectors that emerged during later wars.

Humbert Davis' Military Enlistment Record

When I was four or five years old, we were still living in the apartment on Fletcher Avenue. There was a church a few blocks away from the apartment building, and Mom would drop me off at the church daycare on her way to work in the factory. This was right after the war, and they made us sleep on army cots during our naptime. I remember being terrified whenever they would turn off the lights. It would have been interesting to visit that church again as an older man, but it was renovated into a luxury condominium complex.

When the war was over with, Dad returned to work for a company called Allison's, which was a division of General Motors. Between his job and my mother's job at the factory, our family had two solid incomes, and we were able to save a sizeable amount of money.

Brute Power: The Autobiography of Buggsy McGraw

After living through the depression, my parents were very frugal, and they wanted to make sure the needs of the family would be taken care of under any circumstances. Dad built a block-shaped house for us with a large yard for me to run around in, and our old apartment was later torn down to make room for a new freeway. Despite their frugality, my parents never stopped spoiling me. They bought me all kinds of toys, some of which I still have.

During my childhood, my mother would take me to services at the Seventh Christian Church, which was about half a mile from our house over on 30th Street, but that was just a case of me going to church because my mother made me. I was in Sunday school, and then afterward I'd sit through the regular church service. Once my childhood was over with, I didn't regularly attend church again for a *long* time.

I was never much of an athlete as a child, although I imagine whatever athletic talents I inherited were derived from my father. When he was in high school, Dad held the state record in the quarter mile run, which was a record he maintained for a solid 12 years. He also played semi-pro football, and won the annual 10-mile swim in the White River of Indianapolis. In addition to all of these raw athletic competitions, he also won the soap box derby race.

Surprisingly, even though I came from such athletic stock, my father never pressured me to play football or any other sports. During the early days of my life, I received far more enjoyment from my involvement with the Cub Scouts than I did from any sports-related activities.

I'm sure one of the reasons I shied away from a lot of social and athletic situations while I was growing up is because I had a *severe* speech impediment. There was a kid who lived about a block away from me when I was growing up named Greg Salezi. Greg and these two other kids came riding by on their bicycles, and Greg decided to make fun of my stuttering problem.

"Don't go riding by my house again!" I warned him. "If you do, I'll hit you with a *bat!*"

Greg must not have taken me seriously, because he came pedaling toward my house again just a few minutes later. As I promised, I walked into the garage, picked up the baseball bat, ran out into the street and cracked him in the thigh with it. Greg immediately started crying and rode off in the direction of his house.

Later that day, Greg's parents knocked on our front door and explained to my father what I'd done. After closing the door, my father walked up to me with a very concerned look on his face.

"Michael, did you hit that kid with a ball bat?" he asked.

"Yes, I did," I said.

"Why did you do that?!" he replied.

"Because he made fun of my speech impediment, and I told him if he came around again, I'd hit him with a ball bat," I said. "I gave my word."

"Oh... " my father said. "Okay then."

My speech impediment was one of the primary reasons I started lifting weights. I figured if I transformed myself into a physically imposing guy, I would get more respect from people, and no one would dare make fun of the way I spoke.

Because I grew up in a dual income family back when most homes got by on a single income, my parents typically got me whatever I requested of them. So, one day I asked them for a set of weights.

"Absolutely *not*," Mom told me. "You'll use them for about a week, and then you'll quit. We're *not* buying you any weights."

In spite of my mother's response, I was determined to train myself with weights. I went out and found the largest rocks I could lift and tied ropes around them. Then I pulled the rocks off the ground in a variety of ways by tugging on the ropes. This crudely devised weight set was all I had. Once my parents saw that I was lifting consistently with my homemade weights and refused to quit, they finally relented and bought me a weight set, either because they were impressed, or because they took pity on me. Either way, I was happy.

The first time I ever saw professional wrestling, it was on our living room television set in 1957. Back then, the National Wrestling Alliance shows in Indianapolis were an unmatched attraction. *Everyone* was crazy about wrestling, no matter what age they were. Whether the shows were in Indianapolis, or in the surrounding small towns, massive crowds were being drawn every night, and it didn't matter what day of the week it was. It was a *very* exciting time to be a pro wrestling fan.

Jim Barnett was the owner and promoter for the NWA Indianapolis territory. Undeniably, his top box office attraction was Dick Afflis, better known as "Dick the Bruiser." He was an Indiana native who went on to play football at Purdue University and some other schools. From there, Dick went on to compete in the National Football League for the Green Bay Packers before leaving football because he thought he could make *more* money as a professional wrestler. He was *right*.

The Bruiser is credited as one of the first football players to fully embrace weightlifting. He had a tremendous physique, with a 52-inch chest and a slim waist. Even more important than the Bruiser's physique was how captivating he was as a performer in the ring. When he walked out of the dressing room, the crowd would start rumbling.

From there, Bruiser would walk down the ringside aisle and stand by the first row of ringside with his hands on his hips. The noise of the crowd would crescendo into a roar. All the Bruiser had to do to garner this type of reaction was simply walk toward the ring, put his hands on his hips, and stare at his opponent. Everyone knew, when the Bruiser got into the ring, there was going to be a fight. In fact, even the people from Indianapolis who thought everything about wrestling was "phony" would say, "But *not* The Bruiser. He's *real!*"

I idolized Dick the Bruiser and talked about him incessantly. He had the ability to draw incredible money in a feverish environment that pro wrestlers today could only dream about. Without traveling more than an hour from his home, he was guaranteed to make a financial killing. He could headline a show in a small Indiana town that only had 20,000 people living in it, and still attract a sellout crowd of more than 2,000 people at the local venue.

The Shire Brothers - Roy and Ray - were also big stars in Indianapolis. They once caused a riot so out of control that the cops had to keep them in the building until 4:00 a.m. until the mob dispersed.

Adding to my fascination with wrestling was the fact that my neighbor was Lou Thomas, one of the referees for NWA Indianapolis. Lou lived in the second house over from us, and his younger son was one of my best friends. In addition to being a referee, Lou was also a fighter, and a training partner for legendary world heavyweight boxing champion Joe Louis. Lou even claimed to have "knocked Joe Louis clean out" during a sparring session once, but "no one wanted it publicized."

Despite his involvement with violent sports, Lou was a very kind man. He took his son and I to the wrestling shows in many of the small towns of Indiana like Franklin and Shelbyville. Even in those towns, the venues were packed full of people anxious to see Dick the Bruiser beat somebody to a pulp. Many times, fans would try to storm the ring and attack the wrestlers who'd gotten them so riled up.

Lou wouldn't take much crap from any of the wrestlers even though he was a referee. Every so often you could see the wrestlers do things over the course of a match that would piss him off. In their attempts to deliver a passionate performance, they might go overboard and shove Lou. When Lou got visibly angry, the wrestlers would quickly back down and steer clear of him. Even if the story about knocking Joe Louis out was a myth, it didn't seem like anyone was anxious to take any chances with Lou's right hand.

Right in the middle of one of the wrestling events he'd brought me to, Lou told me, "Hey Mike... I need you to take this briefcase into the locker room."

"What?!" I replied. "No, sir! They'll kill me!"

"Don't worry" Lou insisted. "It will be fine."

After some additional prodding from Lou, I finally picked up the briefcase and walked it into the musty locker room. Usually there would have been someone at the door to prevent entry, but no one was there, so I just opened the door and waltzed straight in. Instantly, I found myself standing in the middle of a pack of giants. Wilbur Snyder, Yukon Eric and Dick the Bruiser were the three who stood out in my mind the most, and I stood in front of all three of them, expecting to get clobbered. I quickly walked over to a section of the dressing room where there wasn't anyone sitting and set the briefcase down on the floor.

"It's from Lou Thomas the referee!" I announced to no one in particular. "Bye!"

Without making eye contact with anyone, I made a beeline for the door and got out of there. To this day, I don't know why I didn't knock on the door of that locker room before I walked in. Back then, "kayfabe" - the code of making sure everyone perceived everything about pro wrestling to be 100-percent real - was taken very seriously. Those guys could have *mauled* me.

By the time I reached high school age, I'd grown to a decent size thanks to my weight training. At Ben Davis High School, I tried out for football, assuming I would be a natural at it. Unfortunately, I was kicked off the team for complaining to the coach before I ever had a chance to put myself to the test.

When I graduated from high school in 1962, I was 6'2" and weighed 175 pounds. I enrolled at Purdue University and officially majored in Economics and minored in Psychology, while *unofficially* majoring in weightlifting. I was in the weight room on a daily basis, and I'd packed an additional 50 pounds of solid muscle onto my frame by the end of my freshman year. At 225 pounds of lean muscle, I was suddenly *very* confident.

I was so confident, in fact, that I almost made a *colossal* mistake. The summer after my freshman year, I was driving in my car on 38th Street in Indianapolis. That's when I looked up and noticed none other than Dick the Bruiser driving in the car behind me.

"I've been working out, and I'm strong as hell," I said to myself, hyping myself up. "I'm gonna *fight* this sonofabitch!"

As we continued down 38th Street, Bruiser tried to pass me twice, but I wouldn't let him. I was doing everything I could to get him to stop so that we would end up in a slugfest at the side of the road. Luckily for me, he pulled over at his destination before I ever got a chance to fight that sonofabitch. If I did get the chance to fight him, I'm now certain that sonofabitch would have *killed* me.

When I returned to Purdue for my sophomore year, I went straight back to the student gym and started pumping iron again. Occasionally, I'd be joined by my roommate from the H2 dormitory, Larry Kaminski - the All-American center from Purdue's football team who later went on to play in the NFL for the Denver Broncos. I'd initially wanted to get larger and stronger to overcome my speech impediment, but I eventually became one of the strongest men in the world on the bench press. During my workouts, I used to go for a high repetition count on the bench press, and my best lifts were 540 pounds for two reps, 525 pounds for three reps, 500 pounds for five reps, 405 pounds for 10 reps, 315 pounds for 35 reps, and 225 pounds for 75 reps.

After three more years of performing this training regimen on a routine basis, I filled out my graduation gown at 6'4" and a solid 310 pounds. At that size, I was *dwarfing* most of the people on Purdue's football team.

Once I graduated from Purdue, I had a pretty clear career path in mind for myself. I applied to law school at the University of Miami, in Florida, and got accepted. During my first term, however, I realized I simply wasn't meant to be an attorney. First of all, my speech impediment made me so self conscious, I couldn't imagine what sort of spectacle I would cause during a court proceeding if I was struggling to spit my words out. Second, I was *constantly* thinking about wrestling. Miami was a major city within the thriving NWA Florida wrestling territory owned by Clarence "Cowboy" Luttrell, who once fought the famous boxer Jack Dempsey, yet I was so preoccupied with my studies that I couldn't attend any of their wrestling events.

After my first term at Miami, I dropped out of law school and drove straight home to Indianapolis. Within moments of returning home, I told my parents, "I'm going to become either a professional wrestler or a professional football player."

"Mike, are you *serious*?!" Dad asked. "That's a *terrible* idea!"

"I already dropped out, Dad," I told him. "It's done."

Dad didn't say anything afterward, but it was clear to me that he was absolutely devastated and disappointed with my decision.

I quickly moved back into my parents house in Indianapolis and got a job working at the Chrysler foundry in the quality control department. It was the same foundry I'd worked for one summer while I was at Purdue. The job at the foundry was a good job, but I just wasn't enamored with the idea of working a typical desk job.

I would sit at my desk in the office and stare out of the window thinking, "There's got to be something more to life than this."

For the next year, while working for Chrysler, I also hounded Lou Thomas to get me in touch with "The World's Most Scientific Wrestler" Wilbur Snyder in the hopes of being able to get trained as a pro wrestler.

By that point, the World Wrestling Association had replaced NWA Indianapolis as the de facto wrestling promotion in Indianapolis, and Wilbur co-owned the territory along with Dick the Bruiser. The Bruiser had become a big national star, and had performed in territories all over the country while winning championships as far away as Hawaii.

In 1964, he won the world championship promoted by the Worldwide Wrestling Associates promotion in Los Angeles, and gave his own territory a corresponding set of initials. After dropping the WWA championship to The Destroyer three months later in Los Angeles, the Bruiser still presented himself as the WWA World Champion in Indianapolis, and he now had the leverage with which to brand himself as a world champion for as long as his territory could sustain itself.

Officially, the Bruiser and Wilbur Snyder bought out Jim Barnett, who then went on to promote wrestling in Australia. Unofficially, the story was that Bruiser and Snyder simply *took* the promotion from Barnett. In essence, there were so many people in Indianapolis who were loyal to the Bruiser that he was able to force Barnett out. The Bruiser was the guy whose name was on the marquee, and he was making money for everyone else who performed on the wrestling card. No one was going to stand against him in Indiana. He was *invincible* there.

My big break in the wrestling business actually came as the result of a bad break for Lou. The WWA's chief referee suffered injuries due to a car wreck, so I went to visit him in the hospital while he was a stationary target.

"Thanks for coming, Mike," Lou said when he saw me. "It means a lot."

"No problem, Lou," I told him. "I'm sorry this happened to you. By the way, do you think you can get me in touch with Wilbur Snyder now?"

Lou's wife, Alice, was standing in the room listening in on our conversation. Before Lou had an opportunity to turn me down again, she spoke up and said, "*I'll* get ahold of Wilbur for you, Michael. I know his wife. I can just call her for you."

True to her word, Alice contacted Wilbur's wife, and they arranged for me to meet with Wilbur at the Snyders' home. When I arrived at Wilbur's house, I briefly sat down with him and explained how I wished to become a professional wrestler just like him and the Bruiser.

"I think we can set something up for you," Wildbur said. "Meet me down at the YMCA and we'll see what you've got."

We set up the date and time. I was thoroughly looking forward to it. Then, on the morning of our meeting Wilbur called me up and said, "Hey, Mike. Sorry… I can't make it. Bye."

That was it. Wilbur abruptly hung up the phone without making any plans to meet up with me again. At the time, I assumed he simply wasn't interested in helping me break into the wrestling business. Later on, other wrestlers told me stories about how Wilbur was a selfish man. I ran into Wilbur at a nightclub later on, and we exchanged pleasantries, but that was it. Neither one of us brought up how he blew me off for our scheduled meeting and training session at the gym.

Still desperate, I went around town and tried to track down some other guys involved with the WWA. After much searching, I finally found someone who would help me. His name was "Mr. Ebony" Tom Jones, a black wrestler who lived in Indianapolis. He wanted someone he could work on holds and throws with, so he found a gym where the two of us could train together.

After placing a thin mat on a basketball court, Tom taught me how to lock up with another wrestler after facing off with him. Then he progressed to showing me how to take holds on someone. From there, he showed me how to react to avoid an injury when a hold was applied to me. After that, he introduced me to the art of taking bumps - or protected falling - by giving me hiptosses and armdrags. Thankfully, he placed a great deal of emphasis on the act of protecting myself when I hit the mat. In retrospect, taking bumps on a basketball court was an *extremely* stupid thing to be doing.

As you might imagine, taking those hardwood bumps didn't feel very good. Every time Tom gave me a hip toss, it *really* hurt. Yet, every time he gave me one, I jumped up off the floor.

"How did that feel?" asked Tom.

"It hurts; let's do it again," I insisted.

We did it again, and unsurprisingly, it kept right on hurting. Putting on a brave face, I got up over and over again.

"Let's do it again," I repeated.

I think I impressed Tom with my toughness and enthusiasm, because after just a few of these training sessions he said, "Let me take you up to meet the Sheik."

"The Sheik" Edward Farhat was one of the biggest stars in professional wrestling during the 1950s and 1960s. Like Dick the Bruiser, he acquired his wrestling territory from Jim Barnett. Unlike Dick the Bruiser, he paid for it legitimately, buying out Barnett and his partner Jim Doyle for $50,000 for the sole ownership and promotional rights to the NWA's Detroit territory.

Sheik's father and mother immigrated to the United States from Syria in 1908 and 1912, just before the outbreak of the first World War. He was born in 1926 and was raised in a large immigrant household in the Lansing metropolitan area of Michigan. Although legend has it that young Ed Farhat attended the University of Michigan and played on one of their national championship football teams, I don't know that anyone has ever found a shred of evidence to confirm this.

At some point after breaking into wrestling, Ed created the character of The Sheik by, frankly, combining some of the worst stereotypes of Arab people into a very sinister gimmick. While there were different iterations of his character, the most remembered features of the Sheik's wrestling gimmick include the turban he wore to the ring, the camel emblem printed on his tights, the curved boots that adorned his feet, and the way he would lay out a Muslim prayer rug in the ring and pray to Allah before his matches while his eyes rolled back in his head. These are all thing the fans saw *before* the Sheik's matches took place!

During the actual matches, the Sheik could be counted on to cheat to gain the upper hand whenever an opportunity presented itself, usually by gouging his opponent's eyes or by kicking him with the illegal-looking tip of his boots. Once the crowd had gotten dutifully pissed off, the Sheik would produce a wooden spike, or some other foreign object from his tights, obscure his opponent's head from the view of the official in the ring, and then *stab* his opponent in the forehead until blood poured profusely from the wrestler's face.

Then, if the crowd hadn't already rioted, the Sheik would light a piece of flash paper and mysteriously "throw fire" into his opponent's face, or finish his opponent by sitting on the man's lower back and jerking his head back as far as it would go. This was the Sheik's dreaded "camel clutch" submission hold.

The Sheik's act was over the top in its villainy, which of course also meant it was pure box office gold in that era. Fans all over the Midwest and Canada paid boatloads of money to see the Sheik in action. Once they'd seen the Sheik for the first time and he'd incensed them so greatly, they would then pay even *more* money to come back one week later in the hopes of seeing him get his ass kicked by the babyface. Over the years, the Sheik made a *fortune* from the fans' desires to see him suffer a miserable death in the ring. He'd also been left with a seriously mangled forehead from having his own blood shed in the ring night after night.

The first time I ever saw the Sheik was when I went to watch him wrestle in Indianapolis. That night, he brought his personal slave girl to the ring - who was actually his real-life wife, Joyce Fleser - and he slapped her in front of everyone and then hovered ominously over her as she cowered in fear. The fans in the arena were livid from watching this makeshift domestic abuse angle play out in front of them. Now that the fuse had been lit, it didn't take much more prompting before the fans stormed the ring to get after him. They *really* tried to kill him that night!

In those days, the Sheik could book himself as the headliner of his own promotion and draw a crowd in Detroit any time he felt like it. He could work a program with practically anybody and sell out Cobo Arena with ease.

Up until Tom mentioned the Sheik to me, my only impression of him was from his act as a pseudo-murderous psychopath, so I had the length of the car trip from Indianapolis to Detroit to recondition my mind to think of him as a competent, professional businessman and wrestling territory owner.

Even though Tom worked for the Sheik's Detroit-based territory, his home was in Indianapolis. "Big Time Wrestling" covered all of Michigan, and much of Ohio, so it was easy for Tom to drive home to Indy after shows in the southwestern Ohio area. While Ohio was largely a spot show state which the Sheik used for shows in fairly small towns, nearly all of the Michigan-based shows were held at Cobo Arena in Downtown Detroit.

After I found a place to park outside of Cobo, Tom and I walked into the building and into the locker room. By now, I was less nervous about meeting the fearsome Sheik I'd watched as a kid, and anxious to make a good first impression on him so that I could hopefully start wrestling soon.

"Hey, boy," the Sheik said, extending his hand for me to shake. "Tom says you want to wrestle."

"Yes, sir!" I said, excitedly shaking the Sheik's hand.

The Sheik was very congenial, but he kept staring at me with those famous Sheik eyes of his. Secretly, I was worried he was going to go crazy and stab me with something.

"He's been doing pretty well in training," Tom said, vouching for me. "And you can see he's got some size on him."

The Sheik looked me over and nodded, and then he broke into a grin and asked, "So you think you're ready, boy?"

I quickly replied by saying, "Yes, sir! I do!"

After that, Tom pulled me aside and said, "Okay, kid... Here's the real deal..."

Tom then explained to me that wrestling was all a work, and that the participants weren't actually trying to harm each other. Even though I always suspected this, I was thrilled to learn it wasn't entirely real. To me, this revelation meant it would be a lot easier for me to earn money without the risk of having to fight off someone who was *actually* trying to kill me! I was shocked to learn how a lot of people who broke into the business had a big problem with the fact that wrestling was worked. They *really* wanted to hurt people!

I told the Sheik I needed trunks and shoes, so he simply said "We'll take you to Carl's in Columbus." Carl's was this shop that made all of the gear wrestlers wore in the ring. Everyone on our roster ordered their gear from Carl's. Because the Sheik decided I should begin my career wrestling under a hood - or mask - I also ordered several masks from Carl's in different colors. When I debuted as a professional wrestler, I would be known as "The Big O." Most of my masks had a big "O" stitched into the center of the forehead.

I didn't realize it at the time, but wrestling under the mask allowed me to learn my craft and get the mistakes out of my system while maintaining my anonymity. Then, once I'd developed my skills a bit more, I could take the mask off and develop a new personality without worrying about fans remembering the green rookie who they'd seen in prior years and holding those memories against me.

In 1967, the Sheik put me in my first official match in Dayton, Ohio against Frank Hickey. By this point in his career, Frank was in his early 50s, and he seemed incredibly concerned about getting stiffed or injured by a massive, unskilled, 300-pound monster with something to prove.

"Hey, boy," Frank said to me when we locked up. "Now remember, boy.... This is a *work*! Don't hurt me, boy. Okay? You got it?"

Frank led through a quick match, and before too long, it was all over.

"You did good, boy!" Frank said after I walked back through the curtain. "You did good!"

Wrestling as "The Big O"

I received a whopping $25 for my first professional wrestling match, which didn't surprise me. I knew I was a rookie who had just completed his first match, and I would have to work myself into a position on the card where I would be more valuable and worth a larger payoff.

The Sheik must have seen potential in me, because he promptly offered me a contract. He ushered me over to his wife, Joyce, who handled the majority of the wrestlers' contracts, and they put me on the minimum salary. I quit my job with Chrysler and never looked back.

In one of my first matches as a full-time wrestler, I found myself in Cincinnati facing off against the veteran wrestler Al Costello, a former member of the world-famous "Fabulous Kangaroos" tag team. Al was 5'11" and 220 pounds at the very most. He was also nearly 50 years old.

Al and I were in one of the opening matches, and I stood there evaluating Al, thinking about how tiny he was compared to me. The Sheik had asked us to do a Broadway, which meant we would go the full 15-minute time limit.

"Fifteen minutes with him?" I thought to myself. "I'm gonna show him just how strong I am."

Unbeknownst to me, not only did Al *actually* know how to wrestle, but he was *exceptional*. You could probably go so far as to say he was a "shooter," which is a title reserved for wrestlers who know how to physically dissect and injure other wrestlers who won't cooperate with them during matches. Clearly, I didn't know what I was getting myself into. For fifteen minutes, we'd lock up, Al would take me down, clamp a hold on me, toy with me, and then set me free.

No matter what I tried, I couldn't do *a thing* with Al. This guy who I outweighed by about 90 pounds would put a hold on me every time we made contact, and every time he did, I was *helpless*. The only time I ever got free from anything was when he *felt* like letting me go! I was so happy when the bell finally rang after 15 minutes, because it had been the longest 15 minutes of my life. I was so blown up. Al did whatever he wanted with me, and there wasn't a thing I could do about it. He was *that* good.

I crawled out of the ring along the floor of the Music Hall where the event was held. I leaned on the side of the ring to hold myself up. In that instant, I literally didn't think I could walk.

I talked myself out of crawling all the way back to the dressing room, because that would have been absolutely shameful. It wasn't that far of a walk, but it seemed like *miles*. Al Costello taught me a lesson that night. I didn't say anything to him about it. I knew better. I kept my mouth *shut*.

In the better part of 15 minutes, I learned there is a lot more to pro wrestling than just being big and strong.

Big O promo photo

TWO – "I don't want to wrestle no *damn* bear!"

I quickly learned to enjoy my frequent trips to Detroit. Back then, Detroit was a very active city. When I went out at night, all of the restaurants and bars of Downtown would remain open well after midnight. The lights of the city were bright, and a lot of exciting things were happening.

The Sheraton Cadillac was the hotel the Sheik booked for the wrestlers to stay in. All of the us got fantastic rates in that hotel, and none of us were required to share rooms. I was only 24 years old, and I was already enjoying a more fulfilling life than I'd ever imagined living when I was staring out of the window of the Chrysler foundry. In fact, I was having so much fun that I didn't even care that I wasn't making any real money to speak of.

No one on the street knew who I was since I wore a hood in the ring, so I had the additional benefit of anonymity. Everywhere I went, I could overhear Detroiters talking excitedly about the Sheik and the hometown wrestling promotion.

Because of the way the territory was structured, I had the luxury of being able to drive directly to most of the cities we were running shows in, work my match, and then drive straight home to Indianapolis. If I didn't feel like driving home after a show, I also had a friend who lived in Columbus who would let me crash at his place.

Since I was a good-sized guy, the Sheik decided to try me out as a main eventer for a few of his shows. When I came to the Sheik's office to have a talk with him about my monetary situation, he pulled out a copy of their in-house publication, "*The Body Press*," and held it in front of my face.

"Look at this," the Sheik said. "Who's on the cover?"

"Me!" I remarked.

"Okay, boy, what do you think?" he said, sliding the program back into his top drawer.

"Looks pretty good to me," I laughed.

For my first main event, they wanted me to work a program with The Mighty Igor, a veteran who'd been working in the business for at least a dozen years by then. His real name was Dick Garza, and he'd been a pretty serious bodybuilder before getting into wrestling. As the story goes, he knocked out the famous Canadian wrestler Brute Bernard during an argument in a weight room. When word of the incident spread, Bert Ruby, the Detroit promoter at the time, sought Igor out and convinced him to get in the ring.

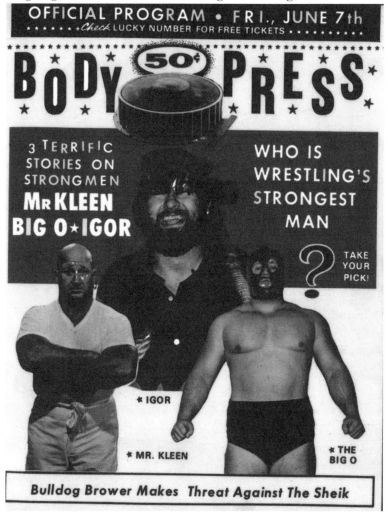

On the cover of "*The Body Press*"

Igor wrestled under a friendly Polish superman gimmick, and he had a manager with him named Ivan Kalmikoff. I quickly learned that you needed to work within the framework of Igor's very specific style, or the match simply wouldn't get over with the fans. Unless you worked Igor's way, he would get lost in the ring and wouldn't know what to do. You'd have to pound on the Polish monster for a while to get him to sell your offense to generate heat with the fans. Then, when Igor was ready, he would act pissed off, stomp his feet, and then get fired up and come back on you.

Working with Igor taught me the importance of selling the offense of my opponents. Igor was respected by the fans as a giant powerhouse, so they believed all of the pain he inflicted on his opponents was real. At the same time, he wasn't afraid to make his opponent look strong in the ring. That way, when he overcame the beating he'd been suffering and made a comeback to win the match, he looked like King Kong in the eyes of the people. In addition, by making your opponent look good, you also make the match look good, and if everyone does everything the way they're meant to during a wrestling match, you can lose right in the middle of the ring and still come out looking like a monster in the eyes of the audience.

One of the incidents that stands out to me from the Sheik's territory involves Jess "Bull" Ortega, a guy I was never too fond of. I'd met Ortega and the legendary Baron Von Raschke at the Sheraton Cadillac, we'd all piled into my car, and I began driving us all to a show in Saginaw, Michigan, which is near the middle of the state's Lower Peninsula.

Ortega said a few things to me during the trip that had *really* pissed me off, and by time we got to Saginaw, I was *steaming*. As wrestlers, we would charge each other "trans" for having provided the transportation services, and since Ortega was only going one way with me during that trip, he needed to pay me once we'd reached Saginaw.

As we all climbed out of my car, I looked at Ortega and said, "Jess, you owe me trans."

Then I quoted him the price for trans, except I intentionally multiplied it by two.

24

"No, that's not right!" Jess objected. "That's double!"

In response, I said, "Okay, Jess. Either you pay me that trans right now, or we're going to have a fight, right here, and right now." Obviously, I was being a jerk, but I was so angry with Ortega that I was pushing the issue with the hope that he wouldn't pay me, thereby providing me with an excuse to kick his ass. To my great disappointment, he paid me what I asked for. Undeniably, it was a bully move on my part, but Von Raschke laughed about it. I don't think he liked Ortega either.

Aside from the Sheik, Detroit had another resident legend: Bobo Brazil. Billed as 6'6" and 270 pounds, Bobo was closer to my height of 6'4". Still, even in his 40s, Bobo had a great, muscular physique. Without a doubt, Bobo was one of the true trailblazers of wrestling as a black star who was often more popular with white fans than many of the white headliners he wrestled against. By the late '60s, Brazil was a worldwide wrestling phenomenon. He'd even traveled to Japan and won the NWA International Championship from Shohei "Giant" Baba - the Japan Pro Wrestling Association's top star - ending Baba's 944-day championship reign in the process.

Although he was born in Arkansas, Bobo had long since settled in Benton Harbor, Michigan, and he had adopted Michigan as his home state. To the surprise of no one, Bobo was a huge attraction in Detroit, and the black fans of Detroit seemed to feel a special kinship with him.

Brazil and the Sheik appeared to have a contentious relationship at times, which was probably over money, but the Sheik clearly loved to have Brazil around because having another international mega star on his wrestling cards was never bad for business. However, the only times I ever saw Brazil was at the Cobo Hall shows. When we held shows in our other cities like Dayton, Toledo, Columbus, Akron and Cincinnati, Brazil was nowhere to be found.

The entire time I wrestled for the Sheik, I still lived at home with my parents. In general, they supported what I was doing. However, I think they were a little concerned when they saw the incessant travel I undertook and the long road trips I went on all by myself. My mother was definitely worried, but she never flat out said "Oh, Michael! This is too much! You're traveling hundreds and hundreds of miles for no money!" To their credit, they never once tried to talk me out of it.

For my first few months with the Sheik, I had Tom Jones as a regular travel companion. Eventually, he departed from Indianapolis to take a job with the NWA territory in Dallas.

One of the guys I hung out with was a part-time wrestler who lived in Columbus, attended Ohio State University *and* ran a bar. Because I was pretty fresh out of college, this guy and his friends proved to be a more natural group for me to want to hang out with than the veteran wrestlers I was working with.

During one of our drinking excursions, we got wasted at a bar and then worked our way over to a restaurant. In our inebriated states, we had the brilliant idea to hold an eating contest, and we selected eggs as the food of choice for the competition. The rules were simple: The eggs could be prepared any way you wanted - poached, fried, over easy, sunny side up, or raw. But, you had to eat the entire egg in order for it to count toward your final tally. My friend downed around 21 or 22 eggs, and I consumed only 20, but I was *still* awarded the championship because I also ate the *toast*, which added bonus points to my score.

As I progressed in the ring, the Sheik found new ways to use me. He put me in the ring with Ox Baker, a 6'5" 300-plus pound former football player from Waterloo, Iowa, because we were both huge guys. In addition to being large, Ox was also bald and loud with a thick handlebar moustache and equally hairy eyebrows. He had a very menacing look, which would serve him well in later years when he was cast in the movie "Escape From New York" with Kurt Russell.

As a worker in the wrestling ring, I would generously rank Ox as a four on a ten-point scale. He didn't look like a very agile wrestler, and in reality, he was *even less* agile than he looked. Guys in the locker room were constantly complaining about Ox and his lofty position on the Sheik's cards. For some reason, they wouldn't take into account how Ox drew consistent money for the Sheik thanks to his unique look and his interview ability. You *don't* kill the golden goose just because he can't fly.

Usually, our matches weren't that great, but sometimes we managed to pull it all together and deliver. Working with Ox Baker was just an early lesson in how to draw money with someone who was very limited in terms of what they could physically do in the ring. I did my best to make him look like the ruthless killer he professed to be, and we'd earn a strong response from the crowd.

Working for the Sheik also introduced me to the tag team of "The Texas Outlaws," Dusty Rhodes and Dick Murdoch. They were two young guys who were willing to work their asses off and bump around for the babyface wrestlers the same way I tried to. In particular, Dusty, the larger and rounder of the Outlaws, had a very colorful performance style, and it was clear he knew how to keep the crowds engaged in the action as the Outlaws sold the violence inflicted upon them by their opponents.

Cobo Arena was an awesome place to work. The wrestling matches I'd seen in Indianapolis were at the Colosseum at the Fairgrounds on 38th Street, and Cobo blew that place away. It was significantly larger than the Colosseum, and it elevated the status of wrestling in my mind in terms of both its popularity with the general public and what my expectations for success in the industry should look like. In short, main eventing in large arenas filled with energetic fans would be what I would look to as the true measurement of success for my wrestling career.

When we wrestled at Cobo, the Sheik had his own personal security team comprising an assortment of former policemen, and he *desperately* needed them. In terms of heat, I don't know that I've ever seen a wrestler consistently piss off fans the way the Sheik could. There were many fans in Cobo Arena who would have killed him if they'd been given half a chance. At a minimum, they would have bludgeoned him, sliced him, or inflicted whatever serious injury upon him they could before security broke it up.

As a rule breaker in Detroit, I was automatically granted an additional level of security to make sure I would come back from the Cobo Arena ring alive. Right before my first Cobo Arena match, the head of the security force caught up with me in the hallway and explained the way things were done in Detroit.

"Here's what we do, kid," he began. "We're going to take you to the ring. When the match is over, you *wait* for us, and we'll take you *out* of the ring. *Period.*"

It didn't take too many matches for me to realize he wasn't messing around. Even as a heel newcomer who fans weren't accustomed to, I still spotted several fans at Cobo who were itching to take a shot at me. When it happened, the security team would smack them right down and drop them back into their seats.

One evening at Cobo Arena, I went out into the building after I'd wrestled and showered, because I wanted to watch the Sheik's match. As usual, the Sheik worked the crowd until they were screaming for his head on a platter. Suddenly, some Detroiter in the crowd hopped the fence, burst through the line of police protection and successfully made it into the ring with the Sheik.

I don't know why, but too many fans seemed to think once they were alone with the wrestlers they would somehow be able to get the upper hand. Little did this guy know, the Sheik was legitimately one of the most dangerous wrestlers around because he would *really* hurt someone if he had to, and he carried weapons with him just in case. Between his robe and his trunks, he typically hid six or seven weapons of various kinds, most of which were bladed.

Once the Sheik saw this guy making his way into the ring, he ran over to the ropes and kicked the guy squarely in the mouth. By then, the police had reached the ring apron, and they caught the fan's limp body as it fell from the ring. Then, they proceeded to carry him up the aisle and back to the locker room as if they were crowdsurfing him through the arena.

I followed the police back to the dressing area and watched as they dragged the intruder into a private room and shut the door. From outside, I heard smacks and thuds for the next ten minutes as this guy screamed for his life. All of a sudden, the commotion stopped, and so did the screams. I was convinced they'd *killed* the man. For all I know, they *did* kill the man. I never asked any questions about it. He'd committed the cardinal sin at Cobo Arena; he'd tried to hurt the Sheik.

For those who know about the early history between the two, it might be a surprise to hear that the legendary Lou Thesz wrestled on the Sheik's shows several times while I was in Detroit. Thesz was one of many special-attraction wrestlers, like Gorilla Monsoon or Dory Funk Jr., who the Sheik would fly in exclusively for the Cobo Arena shows, but who wouldn't travel throughout the rest of the territory.

Lou was actually born in the Upper Peninsula of Michigan, and he still holds nearly every significant record pertaining to the NWA World Heavyweight Championship. His six-year reign as champion back in the late 1940s and early 1950s resulted in every meaningful world championship being unified under the NWA banner. Thesz was picked as the wrestler who could most reliably accomplish this task, because he was legitimately skilled in a variety of dangerous holds and maneuvers. If anyone tried to cross him in the ring and alter the finish to a match, Thesz could easily break one of their limbs and *make* them stick to the plan.

There was a story going around the locker room about how Thesz stopped cooperating with the Sheik in the ring because he didn't respect the Sheik's gimmick and wanted the Sheik to wrestle for real, so the Sheik just left the ring. Thesz supposedly chased the Sheik outside, and the Sheik then hid under a bus until Thesz left. I didn't believe it, so I asked the Sheik about it. He conceded that the story was true, but then he added an additional detail.

"It's not that I was afraid of Lou Thesz," the Sheik said. "I was afraid of what I would have to *do* to Lou Thesz."

"What are you talking about?" I asked. "What would you have done to him?"

"*Stab* him," the Sheik said, smiling.

Then the Sheik pulled open his robe and pulled out all of the weapons he kept hidden inside of it. My jaw dropped.

"It's hard to get work in the wrestling business after you *stab* the world champion!" laughed the Sheik.

Then the Sheik told me a story about a time when he and Thesz were on the same flight. Thesz didn't realize the Sheik was on the flight because he'd fallen asleep as soon as they'd boarded. After the flight, the Sheik walked by a sleeping Thesz, slapped him upside the head, darted in front of the other deplaning passengers, and scurried away. Thesz *never* found out it was the Sheik who'd slapped him.

Almost all of our television tapings were done right across the bridge at the CKLW television studio in Windsor, Canada. It was a standard television studio setup with a few rows of seats which they packed with fans. The lead announcer for the broadcast was Lord Athol Layton, an English wrestler who also worked matches from time to time. By this stage of his life, Layton was in his mid-to-late 40s, and had already experienced the lion's share of whatever success he would have in his wrestling career.

One of the few matches I had involving Layton was a tag match at Cobo Arena which also included Mark Lewin, and they took the fall on me. Layton must've felt like showing off for the crowd that night, because he picked me up to give me another one of his trademarked judo chops even though the match had concluded.

"Don't touch him!" Mark admonished his partner. "Leave him alone!"

Layton didn't listen and decided to judo chop me anyway. I dutifully took the bump for the stiff chop. He picked me up and delivered yet another stiff chop to my chest, and I took another bump on the mat. I'm sure Layton was doing this because I was a rookie, and he felt like he needed to remind me of my place in the business, so to speak. All the same, he wasn't exactly one of the veterans I felt I should be modeling myself after. Layton wasn't very entertaining in the ring, and the only time he ever drew any crowds was when he was working with the Sheik, who was the *true* attraction. Unfortunately, I wasn't able to get into the ring with the Sheik during my time in Detroit, so those giant paydays eluded me.

On the other hand, Mark Lewin was one of the most giving wrestlers in Detroit, and he did what he could to help me get better in the ring. He realized I was green and needed the help, but he also realized I was probably worth the investment. I'd quickly established myself as the kind of wrestler who would do whatever was necessary for the sake of the match, and not the kind of guy who wouldn't sell damage, or who would take advantage of a smaller guy in the ring.

Mark and I were working in Columbus, Ohio, and Mark had me down on the mat. Slowly, he positioned his leg close enough to me that I could reach out and clasp it.

"Grab the leg," Mark instructed me. "Grab the leg."

"What?" I said back to him. I was so green as a young wrestler that I couldn't understand why he would want me to grab his leg.

From that point on, Mark would tease me about that moment whenever he saw me.

"You just *couldn't* grab my leg, could you?" he'd ask through a grin.

Danny Miller was another guy I enjoyed working with, but one time in Cincinnati, he got under my skin. We had a minor altercation in the ring, and I wanted to fight him. He came to me later and said, "Okay, kid. Settle down. It's a *work*."

"If you think you're really tough, we can fight!" I challenged him.

"Come on, kid," he continued. "*Relax*."

Later on, I appreciated his diplomacy, but at the time, I was pissed. I hadn't considered the type of muscle Danny had backing him up.

We went to Fremont, Ohio, which was Danny's hometown, and wrestled at the city fair which was packed with 4,000 people. My partner and I were wrestling the "Miller Brothers," a team comprising Danny and his brother Bill. "Big Bill" was a former Big 10 wrestling champion at Ohio State University. He was 6'6" and 300 pounds, so he certainly lived up to his monicker. I used to watch him wrestle as a kid and I was extremely impressed by him. Not only was he big and strong, but he also had the grace and agility you'd expect from a former Division One wrestling champion.

In the dressing room, I was a little concerned that the Millers might seek revenge for the confrontation I'd had with Danny just a few weeks prior. I didn't want Bill to try to take retribution against me in the ring for what I'd said to his brother.

"Hey, kid… we're gonna backdrop you over the top rope," Bill said. "You can take that move, right?"

Bill posed that question to me almost as a challenge. In that era, a backdrop over the top rope was a *major* bump, and I was a big man to be getting backdropped out to the floor. I *truly* did not want to take that move, and I absolutely didn't want to take that move from two guys who were harboring a grudge against me. But, I also didn't want to show any fear in the presence of the Millers.

I stared at Bill for what probably seemed like a long time, and finally I relented and said, "Yeah… okay."

As if he could read my mind, Bill stared at me, and then his face broke into a grin.

"No, we're *not* going to do that!" he laughed.

I was *thoroughly* relieved. The match went off without a hitch.

Later, I worked with Bull Curry, who was a fairly wealthy man who had also been a former professional fighter in the late '20s and early '30s. He was of Lebanese descent, and he wasn't particularly big, but he made up for it by adopting a menacing, rulebreaking style that caused plenty of riots during his heyday. By the time I worked with him, however, Curry was in his mid 50s, and he had no interest in selling anyone's offense or taking any bumps. Needless to say, I didn't enjoy the experience very much. He was also a firm believer in using foreign objects during all of his matches, so there was no real creativity involved in anything he did.

Another a tag team in Detroit at this time was called the "Hells Angels," Ron and Paul Dupree. Contrary to the gimmick they were using at the time, they definitely were *not* brothers, and it was a poorly kept secret that they were involved in a homosexual relationship with one another. In the ring, the Duprees were great workers who bumped around as much as anyone else in the Detroit territory and tried to keep the fans entertained.

I don't know why, but Bull Curry didn't like the Hells Angels at all. One night in the dressing room, Curry sucker punched one of the Angels and knocked him out. To the best of my knowledge, the Sheik didn't do anything to punish Curry for the incident.

Fred Curry was Bull's son, and he was a favorite of the Sheik's *solely* because he was Bull's son. One night, Fred really pissed me off by not selling any of my offense. He was only 5'11" and 200 pounds. Visually, it looked like I could have eaten him alive if I'd felt like it. For the life of me, I couldn't understand why he thought it was okay to not sell the offense from a man so much larger than him. It made the match look stupid!

"You son of a bitch!" I said to him as I picked him up and slammed him to the mat against his will. If he didn't want to sell, I was going to *make* him sell.

After the match, I was determined to kick Fred's ass. The Sheik came up to me and tried to preempt the ass kicking.

"Listen, boy… I hear you're starting fights," Sheik said. "I don't want to hear about any shit like that from you."

It's a good thing for Fred that the Sheik intervened to save him. I definitely would've beaten his ass that night if I'd been able to get ahold of him.

Later on, in Cincinnati, I took my father to meet the Sheik. The two of them worked their way into a pretty deep and lengthy conversation about religion and ethnic heritage. During their talk, my father asked Sheik about his religious background, presuming he was a Muslim.

"I want to show you something," Sheik said to my dad.

Sheik reached into his pocket and produced a medallion of the Star of David. The Currys were Lebanese, and the Sheik was Syrian, so I was suspicious that the shared ethnic and cultural background was the reason the Currys were both pushed and protected by the Sheik. However, after seeing the Sheik produce a Jewish symbol from his pocket, it seemed he was at least sympathetic to Jews, so I wasn't so sure what to think after I saw that.

Two of my most memorable nights working for the Sheik didn't even involve wrestling with another person. Instead, I was wrestling with a *bear*.

I wasn't as scared to be working with a bear as you might have thought, because I'd actually wrestled with a bear prior to getting my start in the wrestling business. During my days at Purdue, I went to the Indiana State Fair where there was an open challenge to wrestle a bear. My friends egged me on, figuring I could hold my own at 6'4" and more than 250 pounds. So, I raised my hand, answered the challenge and rolled around with the bear for a while. By the time I became a wrestler, all of my bear-related fears were long gone.

Jack Kane was my partner for my first handicap match with the bear. Jack came to Detroit from Amarillo, Texas, and handled all of the bookings and finishes for the Sheik while we were on the road. During one of our shows in Akron, Ohio, Kane and I were slated to wrestle the bear in a handicap match as the semi main event.

As Jack and I stood in our corner, the muzzled black bear confidently crawled into the ring.

"I'm gonna start!" Jack said to me as the bear stared us down.

"Sure!" I responded. "Fine with me!"

I stepped through the ropes out to the ring apron, and I prepared myself to learn the finer points of bear wrestling from Jack Kane.

Jack wasn't a very big guy. He was 5'10" and weighed 190 pounds at the most. Yet, he charged at this bear as soon as the bell rang to start the match, as if he was going to physically dominate the animal. Instantly, the black bear swung its arm and cracked Jack on the right shoulder. Jack *collapsed* onto the mat. When he finally pulled himself together, Jack scrambled over to my corner.

"I'm hurt! I'm hurt!" Jack screamed. "*Tag* me!"

I should have been more reluctant, but I tagged Jack and stepped through the ropes to lock up with the bear. I charged the bear, and fortunately, the bear didn't swing on me like it had swung on Jack.

The black bear was owned by a guy named Tuffy Truesdale, and he'd advised me to keep my hands away from the bear's mouth. Even with the muzzle on, the bear could suck your fingers into its mouth and chomp them off. Early on in the match, I forgot about this advice and got careless. I felt the bear trying to draw my hand into its mouth. I hurriedly yanked my hand away and vowed not to make any more mistakes. We rolled around on the mat for a while and managed to have about as decent a match as you can have between a professional wrestler and a bear that doesn't realize it's supposed to be working a match.

I wrestled the bear a second time at a fair in Springfield, Ohio. The event was held inside of a tent that could hold about a thousand people, and all of the fans in attendance were seated in wooden folding chairs. For this event, I was partnered with a Detroit mainstay named Big Bad John. He was about my size, although not quite as heavy. The two of us didn't know we were going to be wrestling the bear in a handicap match until right before the show started, and John was *pissed* off. John was used to working in main events, so he interpreted being booked with the bear as a demotion.

"I don't want to wrestle no *damn* bear!" John complained in the dressing area. "*Fuckin'* bear!"

When we got in the ring, John insisted on starting the match with the bear the same way Jack had.

"Whatever you want, John," I told him. Far be it from me to insert myself between a black bear and an angry main-event wrestler.

John locked up with the bear, went behind it, and gave it a belly-to-back *suplex*! He dropped the thing right on its head and neck! Shocked and startled, the bear sprang off the mat, tore through the ropes and darted through the center of the crowd! People and chairs went flying all over the place. All the while, I was standing in my corner with my jaw open, thinking, "*Damn*! Look at *this*!"

It was a crazy scene. People were running all through the tent trying to escape from this bear, while Tuffy Truesdale was chasing behind it trying to corral his pet and prevent a full-scale riot.

That might have been the quickest bear match in wrestling history that didn't involve a wrestler getting his fingers bitten off. John was determined to show the bear who the boss was, and he'd done exactly that. There was nothing left for me to do except to walk to the dressing room, because the match was undoubtedly over.

Prior to 1966, Dick the Bruiser's World Wrestling Association had been running opposition shows at the Detroit Olympia Arena. Blackjack Mulligan once worked for the Sheik, and he was made out to be a pretty big attraction. He then switched offices and started working for The Bruiser, and the Sheik was understandably pissed.

Much later, Mulligan told me about how during height of the promotional feud, the Sheik conspired to plant drugs in his car in order to get him arrested. The Sheik was not a trusting sort of guy in general, so it is consistent with his character to think he would have dealt with betrayal somewhat harshly. Still, when Mulligan told me this story, it didn't sound like something the Sheik would do given the kindness he'd shown me. From what I could see, the wrestling business was filled with shady characters, and the Sheik had simply adapted to his environment.

One of the old-school promotional tactics the Sheik would use would be to artificially elevate the status of guys on his roster to "championship" level for the sake of hyping a match. For instance, Mark Lewin, who was Jewish, would be billed as the "Israeli Champion" in his matches with the Sheik in order to publicly pit a Jewish wrestler against an Arab wrestler to capitalize on Middle East tensions.

Another match might be billed for the "World Negro Championship," and feature Bobo Brazil defending his fictional championship against Ernie Ladd. If the Sheik was off working elsewhere and had the United States Championship with him, Bobo could substitute for him as the "Negro Champion" and work at the top of the card. This could also be done to elevate the future matches between the Sheik and Bobo to the level of champion-versus-champion, even if the only official championship up for grabs was the Sheik's U.S. title.

Brute Power: The Autobiography of Buggsy McGraw

Eventually, I was built up to feud with Bobo, and they had me beat Crusher Verdu at Cobo with a reverse bearhug in order to make me look strong heading into my match with the wrestling legend. My parents never saw me wrestle in person until I brought them up to Detroit to see my match with Bobo Brazil. For the occasion, I bought brand new yellow trunks and a new yellow mask. Before the match, Bobo sat with me in the dressing room and walked me through how he wanted the match to go.

"Take your heat, and I'm going to sell for you," Bobo advised me. "Then I'll make the comeback, headbutt you, and take the fall."

For Bobo, it was just another night. I felt a little trepidation about working with a legend, but it wasn't too bad, partially because I knew there was no way I would be winning. My simple objectives were to make Bobo look good, get the match over with the fans, and get Bobo ready for another feud with the Sheik. Bobo's big move was his "Cocobutt" headbutt, which was extremely easy to take. Once he hit that on me, he covered me for the pinfall, and that was that.

My mother got a little *too* excited during the main event match. When Bobo hit me with the Cocobutt, she screamed because she thought I'd been seriously hurt.

"That big, black man looked like he really hurt you!" she told me afterward. When your own mother starts crying and worrying about your safety, that's when you know you're selling a headbutt properly.

I got the concept very early that there were certain guys in each territory who were never really going to leave, and so they always needed to maintain their dominance in the fans' eyes. While Bobo was a worldwide legend, and probably the foremost black wrestler in the world at the time, he also lived in Benton Harbor, Michigan, so the Sheik could rely on him to drive across the state and attract fans whenever it was necessary.

One of the things I appreciated about Bobo was his willingness to sell moves. Even though he was a mythical figure in professional wrestling, he realized he would do better business if he looked vulnerable, overcame the odds, and won despite the adversity he'd been faced with. Because of this philosophy, he *always* attracted fans and earned money, even if he was somewhat limited in terms of the moves he did in the ring.

After beating me, they moved Bobo right back into main event matches with the Sheik. The two of them always found themselves working with one another, on and off, and the two of them at the top of the card almost always drew money. In the meantime, it was clear my job was as a stepping stone to help solidify other wrestlers at the top of the card.

After about a year in Detroit, the Sheik called me into his office.

"I need to send you to work somewhere else so you can learn more," he said. "After you get some more experience, I can bring you back and you can work some bigger programs under another name."

Everything he said made sense. If I was being fired, it was about the nicest way you could ever fire somebody.

"I've made arrangements with Stu Hart to have you wrestle for him," Sheik continued. "His promotion is called Stampede Wrestling, and they're in Calgary."

"Never heard of it," I told him.

"Don't worry about it, boy," Sheik said. "Stu will take good care of you. Just don't let him put any holds on you. He's a shooter, and he likes to test out the young guys."

"Thanks for everything, Sheik," I said, shaking his hand. "You've done a lot for me."

"You're welcome, boy," Sheik replied. "I'll be seeing you again pretty soon."

THREE – "Joe Furnum"

Having accepted my marching orders, I drove back to Indianapolis and explained to my parents that I would be moving to Calgary, Alberta, Canada in the dead of winter.

"If that's what you have to do, it's what you have to do," Dad said. "But you'll need to make sure your car is prepared to make the drive."

Heeding my father's advice, I equipped my car with spikes on its tires, and then I packed up my things and hit the road. As I got through Illinois and Minnesota and into the Dakotas, things gradually got colder and colder. West of Winnipeg, I made a stop for gas. After filling up the gas tank, I climbed back into the car and slammed the door shut.

In an instant, *hundreds* of shards of glass struck me in the face. The Canadian air was so frigid that my window shattered from the simple act of closing my car door! I thought Indianapolis winters were cold, but nothing I'd experienced in my life up to that point had prepared me for a *Canadian* winter. Just my luck, I was driving smack dab into the *worst* Canadian winter in *37 years*.

I made my way to a service station where they equipped my car with a cardboard window, and they also added a clear, plastic section in the center of it so that I could see through it. Finally, I made it to a motel where I checked in and got some sleep. When I woke up and tried to start the car, it was completely dead. The engine was frozen solid; I had to get a block heater to thaw everything out.

I was miserable, but I was certain things couldn't possibly get any worse once I actually started wrestling for Stu Hart. I couldn't have been any more wrong.

When I finally got my car running, I met up with Stu and the rest of the Stampede Wrestling roster. Once I entered the building, I walked to the dressing room and introduced myself to the guys who worked for Stu.

Brute Power: The Autobiography of Buggsy McGraw

By the time I began working for Stampede Wrestling, Stu had already been running wrestling events out of Calgary for about two decades. Stu was born in Saskatchewan to immigrant parents and was a highly successful athlete, particularly in amateur wrestling. Once his Olympic dreams were derailed by the outbreak of World War II, Stu became a professional wrestler, and then returned home to buy the Big Time Wrestling territory there. Over time, the company morphed into Stampede Wrestling.

Stu walked over and looked me up and down. Rather than offering his hand for a handshake, he latched onto my left arm with both hands and started squeezing it.

"Big-a, fat-a arm-a," Stu breathed, and then he chuckled loudly.

The Sheik had warned me about Stu's penchant for tying wrestlers in knots using shoot wrestling holds, so I was leery about him grabbing me like that. I soon heard stories about Stu's famous training facility, "The Dungeon," which was in the basement of his house. Luckily, I never got to see or experience it in person.

I was quickly introduced to Jos Leduc and his brother Paul, and I soon partnered up with them to share driving duties during car trips around the territory. They also got me situated in the same motel they were in after I'd spent my first few nights at a motel in downtown Calgary. The road trips for Stampede Wrestling were *unbearably* long, and the cold weather and ceaseless snowfall only added to the misery we felt during each of those journeys. Some of the cities in Stu's territory were as far as 500 miles away from each other.

Stampede Wrestling was also a step down from the Sheik's territory in another significant way. While working for the Sheik, we could count on being in some decent venues like Cobo Arena. Conversely, most of Stu's events were held at tiny, high-school-type facilities. After starting out in Detroit's Big Time Wrestling territory, the situation in Calgary simply wasn't measuring up.

During a particularly cold night in Saskatoon, Saskatchewan, I was in the first match on the card, and I decided I'd rather sit in the car outside than hang out in the dressing room with the rest of the wrestlers. Unfortunately for me, the Leducs were still holding the keys, and the car was locked, so I just stood outside in the frigid air and looked around. It suddenly dawned on me that ice crystals were suspended in space around me. *Millions* of them were hanging in the air.

Working as a masked man

"I'm either hallucinating, or I'm in the Twilight Zone," I said to myself. It just wasn't natural.

I went back in and asked the other wrestlers about it, and none of them had an explanation for it. Later on, I would learn that what I saw is called "diamond dust." It's one of those phenomenon that's only visible in a polar region as a ground-level ice cloud. This should only serve to underscore just how cold it can get in Canada! It was something you had to be mentally prepared for, because it could *break* you.

Adding to my misery was the fact that Stu's payoffs were even worse than the Sheik's. At best, the payoffs might be as good as $40 for a match, but some were as low as $15, and the average was around $25. By the time you paid for trans and the hotel room, it wasn't uncommon to come back from the Calgary loop feeling like you were in a financial hole. Between miserable living conditions and miserable pay, there was nothing at all enjoyable about working for Stu Hart. After a few loops within the Stampede territory, I was at my wit's end.

After one particularly draining loop of the Calgary circuit, I'd had all I could handle. While sitting on the bed in my dark, tiny motel room, I got on the phone and called the Sheik.

"Sheik, I can't take it here!" I whined. "I can't make any money here, and the trips are just *way* too long!"

"Okay, boy, I'll take care of it," Sheik said after a brief pause. "Give Stu your two-week notice. It's the right thing to do."

The featured guy in Calgary was "The Mongolian Stomper" Archie Gouldie, who wore the belt as Stampede Wrestling's recently crowned North American Champion. On my way out of Calgary, Stu booked me to put Archie over. By the time the week was done, I'd be on the eastern edge of the territory, so it would be easier for me to drive home from there. Frankly, I *couldn't wait* to put Archie over in the middle of the ring, because as soon as it was over I could leave!

Archie was a decent-sized guy who put on some entertaining matches. However, he was as Canadian as a person could get, and was *by no means* Mongolian. Before our match, he pulled me aside in the dressing room to have a one-on-one discussion.

"Hey, kid, with your size and your look, you should really think about working for McMahon in New York," Archie explained, referring to Vince McMahon, the famous promoter of the Word Wide Wrestling Federation. "But to *really* make a splash there, you and I should go as a tag team."

I nodded, but I didn't really give him much of a response. At the time, I figured Archie just wanted to use me as a means of securing a spot on the WWWF's roster.

"Remember, *don't* go there without me," Archie said as he walked away.

It sounded complimentary, but I didn't accept what Archie was telling me with any sincerity. Archie seemed like he was only out for himself. Even he wasn't happy over the money he was making in Calgary, and he was their *top attraction*. That's precisely why he wanted to get out of Stu's territory so badly.

When I arrived back to my parents' place in Indianapolis, I called the Sheik again to see if he'd been able to arrange for me to work in another wrestling territory. Fortunately for me, he was a man of his word

"Pack your gear, boy," the Sheik said. "You're going to Florida to wrestle for Eddie Graham. You should start driving down toward Tampa right away."

My parents were a lot happier with the idea of having their son living in Florida as opposed to freezing to death in the barren Canadian wasteland.

Before I made the trip to Florida, I bought a new red Ford Torino with a white stripe, which I thought was a pretty sharp car at the time. This car was a replacement for the black Ford Torino which had been devastated during my initial drive out to Calgary.

The promoter of the NWA's Florida territory was Cowboy Luttrall, but he was in the process of grooming Eddie Graham to promote alongside him. Eddie had once been a member of a very famous heel tag team in the Northeast with Dr. Jerry Graham, and he then moved on to Championship Wrestling from Florida in the mid 1960s and became a major babyface star.

Being in Tampa during the winter of 1969 was an *undeniable* improvement over Calgary. I immediately checked into a motel on Hillsborough, and then went in search of more permanent accommodations. I soon found an apartment at the corner of Armenia and Buffalo, which was later changed to Martin Luther King Street. Nowadays, there's a bank where my apartment complex used to be.

I wasn't the only new talent arriving in Florida around that time. Homer O'Dell was also new to the territory, and the Championship Wrestling from Florida officials sent him over to visit with me at my apartment complex in the hopes that I could also help him establish a residence there. I had no clue who Homer was, and no one made me aware that anyone was being sent over to see me.

Homer drove into the parking lot, stopped his car, and then stood outside to patiently wait for me to show up. When I finally returned from whatever I'd been doing, I pulled in, parked my Torino right next to Homer's vehicle and climbed out.

"Kay Fabe!" Homer said to me with a smile. That was his way of letting me know he was one of the workers.

Since I didn't know who Homer was, I just looked him up and down as I walked past him and responded by saying, "Joe Furnum!"

With that, I left Homer in the parking lot and walked off in the direction of my apartment. He drove straight back to the CWF office and told Eddie Graham, "I don't know why, but Mike *won't* talk to me!"

Among the first things Cowboy and Eddie did with me was to take the mask off of me and put me in the opening matches as a heel named "Brutus." I was there as a complement to the main heels on the CWF roster like Boris Malenko, and Hans Mortier.

Malenko was Jewish despite the Russian surname he wrestled under; his real name was Larry Simon. Since Florida had been flooded with Cubans who'd fled their home country earlier in the decade to escape communism, Malenko's act as Russian villain made him especially hated in South Florida. Everyone wanted to see him get beaten up, and his matches with Eddie Graham made a lot of money for the both of them.

Leaping from the top turnbuckle in an early Florida match

Aside from Eddie Graham, Jack Brisco was also one of the top babyfaces on the roster. I never would have guessed at the time that some people within the NWA hierarchy were already looking at Jack as someone who should be groomed for a run with the NWA World Championship. He was a handsome, athletic young wrestler, and he was also highly credible. Just a few years prior, he'd become the first Native American in NCAA history to win a national championship in wrestling, winning the 191-pound weight division during his junior year at Oklahoma State.

In a standard week, the CWF would start its tour in Orlando, hit West Palm Beach on Monday, and then get to Tampa on Tuesday. Then we would perform in Miami on Wednesday and Jacksonville on Thursday. In each successive week, the loop would repeat itself.

Fridays and Saturdays were the evenings for spots shows. Sometimes, these included shows in the Bahamas, which were usually in Nassau Stadium. For these trips, we either flew on a commercial airline, or we flew with Lester Welch in his personal aircraft. No matter who we flew in with, the wrestlers always seemed to breeze through customs, so in that respect, we always seemed to get some favor there. If you were a well-liked babyface wrestler, the people would bend over backwards to help you.

Charlie Major owned Nassau Stadium, which wasn't much of a stadium. To be honest, it was more of a bar and restaurant which opened up into an open-air courtyard with a wrestling ring in the middle of it, and bleachers along the side. The ring was also used for local boxing events, so it was like wrestling on concrete. I never got the impression the ring was removed in between our events.

The Bahamian crowds certainly didn't react the same to the wrestlers as the Floridians. If an object wasn't nailed down, the Bahamians would pick it up and throw it at you. This included rocks, whiskey bottles, beer cans, and even chunks of the stadium walls. If you were working as a heel, they didn't mind seriously injuring you.

Another unique feature of the Bahamas is the overwhelmingly black fanbase. For the most part, the black wrestlers in Florida were babyfaces, and they almost always won their matches in the Bahamas. If they didn't, the already high likelihood of a riot would increase tenfold.

Even though Nassau was a resort location, we didn't get a whole lot of time to bask in the tourist-friendly atmosphere. If you flew in with Lester Welch, you typically got up early the following morning and flew straight back to Florida.

Even outside of the Bahamas, it was clear that Florida had a unique character to it. Different ethnic groups predominated different areas of the state, and so the wrestlers who performed at each show might vary based on the demographics of each Florida community. A popular black wrestler like "Sailor" Art Thomas, who was a giant, heavily-muscled man and a huge attraction in South Florida, might be left off the card in other parts of the state where fans weren't too fond of blacks.

After only a short time working in Florida, I was far more knowledgeable as a wrestler than I'd been at the beginning of my career, simply because I was getting so much time performing in the ring, seven days a week, in front of different types of crowds.

No matter what position I was in on the card, *anything* was better than dealing with the cold road trips of Calgary, so I had nothing to complain about. But it also turns out I got my first big break in Florida when they put me in the ring with the Great Malenko. Apparently he liked my work, and he thought we could draw money if we feuded with one another.

"I want Mike to team with me, and then in a few months we can switch him," Malenko told Eddie.

"Sure, Boris," Eddie replied. "If you think it will work, let's do it."

Malenko was a big money draw for the Florida office, which gave him considerable influence with Eddie Graham. When Malenko told Eddie he wanted to work with me, Eddie quickly acceded to his wishes and made it happen.

Boris designed a program where I would be his regular tag-team partner in a heel tandem, and then I would turn on him and become a babyface. Malenko had taken me under his wing behind the scenes, and he wanted that relationship to play out in the ring as well. Week after week, we communicated to the fans through our actions that Malenko thought he was the clear leader of the team, and I was his young understudy who was being unfairly disparaged. Occasionally, he would also slap me around in front of the audience.

Beautiful Brutus in Florida

One night, in Tampa, Malenko's temper slowly became more inflamed as the match wore on. Finally, when we lost the match, he yelled at me and slapped me, and that's when I turned on him and pummeled him. The crowd went *crazy* for it.

When Malenko and I then started competing with one another in the ring, the matches were tremendous. The feud with Malenko eventually culminated in me winning my first championship in wrestling - the Florida Brass Knuckles Championship. No actual brass knuckles were involved; they were more like hardcore matches where we taped our fists. Rather than being represented by a belt, the Brass Knuckles Championship was represented by a trophy.

The referee for my Brass Knuckles Championship coronation match with Boris was none other than the legendary world heavyweight boxing champion, "The Brown Bomber" Joe Louis.

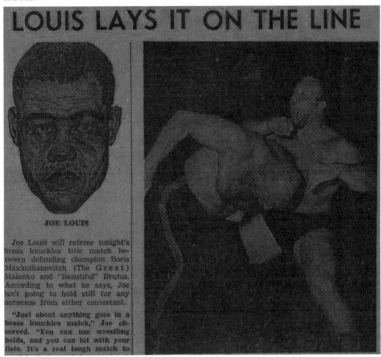

LOUIS LAYS IT ON THE LINE

JOE LOUIS

Joe Louis will referee tonight's brass knuckles title match between defending champion Boris Maximilianovitch (The Great) Malenko and "Beautiful" Brutus. According to what he says, Joe isn't going to hold still for any nonsense from either contestant.

"Just about anything goes in a brass knuckles match," Joe observed. "You can use wrestling holds, and you can hit with your fists. It's a real tough match to

Special referee Joe Louis

Eddie brought Joe into Florida as a special attraction. Unfortunately, Joe was a broken-down shell of the man who had once been a national sports hero. From the first moment I set eyes on him as he shuffled his way into the dressing room, I felt intense sympathy for him.

This disheveled figure, formerly an idol to millions of people around the world, was adorned by an ill-fitting, wrinkled-up sport coat and slacks. Instead of carrying his belongings in a suitcase, the

49

drooping ex-fighter kept his valuables in a standard brown paper sack which would commonly hold groceries.

Joe sat alone with his hands on his knees and didn't really say anything to anybody. It was a depressing image.

Even as a referee, Joe didn't show a great deal of authority in the ring, nor was he particularly animated. This means he didn't lend any heat to the match; he was solely there to have his name on the marquee and attract fans to the event.

Thankfully, Championship Wrestling from Florida was one of the final stops for Joe before he was offered a job in Las Vegas as a greeter at the Frontier Hotel & Casino. At the very least, that new job prevented him from further sullying fans' final memories of him between the ring ropes.

Carrying the Brass Knuckles Championship trophy around was a far bigger pain in the ass than traveling with a belt would have been, because a belt can fit inside of a suitcase, but the trophy would've been broken if I'd attempted to fit it into my luggage. Even so, I liked the idea of the trophy, because it was a visual change of pace from the belts worn by the other champions like the Florida Heavyweight Champion, the Southern Heavyweight Champion and the Florida Tag-Team Champions.

Blading was common during the brass knuckles matches in Florida. I was a little nervous the first time I was asked to "get color" during a match, but most of the nervousness stemmed from the way they asked me to conceal the blade. When some of the guys suggested I carry it in my mouth, I said, "That sounds *really* stupid." If you mishandle a strip of a razor blade in your mouth, all sorts of horrible things could happen. One of the *least* damaging things you could do to yourself would be to simply cut your tongue or your gums. If you *swallowed* the blade, that could be a nightmare.

I usually opted to put the blade in a flap of tape on my finger. You might be wrestling a full 20 minutes before you actually needed to cut yourself or someone else, so the blade needed to be very secure until it was needed. To keep fans from getting wise to the presence of blades, I would commonly tape up four or five fingers so they wouldn't know where to look.

With the Florida Brass Knuckles Trophy

Wrestling without a mask brought changes to my personal life that I hadn't considered before. I was finally recognizable to the public as a wrestler they'd seen on television. To be honest, I wasn't quite sure how to handle it. Not only did I not flaunt or revel in the attention, but I typically withdrew from it as quickly as I could after the autographs had been signed and the photos had been posed for.

Stomping Dale Lewis in Florida

In Florida, there were a *ton* of groupies who would hang around at the wrestling matches, and the majority of them would go after the babyfaces. But don't kid yourself… the heels didn't have *any* problems hooking up with girls if they wanted to. Also, the girls were well aware of the wrestlers' favorite places to hang out after the shows.

When you traveled with guys like Malenko and the other heels, they tended to not hang out in clubs nearly as much as the babyfaces did. Also, Eddie Graham had strict rules about not being seen in public with your opponents, so if the babyfaces staked out a bar or club as their own, there was no way the heels could enter the club and attempt to interact with fans without Graham finding out about it and firing them. I didn't mind this limitation. Despite working in a near main-event-level feud with Malenko, I was still just a shy kid who really didn't understand life. I was still self conscious about my speech impediment, and I preferred to be left alone.

A few times, I traveled with heel midget wrestlers. Little Bruiser and I were cruising home after a show in West Palm, and he was tearing through the back roads at about 75 miles an hour. Out of nowhere, we came across a horse that had wandered into the middle of the road.

Bruiser swerved left to avoid the horse, and then he swung back to the right to get the car back onto the road. Lo and behold, a second horse appeared, and Bruiser repeated his series of swerves. Unfortunately, a *third* brown horse emerged in front of us, and Bruiser plowed into him at about 60 miles an hour. The horse flew clean up over the hood of the car and broke out the windshield in the process. It wasn't long before a state trooper pulled up alongside our wrecked car, and he called someone to give us a ride home. We were very blessed the horse hadn't smashed through the windshield of the car, because it could have crushed us. It almost certainly would have *killed* Little Bruiser.

An average payoff in Florida was between $100 to $200 per match, which was also a hell of a lot better than the $15-to-$25 payoffs I would still have been getting from Stu Hart over that same stretch of time. After I started to make some decent money, I got a nicer apartment at a place called "The River Garden." The River Garden is also where I met my first wife. She was a 5'10" brunette schoolteacher named Elizabeth Mitchell. She came from Griffin, Georgia, where her family had amassed a great deal of wealth due to her grandfather being the founder of the Georgia Power utility company. The family also owned a factory there.

Elizabeth's parents were divorced, and her father had married a young lady who was significantly more attractive than his first wife, which caused a lot of dissention within the family. Unsurprisingly, Elizabeth sided with her mother on most things.

We departed Florida for Georgia after I'd spent about 10 months working for CWF.

FOUR – "Permanent Alimony"

In Griffin, Georgia, Elizabeth's family was like royalty. Their factory employed the majority of the people in the town, and her uncle, who ran the factory, was also the town's *mayor*. Needless to say, if anything happened in Griffin, my in-laws could quickly get it under control.

Our wedding also took place in Griffin. It was nice and traditional, and it was followed with a well-attended reception. Even though having a wrestler as a son-in-law might not have been what they envisioned for their daughter, Elizabeth's parents were always very kind to me, and I never felt as if they had any contempt for my chosen profession.

When I eventually returned to the ring after the honeymoon, it was for Georgia Championship Wrestling. It didn't take very long for me to realize my career had taken a clear backwards step.

Ray Gunkel and Buddy Fuller were the promoters of the territory, and I had no major interaction with them during my time there. Needless to say, neither of them was particularly friendly to me. In most cases, my instructions would come from Leo Garibaldi who was working in matches as well as booking the territory.

Gunkel was a fellow Purdue graduate, albeit is 20 years prior to my own graduation. He'd also been an All-American on the wrestling team. While Buddy Fuller lacked Gunkel's amateur pedigree, he made up for it terms of his professional wrestling bloodline. Buddy's real name was Ed Welch, and he was the son of Roy Fuller, who'd promoted wrestling all over the southern states. Both of them were still active in the ring, which means one or both of them usually had their hands on at least one of the Georgia territory's championships.

Like Fuller, Leo Garibaldi was also a second generation wrestler, having formed a tag team out in California with his father, Gino Garibaldi. Years prior, Leo had wrestled against legends like Gorgeous George and "Classy" Freddie Blassie.

As far as I could tell, Leo handled the majority of the booking decisions. In fact, the only time I ever recall getting instructions for a match from Buddy Fuller was during one of my first appearances. Fuller and Gunkel were wrestling against "The Assassins" and I was the special referee. Like an idiot, I completely forgot what the finish to the match was supposed to be, and my brain fart soon became apparent to all of the wrestlers involved.

"You forgot the finish, didn't you?" Buddy asked me, clearly annoyed.

"Yeah, I sure did," I told him. I clearly wasn't doing very well with my attempts to ingratiate myself with the owners of the territory.

From what I could tell, I'd already blown my opportunity to get pushed as a star in Georgia Championship Wrestling. Having two active wrestlers calling the shots developed Georgia into a very cliquish territory. If you weren't a favorite of Fuller and Gunkel, you had virtually *no* chance of getting pushed. In many ways, wrestling as a heel was one of the safest positions to be in when so many territories were owned or managed by active wrestlers. Since the owners of the territories usually booked themselves as babyfaces, that automatically meant those big-money positions were spoken for. On the other hand, if you wrestled as a heel, you might not get as much attention from the women after the shows, but you had a better chance of earning a big payoff.

The Assassins - Tom Renesto and Jody Hamilton - were always featured on the cards. Of all of the guys in Georgia at that time, Jody was the truest definition of a ring general. He knew what he was doing at all times, and was a very likeable guy behind the scenes. On the other hand, Tom Renesto was a thoroughly detestable guy, and I couldn't fathom why Jody was partnered with him. In my experience with him, Tom was a dishonest man who rarely kept his word.

When it was my turn to perform in matches, they labeled me as "The Spoiler," although they sometimes had me wrestle under my real name as Mike Davis. Although I was only in Georgia for a few months, my time in GCW overlapped with the brief but noteworthy career of the infamous "Killer" Sam Sheppard.

Sam's wife, Marilyn Sheppard, was beaten to death in their suburban Cleveland home on July 4th, 1954. Sam reported that he'd confronted an intruder, only to be knocked out on two separate occasions. He later woke up with half of his body dangling in Lake Erie.

Despite the fact that Sam was very clearly distraught and disoriented, suffered obvious injuries, and several of his most valuable possessions were missing from the house after the incident, local media coverage placed the blame squarely on his shoulders. He was ultimately convicted of second-degree murder and sentenced to life in prison on December 21st, 1954. Within one month of Sam's conviction, his mother committed suicide, and his father died of stomach cancer.

Finally, after serving more than ten years in prison, Sam's case was declared to be a "mockery of justice" by the U.S. district court, and he was released from prison. He married the sister-in-law of the infamous Nazi propagandist Joseph Goebbels, which did nothing to endear him to the American public. Sam was later retried and found "not guilty."

While Sam was in the midst of clearing his name, the television series "The Fugitive," starring David Janssen, was enjoying a four-season run as a popular show on ABC. By 1969, Sam had gotten divorced from his second wife, and had essentially been sued out of the medical profession. He'd gotten married for a third time; his final marriage was to Colleen Strickland, the daughter of wrestler George Strickland.

George trained Sam to wrestle, and he became an instant attraction despite having a strong penchant for alcohol and none of the requisite traits of a professional wrestler, like a good physique, athleticism or charisma.

Despite these blatant shortcomings, Sam was a special attraction for GCW. Typically, Sam would get the hot tag and save the day after the heels had gotten the heat on his partner. Mentally, Sam wasn't all there, and there was nothing he could do to make his offense look convincing against any of the full-time wrestlers. He was *hopeless.*

After one of these piss-poor matches involving Sam, Tom Renesto and I were walking in Sam's direction while we were all positioned alongside the ring out on the arena floor. As we got near him, Sam began to throw some abominable looking punches at us which we struggled to sell convincingly.

"Forget it!" Tom said, frustrated. "Just walk by him!"

Immediately, the two of us stopped selling the punches and resumed our walk to the dressing room while Sam continued to flail away, oblivious to the fact that we were ignoring him and were through with selling his pathetic offense.

It wasn't long afterward that Sam died of liver failure at his home in Columbus, Ohio. Apparently, he was drinking *liters* of liquor every day. Although his professional wrestling career only lasted about 40 matches, his "mandible claw" tongue-depression finishing hold would be revived decades later by Mick Foley and become world famous.

As far as Georgia is concerned, I simply didn't care for it. Florida was a much more cosmopolitan and laid-back place, whereas Georgians came closer to matching the traditional redneck stereotype. Obviously, there were some exceptions to this rule, but my overall experience in Georgia was negative, and GCW just wasn't the place for me.

Fortunately, for the sake of my marriage, I was able to come home almost every night. Only when we wrestled in Savannah did I have to stay overnight in another town. We also had shows in Macon, Atlanta and Columbus.

Fred Ward was the promoter in Columbus, and he had some clear animosity with Fuller and Gunkel. I understood the issue to be over talent exchanges, and a general lack of teamwork as they all attempted to promote in different cities within the same state.

Promotional conflicts aside, I wasn't being used in nearly as many shows as I thought I should have been. Certainly, given the connections I had within my wife's family, I could have easily gotten a job at the factory and supplemented my income, but I was still primarily interested in furthering my wrestling career. I needed a way to escape from that situation.

During a phone call with my buddy Tarzan Tyler, who I'd become friends with in Florida, an opportunity was presented for me to get out of Georgia and reinvigorate my stalled career.

"I'm sure we can use your help here in Omaha," Tarzan said. "Let me talk it over with Joe Dusek and see if we can't get you on the cards here."

Tarzan made good on his word. I gave my notice to Gunkel and Fuller, and I packed everything up and moved with my wife to Omaha, Nebraska, ready to start wrestling for my fourth territory in three years. Elizabeth was surprisingly supportive of my desire to switch promotions and jump to Nebraska. Undoubtedly, she would be much further from the veil of protection provided by her family in Griffin.

Joe Dusek was the promoter for All Star Wrestling in Omaha, and his brother, Ernie Dusek, did a host of things, including refereeing the matches and hauling the ring around. They were both over 60 years old and fervently set in their ways. Along with their brothers Rudy and Emil, they had collectively been part of a famous wrestling family that had dominated the wrestling scene in Nebraska for generations. In the late '60s, they'd affiliated themselves with the American Wrestling Association which was headquartered in Minneapolis, Minnesota and owned by the legendary wrestler Verne Gagne. When that partnership was forged, several of the Nebraska championships were converted into championships nominally sanctioned by Gagne's AWA.

Tarzan Tyler was living in a very nice apartment, and Elizabeth and I got an apartment in the same building because we also wanted to enjoy a high-caliber living arrangement. When Joe Dusek heard about my choice of accommodations, he seemed more than a little concerned about my decision.

"I think that apartment might be a little *too* expensive for you, Mike," Joe warned me. "Or, maybe I should say, it's a little too expensive for you while you're working in *this* territory."

When the promoter of the territory tells you that your standard of living is too high for his territory, it's *never* a good sign! I knew right then and there I was in no danger of getting rich while wrestling for the Duseks in Omaha.

"Beautiful" Brutus in Omaha

In Omaha, I was once again known as "Beautiful Brutus."
The Duseks had me win their AWA Midwest Heavyweight
Championship in April of 1970, and from there I main evented
against guys like "Cowboy" Bob Ellis. Ellis was a guy I watched
regularly during my childhood in Indiana, and he was promoted as
one of the few guys in the area who could give Dick the Bruiser a
stiff challenge inside the ring.

Dropping the big elbow

It soon became all too clear why wrestlers all referred to it as
the "Omaha" territory as opposed to the "Nebraska" territory; the
Duseks rarely ran any shows outside the city of Omaha. In fact,
compared with most territories, the Duseks hardly ran *any* shows at
all!

Occasionally we did some spot shows, like a show we did
out in western Nebraska. The distance from Omaha to that small
town was about 300 miles, and when we got there, a sign posted on
the side of the road listed the town's population as 360 people.

"Why the hell are we coming to a town that only has 360 people?!" I asked my travel companions. No one had a good answer for me.

We pulled up to a high school in the town, and it somehow had more than 1,000 people in attendance. I was shocked. Somehow, they attracted three times the population of the town the venue was in. To me, this indicated the wrestling product was popular in the state, but we just didn't run enough shows to earn money. Outside of working in Omaha and occasionally Lincoln, we spent most of our time sitting around, hating life, and regretting the decisions we'd made to work there. At most, we worked three times a week, and sometimes we would only work *once* a week.

After one of our spot shows, some of the locals decided to take the wrestlers out to get some food and drinks. I absolutely overdid it on the drinking end of the spectrum. When we were finished, I staggered back to my car, climbed inside, and began driving back to my apartment in Omaha.

Whether it was as the result of any speeding or swerving I might have been doing, I can't say, but the manner in which I was driving attracted the attention of a Nebraska State Trooper. Once I'd pulled my car to the side of the road, I recalled the words a veteran wrestler once told me about what I should do in situations like that: "Get out of the car and show the officer that you're no threat."

Intending to capitalize on those words of wisdom, I climbed out of the car and instantly lost my balance. Realizing how *terrible* it would look to the trooper if I couldn't stand upright, I threw myself backward against the car and leaned against it with all of my strength just to stay on my feet. As I struggled, the *shortest* Nebraska State Trooper you've ever seen in your life approached me. He could generously be described as standing five-and-a-half feet tall, which means he was about chest high to me.

The trooper and I conversed for a short while, and I have zero recollection of what words were exchanged, but he unexpectedly allowed me to leave. By the grace of God, I managed to return to Omaha safely. To this day, I can't imagine why the trooper would have let me drive home under my own power.

Realizing Omaha was a dead end, I shifted my focus and started looking for other places to work. I soon got a job working for Dory Funk's Western States Sports promotion based in Amarillo, Texas. They ran far more shows than the Omaha promotion, but the distance between towns was brutal, and the pay was *horrendous*. At least in Georgia the towns were close to one another, but Texas was a traveler's nightmare. The wrestlers would constantly complain about their cars being run to death as they crisscrossed the state.

Elizabeth stayed behind in Omaha while I worked my way through the Amarillo territory to get a feel for whether or not I could stomach working there on a more permanent basis. It would have made no sense to take her with me because I wouldn't have been able to spend any time with her even if I'd wanted to.

Dory Funk conducted himself like he was one of the boys, and I don't mean that in an endearing way. He had a very young wife named Betty, but he was still regularly drinking and chasing women with the rest of the roster. His son, Dory Funk Jr., was the reigning NWA World Heavyweight Champion at that time, and I was actually in attendance when his title reign commenced. Dory Jr. beat Gene Kiniski on February 11th, 1969, which was also my first night with Championship Wrestling from Florida. Despite this lofty achievement of Junior's, the boys all seemed to think the real talent belonged to Terry, the younger of the two Funk brothers. Dory Jr. was such a paint-by-the-numbers wrestler, whereas Terry imbued his matches with far more fire and creativity.

Once I gave up on Amarillo, I returned to Omaha and resumed wrestling for the Duseks, but I was still upset to not be making much money, and I was also upset because I didn't feel like I was improving my skills by working in so few shows. Finally, after constantly hearing about the quality of the wrestling in San Francisco, I made the decision to travel out there to work for Roy Shire, a wrestler I'd idolized in my youth when I watched his matches in Indianapolis. I knew I would improve exponentially if I could find regular work in matches with the legendary performers on Roy's roster, like Pat Patterson and Ray Stevens.

Brute Power: The Autobiography of Buggsy McGraw

I wrote Roy a letter which carefully expressed my strong desire to work for him and why, and he quickly responded and offered me a job in San Francisco. I was *ecstatic*.

By this point, Elizabeth's patience with being a wrestler's wife had all run out. She was tired of my endless travel schedule, my constant career uncertainty, any my rapidly changing life trajectory. The idea of moving to San Francisco on a whim, and living so far from her family in Georgia, was the final straw. Elizabeth packed her things and returned to Griffin, and I never really saw her again.

Soon after, Elizabeth's divorce attorney sent me a simple letter identifying who he was, and requesting "permanent alimony" on her behalf. I was sympathetic to her position, but there was no way in *hell* that was happening!

I contacted a friend who was a former judge; he was working as a lawyer at the time. I read the letter from Elizabeth's attorney to him which explained how my wife was seeking to squeeze guaranteed money out of me and turn me into a wage slave for the rest of my life.

"Ha! I'll take care of *that*!" he said.

I flew home to Indianapolis in the midst of one of worst snowstorms in the history of the region, and the snowfall got progressively worse after I landed. Obviously, my divorce proceedings were vitally important to me, and I was deathly afraid of how the snowstorm might hinder the ability of key legal people to involve themselves in a divorce case that had "permanent alimony" on the line.

It turns out, I was right to be worried; the judge couldn't get his car out of the garage. Fortunately for me, the judge handling my divorce was one of the most conscientious judges I've ever encountered. As a favor to my lawyer, he actually trudged through the snow to a bus stop and took a bus to the courthouse in order to hear my case. Inside the courtroom, the only people who showed up were the judge, my attorney, my father and myself. The snow had kept everyone else away.

After I'd been sworn in, the very next thing the judge said to me was, "So, Mr. Davis... Please tell me about your *wrestling* career."

As luck would have it, the judge was a *huge* wrestling fan, and nearly every question he asked me had to do with wrestling!

When I answered enough questions to satisfy his curiosity, the judge returned to the matter at hand.

"On the divorce," the judge began, as if it was an afterthought, "Is there any chance the two of you might be able to reconcile?"

"No!" I replied.

With that, the judge banged his gavel down.

"The divorce is *final*," he said, before adding, "*No* alimony."

That just proved to me that sometimes it truly does pay to be a pro wrestler.

FIVE – "Heels don't apologize"

Roy Shire's "Big Time Wrestling" company officially joined the National Wrestling Alliance just a couple years before I arrived in San Francisco. Once Roy decided to retire from wrestling and promote shows in the Bay Area, he brought a whole slew of performers with him who he'd worked with in Indianapolis, including Wilbur Snyder, Bob Ellis and his gimmick brother Ray Shire. Once he arrived in San Francisco, Ray would revert to using his real last name of "Stevens," and go on to become a household name in Northern California.

Headlocked by the great Ray Stevens

Brute Power: The Autobiography of Buggsy McGraw

With Ray Stevens in his arsenal, Shire ran the prior promoter in the region, Joe Malcewicz, right out of town. By 1962, he was the undisputed king of San Francisco, and his locker room continued to fill with some of greatest performers in the industry. Right alongside Ray Stevens was Pat Patterson, and the two formed a legendary duo known as "The Blond Bombers." Not only were they financially successful, but they developed a reputation among wrestling industry insiders as the very best tag team in the world, comprising two of the greatest individual ring talents the business had ever seen. As a young wrestler, I felt privileged to have an opportunity to work with them.

In addition to Stevens and Patterson, both the Samoan wrestler "High Chief" Peter Maivia, and the Afro-Canadian wrestler "Soul Man" Rocky Johnson were working in San Francisco when I arrived. There were plenty of Polynesian and black wrestling fans in Northern California, and Maivia and Johnson were very popular with those respective ethnic groups. Shortly after I left San Francisco, Johnson would have a son named Dwayne with Maivia's daughter, Ata. Everyone who follows either wrestling or feature films knows about the successes Dwayne "The Rock" Johnson would go on to have as a megastar in both the wrestling ring and in Hollywood.

Rechristened by Shire as "The Mighty Brutus," I began to work in a Northern California territory that included San Francisco, Sacramento, San Jose and Fresno, and extended as far away as Reno and Las Vegas when we did shows in Nevada every six weeks. Many of the wrestlers lived across the bridge in Hayward to save money on housing, but I decided to find an apartment in Fremont. Located in Daly City, the Cow Palace was the unchallenged headquarters of Shire's major wrestling events. If the local fans found the wrestling card to be intriguing and worth watching, the Cow Palace could easily accommodate more than 15,000 of them.

As of this writing, Pat Patterson has fully disclosed his homosexuality to the world, but in San Francisco, his sexual orientation was not yet public knowledge. During one of his reigns as the United States Heavyweight Champion, he got into a physical altercation at a gay bar with a huge, bull-dyke lesbian. She beat the crap out of him and knocked him out cold.

The San Francisco Examiner actually ran the story about the incident under the headline "U.S. Champ Knocked Out By Woman," which was thoroughly embarrassing for the promotion, and especially for Pat. During my stay in San Francisco, the guys in the locker room were constantly whispering about it, but no one would dare bring it up to Pat; not only was he a top star, but he was also the de facto booker for the territory. If you crossed him, he could find plenty of ways to bury you before Shire sent you packing.

To me, Pat only seemed to be looking out for himself. In the ring, he was one of the best around, although there was a clear talent disparity between Pat and Stevens. No one would dare say Pat was better than Stevens in the ring. I was also never very impressed with Pat's interviews, partially because his French-Canadian accent was so thick, and it made it difficult for anyone to understand what he was saying. On the other hand, Stevens didn't insert himself into any of the affairs in the office. His spot as the ace of the territory was secure, and he took care of his business in the ring.

Despite having a major star who was a homosexual and the image that might convey, Roy Shire was a *pure* alpha male. I don't know if he was compensating for something or not, but he would strut around arrogantly in the locker room, puffing away on his cigar, and speaking to the wrestlers in a very condescending manner. When he passed out paychecks to the boys during our TV tapings in Sacramento, he would call our names individually and then dismissively throw our checks at us one at a time.

Seeing Roy behave this way was personally very disappointing to me. I'd admired Roy and been a fan of his as a child in Indiana. Quite simply, he *wasn't* a pleasant man to be around.

We were on the road headed to a show in Reno, and Pat was riding with Roy. Suddenly, a pack of about a dozen Hell's Angels biker gang members roared by. Unwisely, Roy took it upon himself to act macho and gesture threateningly toward the Hell's Angels while they were in transit. The Angels managed to force Roy's car to come to a stop, and then they yanked Roy out of the car and kicked the shit out of him. All the while, Pat Patterson refused to budge from the front seat or come to Roy's aid in any way.

Plenty of other people retaliated against Roy for his offensive behaviors. The lady Roy was dating when I got to San Francisco was a Playboy Playmate. In order to begin dating the Big Time Wrestling owner, first the girl had to break up with the U.S. Marine she'd been seeing. Undaunted by Roy's reputation as a professional wrestler, the marine waited outside the office, jumped Roy in the parking lot, and beat the shit out of him. After Shire was finished screwing around with the young lady and broke up with her, he decided it was best to remain on good terms with her and sent her a check for $200. A few days later, a truck filled with $200 worth of horseshit pulled up to the Sacramento TV station and dumped manure directly in front of the entrance to the building.

Working in San Francisco gave me the rapid realization that I had to get in better shape if I was going to keep up with the area's top workers. I couldn't just get by on my size and strength anymore. Contending with guys like Stevens, Patterson, Johnson and Maivia, you had to be able to move. Cyclone Negro was another guy on that roster who could also get up and down the ring if he felt like it.

Not only could Maivia move, but he was deceptively strong. During a six-man tag match in Stockton, Maivia and I got into it because he kept making derogatory comments about me. When we went to the mat, he hooked me and tried to hold me down. To his surprise, I grabbed his hands and separated them by simply wrenching them apart. That show of strength caught the High Chief by surprise. He didn't expect me to be nearly that strong.

Sensing that things were about to get ugly, Ray Stevens jumped in the ring to try to prevent a shoot from breaking out. He told me later on in the dressing room that his old-timer instinct kicked in, and he thought Maivia and I were about to have a brawl. Contrary to what Stevens thought, I didn't perceive the situation as being all that serious; Maivia was trying to show the young guy how strong he was, so I needed to prove my own capabilities to him.

The first time I wrestled at the Cow Palace, I encountered the security guards who were waiting at the bottom of the steps to escort me out to the ring. They were attired in full riot gear, complete with face shields and nightsticks. When the officer in charge saw me coming, he asked me only one question: "Are you ready?"

When I answered him in the affirmative, he signaled to his crew to pull down their face shields and extract their nightsticks from their holsters. From there, I was ushered off into the mob. Both to and from the ring, the security team poked and bashed spectators with the nightsticks without hesitation just to keep them away from me. If we didn't have that level of protection, the Cow Palace fans probably would have killed every heel on the roster during every single show. It was a very scary way to have to get to work!

Rocky Johnson and I had a fairly noteworthy feud centered around the city of Sacramento. The two of us were booked for an upcoming main event match there, and I was preparing for my interview at the KTVU television station to promote the match. We did our TV tapings there every Wednesday with Hank Martin on commentary. We had to do separate interviews for each town's broadcast, so we would end up more or less repeating ourselves, and then localizing some of the interview's content for each city.

Roy Shire came to me and said, "You're going to wrestle Rocky Johnson in Sacramento. I want you to get *really* heavy on Rocky during this interview. I want the fans really invested in this match."

"No problem, Roy!" I told him as I walked out to do the interview. "I've got this."

I can't really explain it, but my speech impediment never really kicked in on interviews. I would get focused, start talking, and the words would just pour out of me without hesitation. As I came out on camera, I began puffing away on my cigar, doing my best Dick the Bruiser impression. Then, in accordance with Roy's instructions, I proceeded to unleash a promo on Rocky during which I probably said every superficially racist thing I could think of *without* using any actual racial slurs.

"Rocky, do you *really* think you deserve to be in the ring with me?" I asked him. "Look at how big and strong I am, and then look at you! You should be picking *cotton*! You should be a *janitor* somewhere! You should be working at a *carwash*! Why would you even *think* about wrestling me?"

The TV station aired the interview as planned, and no one said a thing to me after its initial release. However, some members of the NAACP were watching, and they had *plenty* to say about it! A few days later, they marched outside of the station in protest. These actions made the station managers concerned about potential riots, and they relayed their concerns to Shire.

"Mike, what the hell were you thinking?!" Shire asked as he lit into me. "*Why* would you say all of those things?!"

"*You* told me to, Roy!" I replied. "You said to go heavy on Rocky, so I went *heavy* on Rocky!"

The Sacramento Bee also ran with the story about the protest march at the station. These were all good things as far as I was concerned! I did what I was asked to do as a heel in order to attract a crowd and make us all money.

When I went out the next week to do a follow-up interview, Roy was waiting for me at the station.

"You've *got* to apologize," Roy instructed me.

"What?" I said. "Why? *Heels* don't apologize for getting heat."

"*You* do," Shire insisted. "Go out there and apologize for what you said about Rocky."

Fortunately, we constructed the "apology" in a manner that would help me maintain my heel heat. Hank Renner stood next to me and said, "This is the Mighty Brutus. Last week, he said a host of somewhat derogatory things about Rocky Johnson. He said Rocky should be picking cotton, working as a janitor, or working at a car wash."

Renner then turned to me and said, "Brutus, you want to apologize for saying these things; isn't that right?"

"Yes, it is," I said, quickly and sarcastically, before walking away. That just got people even *angrier*!

71

After all of that, the crowd for the actual match between Rocky and I was only mediocre. Shire later told us the match was booked for the time of the month before the state government employees in Sacramento received their paychecks. That was a downer, because I was out to make as much money as I possibly could, and Roy's payoffs were better than most other territories whether you were working in the main event or not. We also didn't run each town every week, which gave us plenty of time off.

Despite my dreams of working with Ray Stevens, I only competed in two matches with him during my initial run in San Francisco. Our first match was in the main event at Sacramento, and we worked a finish where the referee halted the match due to blood loss. Shire had no plans to give me another main event match, so I shared an idea with him in order to get another shot at Ray.

"Can I have a match on top with Ray if I offer up my hair?" I asked Shire.

"And you'll lose, right?" asked Shire.

"Of course!" I replied. "I'll cut it all off. I don't care. I just want the match."

"Okay… yeah!" Shire agreed. "That would be great!"

Stevens and I had our rematch in a best-of-three-falls match in Sacramento. I scored the first pinfall, but Stevens secured the win by taking the next two falls, with the final fall coming in disputed fashion as all four of our shoulders were pinned to the mat. I had the dominant position, but the referee conveniently couldn't see it. When the barber entered the ring, I fled the scene and ran up the aisle, only to be met by Maivia, Martin, Johnson and Parisi. The babyfaces all ushered me back to the ring and held me down to the mat while the barber shaved my head to the delight of the crowd.

Maivia and Johnson restrain Brutus for a haircut

It was also in San Francisco that I first started hanging out with Lonnie Mayne. Shire booked us as a tag team and Lonnie quickly became one of the best friends I would ever have in the wrestling business.

Lonnie's real name was Ronald, and he usually sported an unkempt, blonde beard to go with his equally mangy hair. Before coming to San Francisco, Lonnie had an absolutely legendary run as a main eventer in Portland. Between 1966 and 1970, Mayne held the NWA Pacific Northwest Heavyweight Championship - the top title in the territory - 11 different times. This overlapped with 12 separate reigns as one half of the NWA Pacific Northwest Tag Team Champions. Years later, when assessing the performers of the era, *Ring Around the Northwest Newsletter* retroactively awarded Lonnie the title of "Wrestler of the Year" for every year between 1967 and 1970.

More than any other wrestler, Lonnie might have been the biggest influence on my wrestling style. He had a reputation as a *big* bump taker for that era who always made the babyfaces look amazing. He would even take bumps from the top rope out to the concrete floor. Undeniably, Lonnie was a crazy man both in and out of the ring, and when I was out with him, I'd get crazy as well.

Our time in San Francisco overlapped with the murder spree of the famous Zodiac Killer. When Lonnie and I were drunk and driving around town one night, Lonnie suggested that we go out to the Fillmore neighborhood of San Francisco and try to look vulnerable so Zodiac would try to take a shot at us and we could beat his ass and bring him in.

"That son of a bitch is out here killin' people!" Lonnie slurred. "You and me can put a stop to this! If we go looking for him, we just might find him!"

"Sure!" I responded back to him. "Let's go!"

Keep in mind, the *police* wouldn't even go to the Fillmore during the early '70s. We must have been the right combination of drunk, stupid and bored, because we spent the better part of the night driving around San Francisco as vigilante crime fighters hoping a *serial killer* would take a shot at us so that we could take him into custody.

Without question, Lonnie was the epitome of an alcoholic, and nearly every time I was around him, liquor was involved. When Lonnie and I drove to our events in Fresno, Lonnie would customarily down an entire pint of Southern Comfort during the two-and-a-half hour car ride. Then he would wrestle completely stoned. On the way back to San Francisco, Lonnie would finish off either a quart of Southern Comfort or a quart of vodka. He would replicate this on *every* trip.

Even Lonnie was shocked by the quantities of liquor he could consume. He once enlisted my aid to see if we could determine exactly what his limits were. I went to Lonnie's apartment and supervised while he consumed three quarts of vodka before passing out. An average individual would have been dead *long* before then.

Another time, Lonnie got into a drinking contest with some *really* big guy at a local bar, and the rules of their game permitted you to drink whatever you wanted, and the other person had to match it. When Lonnie realized he might not be able to outdrink this guy when it came to liquor, he reached for a quart of motor oil and drank that instead. The other guy quit *immediately*.

Lighting up after a match in San Francisco

SIX – "I'll have you blackballed"

After 10 months in San Francisco, I decided it was time to move on again. Shire did me a favor and arranged for me to work for his old Indianapolis promoter, Jim Barnett, who was now running shows in Australia. Once he left behind his wrestling territories in the mainland United States, Barnett founded World Championship Wrestling in Sydney, Australia in 1964, and started promoting under the International Wrestling Alliance name. After nearly six years of operating as a territory with its own world champion, Barnett's WCW finally joined the National Wrestling Alliance in 1970 and the world championship was downgraded from a "world championship" to the NWA Austra-Asian Heavyweight Championship. Perhaps having the level of their championship devalued was a disincentive for Australian wrestling fans to attend events. Whatever the reason was for the decline in interest, Barnett was having tremendous difficulties in Australia when I arrived. His business had taken a massive downturn, and he was trying to cut costs everywhere.

His partner, in both a business sense and a relationship sense, was named Lonnie. During my first week in Sydney, Lonnie was stomping around the dressing room yelling at us all, saying, "I'm telling Jim to close the territory down!" This wasn't welcome news to a guy who'd just traveled a very long way from home with dreams of furthering his wrestling career!

The first few weeks I was in Sydney, I stayed at the Plaza Hotel, which was *not* a great place to live. Later on, I moved into a room at the Texas Tavern, which was a large building that contained several bars and restaurants.

The distance between Australian cities was extraordinarily long for it to honestly be considered a cohesive wrestling territory. From Sydney to Melbourne alone was a 500 mile trip, and then we'd go another 450 miles to Adelaide. That alone would be comparable to a trip from the Sheik's office in Detroit, Michigan to Eddie Graham's office in Tampa, Florida. Occasionally, we would also perform in Hobart on the island of Tasmania. Thankfully, Jim arranged for us to fly almost everywhere, because driving those distances on a regular basis would've *killed* us all!

Right away, Jim put me in main event matches against Mario Milano, who'd established Melbourne as his home. We worked for an hour every night, doing one-hour broadways in every town we visited. Mario was an Italian whose real last name was Bulfone. He'd grown up in Venezuela, moved to Australia on what was initially a three-month deal, and loved Australia so much that he never left.

As a young guy in the business, I was very concerned about the rumors Lonnie was spreading about the territory potentially shutting down. The shows weren't well attended, and Milano and I were the only two who seemed to be holding the company together.

After a few weeks, I phoned Ed Francis over in Hawaii and asked, "Ed... can you get me on your cards out there?"

"Absolutely!" Ed said. "We'd be happy to have you. Give Jim your notice."

I immediately went to the office to see Jim and told him, point blank, "Jim.... I'm leaving. I'm going to wrestle in Hawaii."

Jim's face flushed with anger.

"No, you're *not!*" Jim replied, gruffly.

"Yes, I am," I reiterated. "It's already done. I already talked to Ed."

"Well, I can talk to Ed and let him know you're *not* coming!" Jim yelled.

"Jim, I *already* told Ed I'm leaving," I said. "I've *got* to go!"

"If you leave me, I'll have you *blackballed!*" Jim threatened.

Coming from a powerful, well-established promoter like Jim Barnett, the threat of being blackballed from the industry was palpable. If he was determined to make my life miserable and to keep me from getting booked as a wrestler, he could almost certainly accomplish his goal.

"Okay; I'm staying," I relented. "You win."

If I tell someone I'm going to do something, I do it, so having to bail on my agreement with Ed Francis bothered me immensely.

Shortly after my argument with Jim, I was approached at the bar of The Texas Tavern by a very attractive lady. The two of us hooked up and began seeing each other regularly, but the relationship died out after only a few months. Once we stopped seeing one another, this woman became very friendly with some of the other wrestlers in the promotion, and she wasn't really making any efforts to hide it from me. I later learned from one of the WCW announcers that this woman was a professional prostitute who'd been hired by Jim Barnett to "keep me happy" while I was in Australia. This was apparently a regular tactic Jim used to make the talent forget about their homesickness and other problems.

On one occasion, I even overheard a conversation between Jim and one of the other announcers as they discussed the likelihood that one of the boys might have been leaving Australia and looking to ply his trade elsewhere.

"No, I don't think he's going to be leaving," Jim smugly told the announcer. "I know who he's been *fucking*."

The night before, the wrestlers had all been at The Texas Tavern, and when that same wrestler got up to leave, the prostitute I'd been in a relationship with immediately shot out of her chair and said, "I gotta go!" She darted after the departing wrestler as if it was her job, because it literally *was* her job.

I certainly didn't enjoy being manipulated by Jim, but the way I viewed it, the real manipulation came when he threatened to blackball me from the industry and forced me to break my promise to Ed Francis. In Jim's eyes, the prostitute was just a backup plan. If he'd *really* wanted to make me happy, he would've figured out a way to make me some more money!

My program with Milano eventually began to turn things around for Jim at the box office, because Jim began bringing more wrestling talent to the territory, including Killer Karl Kox. When Kox showed up, that's when the territory *really* started to pop. Kox was one of the true brilliant workers in our profession, both in and out of the ring. He truly excelled at talking fans into the building. He also excelled at convincing Jim Barnett to do what he wanted. Any time I wanted a key piece of information from Jim, I would bring Karl along with me, because Jim would *never* lie to Karl.

Dropping elbows on a VW with Killer Karl Kox

Jim had Karl and I work a lot as a tag team, which created an opportunity for Karl to take me under his wing. It was a pairing I relished being a part of. I was the young guy of the tandem, flying around the ring and taking all kinds of bumps for the sake of the team. Between the two of us, I was absolutely taking the lion's share of the bumps during our matches, but I didn't care at all; I was having a *great* time. When we were in the ring, I would listen to Karl and watch everything he did, like an apprentice watching a master craftsman. After matches, I would listen to Karl's critiques and ask him questions about why he did what he did when he did it. I didn't know when I'd ever have the opportunity again to be partnered up with someone who was such an outstanding veteran worker, and I wanted to learn everything I could while I had the chance!

Karl was so skilled at getting under the fans' collective skins that he could start a riot with a simple piece of *tape* from his hand. He would wrap the tape around the palm of his hand, and then put a few of his opponent's fingers inside of the tape. When that wrestler would overpower Karl and try to break a hold, he wouldn't be able to get away completely because his hands were wrapped in the tape, and Karl would yank him back into a hold. Simple tricks like this helped Karl raise the ire of the fans and draw a lot of money. Once the promotion and the boys were all making more money, working in Australia was a *blast*.

With WCW now humming along, Jim brought in Haystacks Calhoun, and also brought veterans Mark Lewin and King Curtis Iaukea back to the territory. Lewin and Iaukea often traveled together from promotion to promotion, so booking them was often a package deal.

During our time off, Karl and I would hang out at Bonsai Beach with some of the friends he'd made during prior visits to Sydney. Bonsai Beach had signs on it that said "no dogs allowed" which had me curious as to why there wouldn't be dogs allowed there. I was later told about how sharks were able to detect the odors of dogs more readily than they could detect the scent of humans, and the smell of dogs would then attract sharks to the beaches. I was still going to the gym to lift weights whenever I could, and I also got involved with another lady for awhile. To my great relief, this one *wasn't* a prostitute.

Whenever I met someone in public and thought there was a chance of becoming a true friend with them, I would loosen up.

However, if I was interacting with random people on the street, I would give them a bit of a show and remind them I was a heel.

Hunting kangaroos with the midget wrestlers

My oddest day off in Australia involved the time I went kangaroo hunting in the Outback with the midget wrestlers. Little Bruiser, Little Crusher and I actually managed to shoot and kill a kangaroo only to discover it was a female with a joey in its pouch. The discovery of the joey actually depressed me a little bit. When we pulled it out of the pouch, the joey became scared and unleashed a stream of crap all over the place.

As we were deciding what to do with this orphaned joey, an Australian guy on horseback came upon us out in the forest.

"G'day, gents," he said. "What've you got there?"

I held out the joey and showed it to the man.

"We just shot his mom," I explained. "I'm not sure what to do with him."

"Give him to me," the guy instructed me. "I'll take care of him."

"You're not going to eat him are you?" I asked, glancing at the .22 caliber rifle slung over the man's shoulder.

81

"Hell no!" the man said. "Only part of a kangaroo that's good to eat anyway is the tail. The rest'll have worms in it."

The man followed the gaze of my eyes over to his rifle, glanced down at it, and then looked back up and grinned.

"I shoot rabbits with this," the man said, raising the rifle. "That's how I earn a livin'. I don't hunt kangaroos. You can trust me. I'll take good care of him."

Clearly, I didn't have designs on doing anything with a baby kangaroo, and handing the joey off to this man seemed like a much better idea than leaving it in the Outback to fend for itself. I passed the joey to the man as it kicked its feet frantically. The rabbit hunter pulled the kangaroo into his lap, nodded to me, and then turned and rode off with his new pet.

With his business now running smoothly, Barnett ultimately warmed to the idea of allowing me to move on to another territory, but he would only let me go after WCW's seasonal swing through Hong Kong and Malaysia. The Malaysia trip was a transitional trip for incoming and outgoing talent. Newcomers came in, and those who were leaving would depart for their next territories.

In Hong Kong, we wrestled at the outdoor soccer stadium, which was a *massive* venue for a wrestling event. It could've held 50,000 people if it was filled to capacity. Jim always made sure there was ample security on hand in the form of the British police, which is something we *absolutely* required while we were there. I don't know if we truly sold out the soccer stadium, but it *definitely* looked like it was full. The ring was dead in the center of the soccer field. When I was through wrestling, I was escorted back to the dressing room by a six-man British police escort: Two in front of me, one on each side of me, and two behind me. Right before we reached the dressing room door, one of the Chinese fans chucked an orange in my direction with a perfect arc to his throw. The orange bent in its flight and struck me directly in my right eye.

The force of the blow to my eye dropped me straight to my knees. In that sea of humanity, I was a sitting duck. Without hesitation, as if this sort of thing happened all the time, the two guards at my sides each put an arm under my shoulders, scooped me off the ground, and propelled me forward. I don't think I was even down on the ground for even more than one second. Those guards were fearless, and completely unphased.

After his men dragged me the rest of the way into the locker room, the captain of the guard approached me while wearing his flared pants and his riding crop. He was pounding his leg, clearly pissed off because this whole ordeal had made his security team look ineffective.

"You go out there and you *find* that little son of a bitch, *now!*" he screamed to the subordinate guards.

Dutifully, the security team turned and ran back through the door in search of the offender; I have no idea if they ever found that guy or not, but if they had, they should've signed him to a major league baseball contract considering how hard and precise that throw was.

Our tour moved on to Singapore. Barnett loved to have meetings, and he expected everyone to show up on time or he would get enraged. Thankfully, the meetings during the tour would usually take place in one of the hotel rooms, which no one minded because Barnett was always sure to set us up in some of the best hotels when we toured. That was one of the major perks of working for Jim.

Curtis Iaukea and Jerry Brisco were late to the meeting, which clearly irritated Barnett.

"Where are Curtis and Jerry?" Barnett kept asking. "Have any of you boys seen them?"

After Barnett said that for about the eighth time, Curtis and Jerry walked in, and it became clear why they were late to the meeting. The two of them had managed to find a shop in town that sold opium cigars, and they were both as high as you could possibly be. They leaned up against the wall and slid right down to the floor.

"Sorry, Jim," Jerry said, in a very relaxed voice. "We're here."

Later in the tour, I wrestled Jerry in Kuala Lumpur. For the record, he managed to abstain from opium during that leg of the trip, and it was good thing, too. Malaysia was one of the *hottest* places I've ever been to in my life, and it was impossible to keep yourself from sweating. Of course, Barnett asked Jerry and I to do a 20-minute Broadway in the most *ridiculous* heat we'd ever encountered.

Carrying fans around during a tour of Southeast Asia

"You two are going to go 20 minutes through," Barnett informed us. I just shook my head and wondered what I'd done to piss Barnett off. If he was angry with Jerry for showing up late and high to the meeting, that was fine, but he didn't have to take it out on *me*!

Before the match even started, Jerry and I were both dripping with sweat, and by the time it was over with, we'd each probably lost 15 pounds of water weight. The first thing I wanted to do when I got back to the locker room was to get a drink of water, but *no one* had any!

Brute Power: The Autobiography of Buggsy McGraw

I hopped in the shower as soon as I got back from the ring. We'd all been told not to drink the water in Malaysia under *any* circumstances. Well, the water in the shower had the fresh smell of well water to it, which was very inviting. It took every ounce of self control I could muster not to take in a few sips! Once my shower was finished, I left the dressing room, which was located at the top of the stands, and I looked through to the other side of the fence and saw a Coke machine, which got me pretty excited.

In Malaysia, Jim's security force was hired directly out of the Malaysian army. They were a non-nonsense group armed with handguns and rifles, and they patrolled the premises in military trucks. I motioned to one of the guards to come over to the fence, and then I tried to pass him some money through the dirty steel wire.

"Coca Cola!" I told him as I handed him coins and pointed to the machine. "Thirsty! Thirsty! Coca Cola!"

The guard didn't seem to comprehend anything I was saying to him, which was quickly making me irate. I was thirstier than I'd ever been in my entire life, and this guy could have remedied that thirst with a single trip to a Coke machine!

"*Please!*" I screamed at him. He stared back, blankly.

"Okay, then… The hell with you!" I said to him, and I began to scale the wire fence.

Alarmed, the guard jerked his rifle up into the ready position and aimed it at me. Realizing a can of Coke wasn't worth taking a bullet over, I descended back to the ground and raised my hands into the air in compliance. The guard lowered his weapon. Defeatedly, I was forced to cope with my insufferable thirst until we arrived back at the hotel.

I hung around with the Von Steigers - Kurt and Karl - during that trip. As opposed to the Nazi thugs they portrayed in the ring, their real names were Lorne Corlett and Arnold Pastrick from Canada. The Nazi schtick was simply a gimmick. It's often said nowadays that wrestlers should be a version of themselves with the volume turned up, but many of the legendary wrestlers from my era didn't do that, because this is almost impossible to do when you're a gimmick wrestler. This included all of the Nazi-esque characters portrayed by guys who weren't even German, but who were still convincing and drew big money. In my career, I was *always* trying to portray a unique character who didn't necessarily reflect who I was in real life. I worked long and hard to refine and perfect the image I was presenting to fans.

When it comes to wrestling, you want to project the *character* you want to project, but not necessarily who you *are*. When you master that skill of projection, you can move the emotions of the crowd wherever you want. Even at this early stage of my career, I'd learned how to project that I was certifiably crazy and make it believable so that most people would stay away from me, even on the street. Plenty of wrestlers over the course of wrestling history had made incredible careers out of portraying a gimmick, and I was anxious to add myself to their number.

SEVEN – "You bastard Americans!"

In 1972, right before I went to Hawaii, I traveled to Japan for the first time as a participant in what turned out to be the Japan Pro Wrestling Association's last ever World Big League tournament event. The tour was seven weeks long, which was a very long trip.

The JWA was in a state of transition, and two of the biggest names in the history of Japanese pro wrestling - commonly referred to as *puroresu* - were involved. The godfather of Japanese pro wrestling, Rikidozan, had been murdered in 1963. He was a Korean ex-sumo wrestler who propelled American-style professional wrestling to tremendous popularity in his adopted home country, and his scripted victories over American adversaries helped to restore the pride of Japanese wrestling fans in the wake of their loss to the United States during World War II.

Rikidozan was essentially unbeaten by any Japanese wrestlers during his career, and his exceedingly rare losses were to American stars like Lou Thesz, Freddie Blassie and The Destroyer, all of whom held recognized world championships at different times. Rikidozan even won the World Wrestling Associates World Heavyweight Championship from Blassie in Los Angeles more than two years before Dick the Bruiser defeated Blassie to capture the same title.

When Rikidozan died, he hadn't passed the torch to the next generation in the traditional sense of putting an up-and-coming wrestler over and being publicly defeated by the young talent in the ring. However, he had handpicked two wrestlers who he identified as the standard bearers for the next generation: Shohei "Giant" Baba and Kanji "Antonio" Inoki. Of the two, the 6'8" (billed as 6'10") Baba was the clear favorite to ascend to Rikidozan's throne atop the JWA, and in 1965 he would win the NWA International Heavyweight Championship, the title Rikidozan had cemented as the symbol of wrestling superiority throughout Japan.

The only problem with this was Antonio Inoki was usually recognized as Japan's most exciting wrestler. After being wooed to Tokyo Pro Wrestling by Michiharu Toyonobori, Inoki feuded with the legendary Johnny Valentine. Shortly thereafter, Inoki was brought back to the JWA and Tokyo Pro Wrestling folded, but Inoki had established himself as an exciting, main-event-caliber talent who was more agile, exciting and relatable than Giant Baba, whose giant head, hands and feet, massive torso and buggywhip arms gave him the appearance of a sideshow freak, and also compromised his in-ring movement. Even if he could match Inoki move for move, Baba would never be able to execute the moves as crisply as Inoki could.

Lifting Shohei "Giant" Baba off his feet

By late 1971, Inoki was clearly tired of playing second fiddle to Baba, especially when he considered himself to be the superior worker and athlete. Many others also shared that opinion. When his attempt to take control of the JWA failed, Inoki founded New Japan Pro Wrestling in early 1972, and he was the unquestioned native ace of his new promotion. Free from the shadow of Baba and the constraints of the National Wrestling Alliance, Inoki won what was billed as the "Real" World Heavyweight Championship from the legendary shooter Karl Gotch in April of 1972.

As the "world champion" of the NJPW, Inoki had a nominal distinction that Baba could never match under NWA regulations, which prohibited member companies from promoting their own individual world champions. And, unlike the IWA World Heavyweight Championship held by Strong Kobayashi of International Wrestling Enterprise, the NJPW Real World Heavyweight Championship around Inoki's waist represented a true threat to Baba's supremacy. As a disciple of Rikidozan and as the owner of NJPW, Inoki could claim equivalency with Baba, and he also controlled his own destiny. No one could ever push Inoki down the card or force him to lose to anyone. He *wasn't* going away.

In the wake of Inoki's departure and initiation of a true promotional war, Baba was in the midst of plotting his own departure, the creation of a new company called "All Japan Pro Wrestling," along with a new sanctioning body called the "Pacific Wrestling Federation," and a series of matches to crown himself as the new PWF World Heavyweight Champion. However, none of us were aware of any of this as the 1972 World Big League tournament began.

Gorilla Monsoon was the leader of our group of *gaijin* - the foreign wrestlers who were participating in the World League tour. Also included were Dick Murdoch, Abdullah the Butcher, Jose Lothario, Salvatore Lothario, Jos Leduc, Tim Brooks and Cyclone Negro, who was working as "Calypso Hurricane." The top Japanese wrestlers featured on the show were Baba, Seiji Sakaguchi, Masa Saito and Kintaro Ohki - who I always referred to as "hard head" because his offense in the ring consisted almost exclusively of headbutts.

Gorilla's real name was Robert Marella, but we all called him "Gino." His ring name was an appropriate one. At 6'5" and 400 pounds, and with long, gangly arms, Monsoon truly looked like a giant, hulking gorilla, yet he was stunningly agile and possessed the athleticism befitting a former NCAA All-American. He'd been the runner up in his weight division for Ithaca College at the 1959 NCAA Wrestling Championships.

By 1972, Monsoon had been a star in New York's World Wide Wrestling Federation for nearly a decade, and he also owned 1/6th of the company. Maintaining that level of influence in such a lucrative territory made Monsoon one of the most politically powerful men in the wrestling business.

In Japan with Gorilla Monsoon and Jos Leduc

In preparation for the event, the *gaijin* wrestlers staged a number of photos for the Japanese press. These included photos of all of us working out and lifting weights together, because apparently the Japanese fans believed all *gaijin* wrestlers were a cohesive unit, even if we were all from different nations. The photos also depicted

Monsoon as the clear leader of our group, who helped us train and organized our wrestling exercises. Socializing in Japan was very difficult at times. Even though all the children in Japan were required to learn English, a lot of the Japanese citizens would pretend they didn't know how to speak any English whatsoever. Many of the older Japanese people were still ashamed of the loss they'd suffered during World War II, and so they had no interest in fraternizing with American tourists no matter who the Americans were or why they were there. While in Japan, we traveled across the country using every method available to us, including buses, planes, trains and boats.

The "gaijin" wrestlers in the 1972 World Big League

From an organizational standpoint, JWA might be the most professional wrestling company I ever worked for, but inside the ring it was a different story. Baba and Sakaguchi, who seemed very sure of themselves and very secure with their positions in the company, had no problem working give-and-take matches where they would convincingly sell the offense of the opposing wrestlers. On the other hand, the younger wrestlers wouldn't sell worth a damn because they

Brute Power: The Autobiography of Buggsy McGraw

didn't want to look weak in front of the Japanese audience, and their chops and kicks were *stiff as hell.* They would feel you out and then get heavy handed with you to see if you were willing to struggle with them for control of the match. If you weren't willing to stand your ground, they would eat you alive in a hurry. If you were scheduled to take the pinfall on them, their resistance would be even more aggressive, and you had to lay your shots in as hard as you could just to keep them down.

In the U.S., the sign of a great worker was that a guy's punches and kicks looked like they might take your head off, but the person on the receiving end wouldn't even feel them. In Japan, none of that mattered; you *had* to hit them for real. Don't get me wrong, the Japanese wrestlers weren't stupid. If they actually tried to inflict serious injuries on the American wrestlers, we would have had every right to retaliate in the ring. Outside of the ring, they would also have had to answer to Baba and other people in the JWA hierarchy who had *serious* political power.

In particular, Kintaro Ohki, who was actually from Korea, stood out as the JWA wrestler who sold the least amount of offense from any of his *gaijin* opponents. At the time, he seemed to be number three or four in the pecking order of the JWA, so he seemed to be working extra snug to try to force his way into the upper-echelon positions occupied by Baba and Sakaguchi.

All of us were expected to work at least one match with each top Japanese star, and it was our job to put them over as best we could. This was true for all of us except for Monsoon, who was given victories even over each of the top Japanese stars, with the sole exception of Baba. Not only was Monsoon positioned as the top *gaijin* wrestler during the tour, but he was also the leader for our group behind the curtain. He always kept us apprised of things that were happening, and if he didn't like the finishes that were planned for our matches, he would negotiate with the JWA bookers to have the finishes changed to our benefit.

Aside from Monsoon, Abdullah the Butcher was the only other non-Japanese wrestler the JWA seemed to be attempting to feature. Abdullah's real name was was Larry Shreeve, and he grew up in Windsor, Ontario, Canada. His mother was an African-American from Ann Arbor, Michigan, and his father was an Afro-Canadian. Despite being on the other side of the Detroit River, Windsor is essentially part of Metro Detroit. In fact, Cobo Arena sat right on the riverfront, and Abdullah had *clearly* been influenced by the Sheik. His curved boots and use of a fork to stab opponents in the forehead were both clearly borrowed from the Sheik's act.

On the bus with Abdullah The Butcher

Since his relatively dark skin precluded any attempts to pass himself off as a Middle Eastern wrestler, Abdullah was billed as being from The Sudan, where the people speak Arabic, and which dips into Sub-Saharan Africa. However, anyone who has met someone from The Sudan knows the people there are several shades darker than Abdullah the Butcher. In terms of performance, the only clear difference between Abdullah and the Sheik is Abdullah actually threw a few more true wrestling moves into his routine than the Sheik would, including his elbow drop finishing maneuver.

Abdullah always seemed like he was out for himself and didn't hang out with most of the other *gaijin* wrestlers during his free time. Years later, he became morbidly obese, but during this trip, he was only mildly overweight. Even then, his forehead was such a mess of scars that it practically looked like a roadmap. Not to be outdone, Jos Leduc's forehead had nearly as much scar tissue as Abdullah's.

During our free time, we all split up into very different groups. I spent most of my time with Jos Leduc; the Lotharios hung out together; Murdoch hung out with the Japanese wrestlers. Jos and I were a natural pairing since we'd traveled through Alberta together during my brief and miserable run with Stampede Wrestling.

Early in the tour, Jos pushed away his seat from the hotel bar and said, "I'm going to the other hotel to see my buddy, Andre the Giant. You want to come?"

"Hell yeah, I do!" I said, anxious to meet the biggest global star in all of professional wrestling. When I say that Andre was the biggest star in wrestling, I mean that both literally and figuratively. He stood at a legit 6'10" and weighed close to 300 pounds back then, and he was much fitter than most people remember him.

Andre was in Japan at the time working for International Wrestling Enterprise and wrestling against their IWA World Heavyweight Champion, Strong Kobayashi. As a French-Canadian, Jos could obviously communicate with Andre in the Frenchman's native language. Jos and I took a cab over to the opposition's hotel, and we had lunch with Andre at the interior restaurant. It was a very comfortable meeting, aside from the fact that Andre's control of English was almost non existent back then. I spent most of my time marveling over his massive head and hands while he and Jos conversed in French.

We were often recognized as wrestlers no matter where we traveled in Japan, including the most remote parts of the country. As our tour extended to the more rural areas, Jos and I made the most of our opportunities. In one of the small towns we went to, Jos and I decided to go swimming in the local river. In Hiroshima, we stopped at the museum dedicated to the victims of the Hiroshima bombing, and stood in a huge line. While we were standing in line, a Japanese man pointed an accusatory finger at us and said, "You bastard Americans!"

Jos turned toward the man and said, in broken English, "I'm *not* bastard! I'm *Canadian!*" I don't think the Japanese man cared about the distinction, but I was laughing so hard, I could barely stand. By his own logic, being a Canadian meant Jos wasn't a bastard.

Inside the the memorial, there was a book that visitors were encouraged to sign. One of the Americans ahead of us had written, "I'm ashamed that I'm an American." That sentence really *pissed* me off. Right underneath his sentence I wrote, "If you fuck with the bull, you get the horns." To this day, I have zero regrets about writing that. Dropping the bomb made the Japanese surrender, and it prevented us from having to send more American troops to die in Japan. Sometimes you have to look out for the lives of your own country's people before you start considering the lives of others… especially when more than 400,000 of your people had already died, and the other side had started the war in the first place.

In Nagasaki, the site of the second bomb drop, Jos and I went out to eat after the matches, and I'm convinced we were *poisoned* at the restaurant. After our meal, we got back to the hotel and went right to sleep, and I was awakened by a fiery, agonizing pain in my intestines. This was followed by crippling diarrhea, and the inability to eat for an entire day. Jos had a similar problem, although it wasn't quite as bad as mine. However, wrestlers don't get days off, so we still had to wrestle our way through the agony.

When we arrived back in Tokyo, Jos and I went to see a sumo match and learned all about the preferential treatment and reverence the sumos receive in Japan. In essence, the top sumo champions got whatever they wanted. It wouldn't have been at all out of the ordinary for a sumo wrestler to receive $100,000 in an envelope as a gift from a wealthy Japanese businessperson who would simply say, "Please, take it." The donor would consider it a true honor to be able to bestow a large monetary gift upon the sumo champion.

As professional wrestlers, we also had donors in Japan, although not at the level of the sumos. A local businessman took Jos and I to a sushi dinner at the Imperial Hotel, which was the most expensive hotel in the world back in 1972. Our donor encouraged us to eat and drink to our heart's content, and every time we cleared our plates he would ask, "You want more?" before summoning a server from the restaurant to bring us more raw fish and sake. This routine continued itself for several hours until we were stuffed.

Out for dinner at Tokyo's Imperial Hotel with Jos Leduc

Joe Haguchi told us early in the trip that we needed to make sure we were back to our hotels by midnight. In the early '70s, there was an unspoken rule that Japanese cab drivers would not pick up Americans in cabs after midnight, simply because they didn't like

Americans. Well, Jos and I stayed out with our donor well past midnight, and when our meal reached it conclusion, we stood next to our donor and attempted to flag down cabs in front of the Imperial Hotel. There were at least 20 cabs out front. One by one, the cab drivers looked at us, shook their heads, and simply said, "No."

After several refusals, our donor walked up to a cab driver, got in his face, and the two of them got into an intense screaming match using words I couldn't understand. For a few moments, it looked like Jos and I would have to break up a physical altercation between our donor and the driver. Finally, the driver put his head down in either shame or submission, and permitted us to climb into his cab. Without a word being uttered, he drove us back to our hotel, and we were finally able to get some rest.

Obviously, Baba was the number-one remaining attraction for the JWA. Having been in the ring with him, I can attest to the fact that he was a solid worker and seller with offense that looked pretty good, and was also very easy to take. However, by no means was he a great athlete. During our matches, I would feed to him the same way I would feed to Ox Baker, with the only difference being that Baba was easily *ten-times* the worker that Ox Baker was.

The JWA paid all of the gaijin wrestlers a weekly salary while we were there, and historically the pay the wrestlers received in Japan was substantially more than we could have made in the United States. That Japanese were prepared to pay top dollar for the best American talent. If you could cope with living in a non-English-speaking country for much of the year, you could earn a much larger salary than you could earn by working for an American promoter, and you could earn it all while working far fewer dates.

When the tournament was all over with, Baba defeated Monsoon in the finals to win his sixth World Big League Tournament Championship in seven years. Shortly after the conclusion of the event, the JWA was finished as a functional wrestling promotion. Baba left to start All Japan Pro Wrestling and vacated the NWA International Heavyweight Championship in the process. The JWA briefly put the championship on Bobo Brazil just so that Kintaro Ohki could beat him for it. However, Ohki was no

Giant Baba, and when the JWA shut down shortly thereafter, Ohki *stole* the championship belt and took it with him to Korea for nearly nine years until the NWA forced him to return it.

As for me, I was finally off to Hawaii to make good on my promise to Ed Francis, but first I had to stop in Los Angeles. Lonnie Mayne had set up a single-shot appearance for me with the NWA promotion in LA, which also happened to be the first time I met "Rowdy" Roddy Piper. In LA, Piper was far skinnier than most people remember him, and he was just on the verge of beginning his legendary run as a heel there, where he would insult Chavo Guerrero and every other Mexican in Southern California for the sake of getting heel heat. At his peak, Piper was one of the most fearless heels of all time, and he would stoop to *any* level to get heat.

Of course, Lonnie quickly decided that he needed to pull some kind of rib on "the guy in the kilt," so when Piper walked past us, Lonnie slid in behind Piper with a cigarette lighter and lit his t-shirt ablaze. The shirt went up in flames instantly, as if it had been soaked in gasoline. Piper ripped the shirt off as fast as he could, then stomped it out on the floor. Once the flame was out, he turned to face Lonnie, fully prepared to start swinging. All Lonnie did was laugh right in his face. Realizing he had no chance of taking Lonnie in a real one-on-one fight, Piper just turned and walked away.

"Geez, Lonnie… you really could've hurt him! I said. "You could've burned all his hair off or something."

"Oh well!" Lonnie shrugged. "He'd probably look better bald anyway!"

EIGHT – "We've gotta call the cops"

By the time Ed Francis purchased the NWA's Hawaii territory from Al Karasick in 1961 and renamed it "50th State Big Time Wrestling," it was already established as one of wrestling's vacation territories. There wasn't a great deal of actual wrestling going on in Hawaii compared with most of the other territories; three days of wrestling in a week was considered a busy week. Most weeks, the promotion put on only two shows. No one made any real money there, but there was plenty of fun to be had. The shows were run at the Honolulu International Center, and at the Schofield Barracks. No matter where we were, there were always plenty of military personnel at the events. Occasionally, we'd also run shows on some of the outlying Hawaiian islands.

Fortunately, Francis was a forgiving man and didn't hold my tardy arrival against me. He was aware of what Jim Barnett had done to keep me in Australia after we'd struck our agreement for me to wrestle in Hawaii. Ed got me a terrific rate in a great room at the Ilikai Hotel, which was right on the beach and had picturesque views.

With all of the free time I had on my hands that came with working in Hawaii, I filled most of it by hanging out with the local owner of a motorcycle shop, and the two of us spent afternoons driving around the island on his motorcycles. The guy also gave me a car so that I'd have regular transportation around Oahu.

I was also reunited with my friend, "Moondog" Lonnie Mayne, who was the star heel in Hawaii. With our social pairing restored, we resumed the wild, crazy, and often self destructive episodes we involved ourselves in during our run in San Francisco. For instance, when we found "Superstar" Billy Graham's car unattended outside of the gym, Lonnie saw it as an opportunity for the two of us to pull a very nasty prank on him.

"Let's fill it up with garbage!" Lonnie said.

Of course, that's exactly what we did, but that wasn't enough for Lonnie, who then said, "Let's see if we can cave the roof in!"

The two of us then jumped up and down on the roof of Billy's car until the metal frame had caved in to the point that it was resting on the front seat. Within seconds, we'd made it impossible for Billy, or anyone else, to get into his car and drive it. It was pure vandalism.

I started to feel a little guilty for what I'd done, so after Lonnie left I waited for Billy came out and evaluate his car. When he saw how the roof on his car was caved in, and then he opened the door and garbage spilled out, the look of shock on his face was priceless. He just stood and stared as if he was looking for the invisible tree that had landed on the roof of his vehicle.

"Here, let me help you with that," I said to Superstar as I walked up behind him.

Moving past Billy, I reclined the seat and slid into place. Then, I propped my feet up as if I was doing a leg press movement in the gym, and I jacked the roof of the car back into place. It wasn't easy, but I got the roof of the car more or less back to its regular dimensions. True to his good nature, Superstar laughed the whole thing off.

As I mentioned before, Lonnie had a tendency to bring out the worst in me. We were invited to a polo player's horse ranch, and the player began to demonstrate his riding prowess to us. He began at one end of the field and began riding toward us quite briskly.

"Hey, Mike," Lonnie said to me, "Do you think you can stop that horse?"

"Absolutely!" I said, accepting his challenge.

I ran straight at the horse, and the startled stallion came to an abrupt stop. I guess he wasn't used to people charging back at him, and he was confused by my tremendous bravery, or my incredible stupidity. Another time, I was with Lonnie at the airport dropping off a friend from Oregon. We got into a verbal altercation with some guy in a van, probably because the guy didn't care for the way we were driving near the airport terminal.

After we exchanged a few volleys of curse words, the situation was primed to escalate into physical violence. The driver of the van opened his door, but instead of simply climbing out to exchange punches, he reached into his center console and pulled out a .45-caliber handgun.

"I'll shoot you, you son of a bitch!" he said.

"Do it!" I said, and I stupidly charged at him.

I guess the guy didn't actually want to have to shoot somebody, because he quickly closed his door and drove off.

I know it's hard to believe, but there was rarely any alcohol involved in these situations. I *wish* I could blame it all on alcohol, but we really were just *that* stupid. Lonnie and I were constantly winding one another up to do crazy things. Our games of "Can You Top This?" were out of control. Under normal circumstances, I wasn't the type of person who would be so susceptible to peer pressure, but when I was with Lonnie, the more reckless the idea was, the better the idea seemed. He was a highly gifted instigator.

With Lonnie Mayne in Oregon

Lonnie brought me to Oregon with him on his way back from Hawaii. In the Pacific Northwest, Lonnie had already minted himself as a legend, and there was almost nothing promoter Don Owen wouldn't do as a favor for Lonnie, even if it meant taking a chance on a wrestler like me who he'd never really heard of, and who had yet to have a substantial main-event run in any significant territory in the mainland United States.

Don Owen's father, Herb, had been a boxing and wrestling promoter early in the 20th century, and Don eventually took full control of Pacific Northwest Wrestling in 1951 following his father's death. The majority of his shows were held in the Portland Sports Arena, which was a bowling alley that Owen repurposed into a suitable venue for his wrestling events. Outside of Portland, Don's brother, Elton Owen, handled the booking for most of the other towns in the territory, which included Portland, Eugene, Medford and a host of smaller towns.

Giving a hip toss to Dutch Savage

When I first arrived, Lonnie told me to check into a hotel called "The Bomber," which was so named because of the large World War II bomber parked in front of the building. Within days, I'd moved into an apartment owned by a wrestler named Tony Borne. Tony would rotate wrestlers in and out of the apartment and

collect rent from those who stayed there. The apartment was in a
duplex right behind Tony's house, so he could easily check on his
investment, and also see if his tennants needed anything.

Despite being a legendary heel character, Lonnie was
working as a babyface when he brought me to Portland. He assumed
we'd have great in-ring chemistry, and he thought I would be a solid
heel opponent for him. With Lonnie's endorsement, and with the
new name of "The Skull," I was intended to work alongside Bull
Ramis as one of the top heels in Pacific Northwest Wrestling.

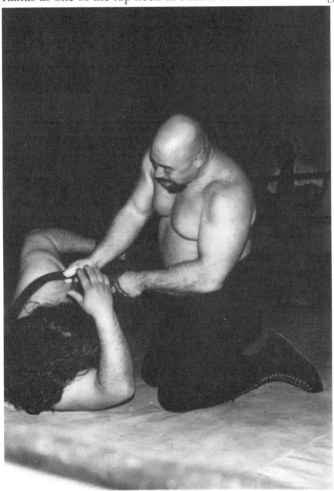

Dishing out punishment in Oregon

Despite his strong relationship with Lonnie, I didn't jibe with Don Owen that well. The other top babyface in Oregon was Dutch Savage, whom Lonnie didn't seem to trust very much. In my limited interaction with Dutch, he did seem to fall into the category of wrestlers who are only out for themselves and couldn't be trusted. Together, Lonnie and Dutch were the NWA Pacific Northwest Tag Team Champions until Tony Borne and I beat them for those titles on September 2nd, 1972. The in-ring style of Oregon was a bit less mat based than what I'd gotten used to in Australia, but I adjusted quickly.

Tony had worked in Oregon for nearly his entire career, and he was a member of the cadre of guys who Don Owen trusted implicitly. This meant Tony had a strong influence over how favorably we were booked together even if I wasn't among Don Owen's favorite guys on the roster. Tony also acted as my mouthpiece during all of the interviews, which meant I simply had to stand there, flex my muscles, and look intimidating.

Tony had a teenage son named Matt who saw me working out in the gym and was blown away by my strength. He saw me hitting multiple reps at 500 pounds on the bench press, and he began *begging* me for workout tips so that he could pack on muscle. Eventually we started working out together, and I did my best to teach a 15 year old how to emulate my workouts without killing himself. Although he never got to be massive, Matt eventually became a successful wrestler using several different personas in Mid South Wrestling, World Championship Wrestling and the World Wrestling Federation.

Another famous wrestling bloodline in the area belonged to Sandy Barr, who was another constant presence in the Pacific Northwest. His sons Arthur and Ferrin both became wrestlers as well, with Ferrin taking the name Jesse Barr and wrestling in Florida before jumping to New York as Jimmy Jack Funk, the fraudulent third Funk brother next to Dory Jr. and Terry.

Arthur Barr went on to become one of the hottest young wrestling prospects in the world as Art Barr, one half of the "Los Gringos Locos" tag team with Eddie Guerrero. Tragically, he was found dead in his Oregon home in November of 1994. To this day, no one is quite certain as to what killed him, but drugs and alcohol are the most commonly assumed culprits for his death.

Don Owen's territory was very healthy, and we were doing tremendous business. We didn't go to large venues; I'd estimate our average venue held somewhere between 1,000 and 3,000 people. No matter where we performed, all of the venues appeared to be filled to capacity. Everyone on the roster was making solid money and seemed happy, and Elton Owen would even pay you extra if you were asked to bleed during a match. Also, the girls of Portland were always very happy to be seen around town with us.

Conversely, the weather in Portland was *abysmal*. The rain was incessant, and I probably would have been depressed if everything hadn't been going so well inside the ring. Oregon's suicide rate is consistently higher than most other areas of the country, and I'm convinced the abhorrent weather is a major contributor to it.

During a match in Salem, I was standing on the floor at ringside when a pretty big guy ran up behind me and tried to kick me in the groin. His blow landed one inch short of its intended target, fortunately, and the flat of his foot hit my groin instead of the tip of his toe. Of course, I got *super* pissed off.

"You son of a bitch!" I said, and started chasing him.

My assailant spun around and ran straight up the aisle, so I pursued him all the way up the aisle, out the door of the building, and down the street for about 30 yards. That sucker was *too* fast.

"The hell with it!" I said.

I turned around and walked back up the street, through the door, down the aisle, and back into the ring to finish the match, and we resumed the action in the ring as if a random fan hadn't just kicked me in the balls out on the arena floor.

In a separate incident, I sprained my ankle during a match in Eugene when Bull Ramis threw me out of the ring and I landed wrong. This was one of those classic cases where it would actually have been better for me if I'd broken the ankle outright.

"I *can't* work on this!" I told Don after the match.

"Do you think you can work outside the ring as a manager?" he asked me.

"Of course," I said.

So, I made my managerial debut in Golden, Oregon, in the corner of Lonnie's opponent. I stood at ringside on crutches and screamed a variety of insults at Lonnie. In the middle of the match, I used one of my crutches to hook Lonnie's leg and trip him to the mat. Since this was Oregon and I'd interfered with a match involving Lonnie, of course a full-scale riot ensued. People descended upon the ring from every corner of the building. There I was, holding on to one crutch for balance while swinging the other crutch around like a maniac to fend off the mob.

In the midst of the melee, some kid grabbed a wooden chair and used it to bash me in the head from behind. It split me *wide open*. I was bleeding like a stuck pig. My shirt and pants were completely soaked with blood. Incredibly, once order was restored, we finished the match while my blood dripped all over the ringside floor.

When we got back to the locker room, I was drenched with my own blood, and Tony drove me to the hospital to get sewn up. Apparently bleeding helps you to work up an appetite, because after my medical visit concluded, I realized I was absolutely starving and started whining to Tony about it.

"You want to go get something to eat?" Tony asked.

"Of course I want something to eat!" I said. "Haven't you been listening?!"

"Okay, okay... I'll take you," replied Tony.

So, Tony and I stopped by a local diner and ordered food. I sat there eating eggs and pancakes, covered in blood, with crutches next to me, looking like a horror show. I'm really grateful to the restaurant staff for letting me in and serving me while I looked like that.

On the one hand, when the crowd riots, it's a tremendous compliment. It's the ultimate reaction from an audience. You've worked them to the point where they've completely bought into what you're doing, and they're foaming at the mouth to make you pay for your misdeeds. Literally, they can no longer stay in their seats without getting involved to right the wrongs taking place in front of them.

On the other hand, riots are *extremely* dangerous. I know guys who have worked in Africa, India and some Middle Eastern countries, and in those places, you have to do everything you can to *avoid* getting the crowd riled up, because if a riot occurs, they *will* kill you.

As a case and point, George Gordienko once told me about a best-of-three-falls match he wrestled in Saudi Arabia. When he took the first fall, the crowd started to stir a little too ominously, so George had the other guy take the next two falls inside of two minutes in order to prevent a riot and save his own life!

Working in Oregon occasionally provided me with opportunites to pay Lonnie back for some of the ribs he'd initiated against other people, including both me and "Superstar" Billy Graham. When Tony and I were leaving Salem, I noticed Lonnie's Corvette parked at a convenience store. As Lonnie's close confidant, I was well aware that he would fearlessly leave his keys in the car's ignition as if he was somehow immune to the threat of auto theft.

"Stop!" I ordered Tony.

I got out and peered inside the car to confirm Lonnie had the keys in the ignition. Then I climbed in, started the car, and drove it up the street to park it. Then I got out, got back in the car with Tony, and rode with him to a parking lot on the other side of the street to see what would transpire. A few moments later, Lonnie came out of the store, accompanied by Rick Hunter. They both walked to the middle of the lot and then looked around frantically.

"We've gotta call the cops, Lonnie!" Rick said. "We've gotta call the cops!"

"Shut up!" Lonnie commanded him.

Lonnie then walked out onto the street and looked up and down until he found his precious car. When I confessed my transgression to him later on, he just shrugged and said, "I figured it was you, you *bastard*!"

I eventually became so popular as a heel that I was chosen as the face of the opposition to a statewide tax initiative. I appeared in a local advertisement as a monstrous figure taking a *huge* bite out of a cake to symbolize the magnitude of the tax increase.

Over the course of my time in Oregon, Don Owen loaned me to Gene Kiniski a handful of times. Gene must have liked what he'd seen of me in action, because he asked Don if he could have me on a full-time basis at the start of 1973. I didn't know much about Vancouver, and I was making more than enough money in Oregon to get by. I honestly didn't want to go.

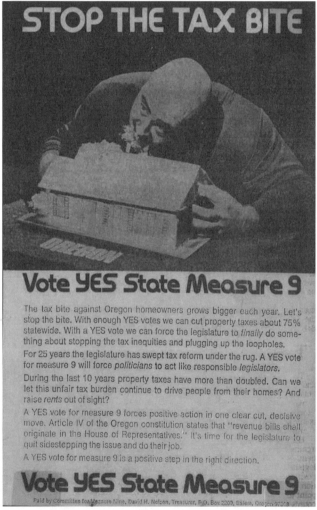

Oregon anti-tax ad featuring "The Skull"

"Why don't you just try it?" Don said. "If it doesn't work out, you can always come back here."

I had no way of knowing I was about to have my greatest success to date, and I would be spending the next two years of my life in Vancouver as the wrestling star that *everyone* across Canada would be talking. I'd been watching and learning for years, and this would finally be my chance to be a star. By now, I could work, talk and bump, and I would soon combine all of these skills, capitalize on the knowledge I'd collected over the years, and draw main-event money everywhere I went.

Flying onto Dutch Savage

NINE – "You Canadians don't think correctly"

When I arrived in the Vancouver territory, it was owned by
Hungarian wrestler Sandy Kovacs and former NWA World
Heavyweight Champion Gene Kiniski.

In his prime, Gene was a massive pro wrestling star. He got
his start as a defensive lineman for the Edmonton Eskimos of the
Canadian Football League, and transitioned to becoming a full-time
professional wrestler after tearing his kneecap. Billed as "Canada's
Greatest Athlete," Gene embarked upon a legendary heel campaign
that saw him enjoy a three-year reign as the NWA World
Heavyweight Champion, and also brief reigns as world champion of
the AWA and WWA. Even in his later years as a worker, Gene was
in tremendous shape. His superior conditioning had been readily
apparent to me during my very first night in Florida when Gene
dropped the NWA belt to Dory Funk Jr. in Tampa.

By this point, Gene was working as a regular in his
hometown territory while making regular feature appearances for
other promoters as a famous, former world champion. In the locker
rooms, Gene was very talkative and enjoyed telling us stories about
how the business used to be, and he would also share his opinions
on the latest wrestling trends. At the same time, Gene's traveling
schedule meant he wasn't always around. We would see him at a few
shows here and there before he would head out on the road to again.

Don Owen sold me to Gene as a big man who could not
only work and take bumps, but who was also in surprisingly good
cardiovascular shape. I quickly learned it was essential to be in good
shape if you were working in a program with Gene Kiniski, or he
would run over, around and *through* you. Even against stronger
opponents, Gene would wear them down and then take over every
element of the match, laying in his shots and beating the hell out of
the guys. He did this with *everyone* like it was a baptism into wrestling.

Luckily, I was also in great shape and could keep up with
Gene. Whenever he got heavy handed with me, I would respond by
getting just as physical with him. If Gene felt you weren't putting up

110

a good showing, he would yell at you, "Lay 'em in!" Of course, you don't want to lay them in too hard when you're working with the promoter, and the general idea of being a good worker has always been to make your kicks and punches look as good as possible without *actually* hurting anyone. I would still exchange shots with him that were stiff enough to get him to stop egging me on to hit him so hard, and he seemed very happy with our matches afterwards.

"The Brute" hits Vancouver

One time, I worked with Gene in Vancouver, and a host of guys came out to watch the match, with Sergeant Slaughter and Larry Zbyszko among them. At one point, I was crawling across the mat on my hands and knees, and Gene kicked me *so* hard, the crack of the boot striking my abdomen echoed throughout the arena.

Slaughter turned to Zbyszko and said, "Oh *man*! That *had* to hurt!"

It *did* hurt, but I wouldn't give Gene the satisfaction of knowing it. I got up and retaliated. I never complained about things like stiff punches and kicks because I wanted to be considered a true professional. In my mind, a complainer could never be considered a great worker, because guys wouldn't want to work with someone who complained all the time. To be considered a great worker by my fellow wrestlers was an ultimate goal of mine.

Besides, Gene would *never* complain about anything you did to him in the ring no matter how rough you got with him.

There were times when I would lock up with Gene and he would immediately start shoving me around, so I'd get a headlock on him and say, "Oh yeah? You're trying to get rough with me? Is that what you think you're doing tonight?" Then I would take him and run his ass right into a turnbuckle to see how he felt about that. Gene would just laugh it off. He didn't care at all.

When I arrived in Vancouver, they didn't have any managers around to pair me with, and they didn't have anyone slotted to take over the top heel position.

"Brute… we're going to have to put the load all on you," Gene told me. "You've got to hold up the heel side of the card. It's all on you."

It wasn't like Vancouver had a dearth of heel talent. As I mentioned, Larry Zbyszko was on the cards working under his real name of "Larry Whistler," and Sergeant Slaughter was also there working under his real name as "Bob Remus." Obviously, these are future wrestling legends who were working in the territory alongside me, but they were even younger than I was and still inexperienced. True to his word, Gene put the weight of his promotion entirely on my shoulders. I could say whatever I wanted to on interviews, and I got over unbelievably well with the people of Vancouver.

I realized if I talked only about wrestling during my wrestling interviews, or I just spoke about how I was tougher than my opponents, I would end up sounding like everyone else and risk getting lost in the shuffle. So, I learned to differentiate myself to be memorable and creative, and to get inside the heads of the fans so they couldn't forget my interviews even if they wanted to.

If I was told I had three or five minutes for an interview, I could roll with it. And, when I worked with Gene Kiniski, the content of my interviews came to me quite easily. All of the Canadian fans knew Gene was a former world champion and a tough customer, so I had to attack that image.

"I realize all of you people like Gene Kiniski," I would begin. "He's Canadian. He's your hero. You *really* think he's something. I'm going to show you how much of a something he is. You Canadians don't think correctly. Gene is old. I'm young. I'm fresh. I'm going to stick my foot way up his A-S-S. You can count on that, and then you can take your Canadian flag and help him wipe his A-S-S with it, because when I'm done with him, he's going to need your help. Do you understand me? I'm not just talking to Gene Kiniski; I'm talking to you sitting at home, drinking beer because you have nothing else to do! The best thing you can ever do is listen to me, because I'm making more sense than Gene can ever make! Gene is just like you! He's Canadian! That means he's a *LOSER!*"

When I gave interviews like that, fans showed up in droves hoping to watch me get beaten. More often than not, the exact opposite happened. After only a couple months in the Vancouver territory, I won the Pacific Coast Heavyweight Championship from Gene on March 29th, 1973. From that point on, we started drawing money everywhere we went, and I was almost always the guy on top.

Gene also started me out in a tag team with Mike Webster, a former professional football player who'd played for the B.C. Lions and was very well known in the area. As a newcomer transitioning to professional wrestling from football, Mike was *extremely* green.

Gene was looking to create the next Gene Kiniski, and he had designs on inserting Mike Webster into that top babyface role. With no real projections as to how long I would be in the Vancouver territory, the goal was to use me to make Mike into Vancouver's next major babyface star. Overall, Mike was working extremely hard and giving it his best effort, but I was clearly the one drawing the money. Mike's heart just wasn't in it. Eventually, he left wrestling to get a degree in psychology. On the flipside, wrestling *was* my passion, and I was willing to do whatever it took to get better.

THE NEW TAG - TEAM CHAMPIONS

THE BRUTE
305 Indianapolis
&
MIKE WEBSTER
285 Vancouver
(New Canadian Tag-Team
Champions)

NORTHWEST WRESTLING PROMOTIONS

Tag Champs – "The Brute" and Mike Webster

Years later, in an article written for a Las Vegas publication, Webster said that I didn't have a lot of social graces and was difficult to get to know. When we started out, we traveled together a lot, but then he broke off from me and began to travel with other guys. I could tell he wasn't someone I was going to be close with. If I could do things over again, I would have tried to have been a better friend to him. To be fair, when Mike and I teamed together, our tag-team matches were generally pretty good.

I don't know what Kiniski was expecting when he decided to book me, but suffice to say I exceeded his greatest expectations.

The Pacific Coast Heavyweight Wrestling Champion

Invariably, when you're getting real heat from the crowds, you get truly violent reactions as well. I was involved in a singles match with Dutch Savage at the fairgrounds of Vancouver. In the middle of the match, some guy from the crowd charged the ring and pounced up onto the ring apron with a wooden chair in his hands, intent on injecting himself into the match. He slid the chair into the ring and then tried to climb through the ropes, and as soon as the guy stuck his head through the ropes, I tossed Dutch to the side and charged the guy. If at all possible, when a fan is charging the ring, you want to keep him out on the floor or out on the apron.

You *never* wanted a fan to actually make it into the ring and get his bearings. Thankfully, I was able to dip my shoulder into the guy and knock him off the apron into the arms of the awaiting police officers who carted him away.

Another time, we were at a spot show in Cloverdale, a town south of Vancouver in Surrey. A full-scale riot broke out while I was standing by the turnbuckle. At first I didn't realize what was happening, until some guys grabbed my legs and yanked me down to the mat. I quickly came to the realization I couldn't move a muscle. Three men were holding onto each of my legs, and they jammed my groin into the ringpost.

It dawned on me immediately that these guys would *seriously* hurt me if they got the chance. This was one of those cases where I had to control my circumstances and not let my circumstances control me. In total panic, I started kicking and screaming with everything I had. Freeing myself from their grasp, I rose to my feet, and the adrenaline kicked in. I was prepared to fight every one of those six men, even if it meant I was facing six-on-one odds.

"Okay, you *motherfuckers!*" I screamed at them. "Let's go!"

The men all scattered. I chased them all around the ring until they bolted up the aisle, at which point I eased up and let them leave. Chasing a fan up the aisle is always stupid, because you're only getting further and further away from a space you have control over. You never want to threaten or fight a fan, but when you're faced with a serious injury, you have to take matters into your own hands.

After a riot like that, it was usually eerily calm behind the scenes, at least in my experience. You have to shrug it off and simply say, "That's life," without dwelling too much on the fact that you might have been seriously maimed or injured by the events that just transpired. This is one of the reasons why it can be so helpful to hint to fans that you're truly dangerous and insane during your interviews, as opposed to simply being a mean person. People are less likely to take a shot at a crazy wrestler, so projecting your insanity through the camera might actually save your life!

As I was building all of my momentum as a heel champion, I hurt my knee and was left with separated cartilage.

"We'll take care of your surgery and get the cartilage removed," Gene said. "Don't worry about it. It's on us."

"That's great, but how long will I be out?" I asked.

"Probably six weeks," Gene informed me.

Missing out on six weeks of main event income wasn't really something I could afford to do at that time, especially since I was succeeding beyond everyone's wildest expectations.

"You know what… forget about the surgery," I told him.

Instead of surgery, I opted to buy a bike. I figured I could still work matches, and then I could ride around on the local hills in an attempt to rehabilitate my knee. It seemed far less costly than going under the knife and then sitting around doing nothing for a month and a half. Before matches, I would either tape my knee, or wear a knee brace, and then I would try to grin and bear the pain. Repeatedly bearing that level of discomfort really earned Gene's respect and elevated the trust he had in me as a wrestler he could invest in.

Because I was the number-one attraction in Vancouver, I was unofficially in charge of the promotion. As the main eventer, I could generally get whatever I wanted if I told Gene I thought it was in the best interest of the company. I was the big dog; nobody compared to me in terms of power within the promotion. I even managed to get a couple friends of mine from San Francisco booked on Vancouver cards when they felt like vacationing in the area. Their names were Jerry Monte and Pablo Mendoza.

One of my favorite photos is a photo of Pablo working with Gene Kiniski, and Gene is in the process of kicking the absolute crap out of him. Gene acceded to my wishes and brought my friends to Vancouver, but Gene always liked to give the new guys a baptism by fire in the ring. His message was, "If you can't take it… *leave*!"

I didn't blame Gene for it, either. Plenty of rookies came into the business and complained about the veterans being too stiff with them, but the business is tough by nature, and everything needed to look real back then. Guys needed to be able to absorb a beating every once in a while if they were going to be successful as professional wrestlers. If it was too tough for you, you had to go.

Unquestionably, my entire situation in Vancouver was light years better than my previous stint as a wrestler in Canada, right down to the money I was making. After wrestling for Stu Hart in Calgary, I swore I'd never work in Canada again. When you enter the business, you're taught you have to save your money, but when I worked for Stu, I was spending every dime I made simply trying to survive. After paying the hotel, food and trans, there was nothing left over to put in the bank.

In Vancouver, I was on top of the card, and I was making *great* money. That experience of working for Gene completely redeemed Canada in my eyes. I started out living in Blaine, Washington during my first year working for there, but by the next year, the territory had grown on me so much that I moved to Victoria, which was a city we had shows in every other week.

When my parents came to visit me in Vancouver, they could see I was on top of the promotion. They watched me wrestle Dutch Savage one night and leave him bloody. Dutch would routinely get color during his matches, and on that night he came to the ring with the medical dressing already on his head. Over the course of the match, I targeted his bandage, then ultimately tore it off and began pummeling his bloody wound. After pounding on him for a while, I hit him with "The Pulverizer," my running powerslam finisher.

"I can't believe you would do something like that to another man!" my mother said, clearly disgusted by the actions of her son. I was such an effective heel; I could turn my *own mother* against me!

I was working a program with a wrestler from Ireland named Sean Regan, whose real name was Gene Murphy. He worked the English style very well, but once I got him accustomed to the American style of working a match, he became very popular with the Vancouver fans. After getting Regan accepted as a main eventer by the fans of Vancouver, I took a month-long trip to Japan.

Brute Power: The Autobiography of Buggsy McGraw

After Rikidozan's death at the end of 1963, the sales manager of the Japan Pro Wrestling Alliance, Isao Yoshihara, broke away from the JWA and ultimately founded International Wrestling Enterprise. The IWE was intending to offer an alternative to JWA given the air of uncertainty caused by the death of Rikidozan, alongside the initial doubts that the JWA would be able to duplicate its prior success without him. Yoshihara established the International Wrestling Alliance as the sanctioning body for the IWE, and he created the IWA World Heavyweight Championship as his company's top championship, which gave the holder of that title a nominal edge over the top star of the JWA.

Since the JWA was a member promotion of the NWA, it could not recognize a "world" champion other than the NWA World Heavyweight Champion. With no one to govern him, Yoshihara could call his top champion whatever he liked.

Unfortunately for Yoshihara, much of the top foreign wrestling talent was off limits to him as the JWA had an exclusive relationship with the NWA. After being turned down for NWA membership in 1970, Yoshihara formed a relationship with the owner and top star of the American Wrestling Association, Verne Gagne, to maintain a steady stream of foreign talent flowing into the IWE the same way the NWA territories had been funneling American wrestlers into the JWA.

Not only was Gagne accepting of the IWE's claim to have a world champion, he welcomed its existence as an opportunity for some of his own stars like Billy Robinson, "Superstar" Billy Graham and "Mad Dog" Vachon to inflate their resumes by winning a world title while never interfering with the reigns of Gagne or Nick Bockwinkel as the AWA World Heavyweight Champion.

The top star of the IWE had been Shozo "Strong" Kobayashi, a bodybuilding type of guy who was visually quite a stylistic change from the top Japanese stars of the past. However, Kobayashi left the IWE in 1973 without losing the championship and jumped to New Japan Pro Wrestling to make more money feuding with Antonio Inoki. Without a legitimate ace or a champion in his promotion, Yoshihara reached out to Giant Baba and All

Japan Pro Wrestling to save his company and to do some co-promotion in 1974, and it was this cooperative tour that I wound up participating in.

Throughout late March and most of April, I spent much of my time losing matches to Baba, or losing steel cage matches to Rusher Kimura and Great Kusatsu. When I appeared in tag team matches, I usually had either AWA star Jim Brunzell or Sailor White as my partners. Roughly one year after this cooperative tour between IWE and All Japan, Kimura emerged as the true ace of the IWE and was crowned the new IWA World Heavyweight Champion.

During my absence from Vancouver, Gene pitted Sean Regan up against Mike Webster. I knew this would be their first attempt at a big push to position Mike Webster as the top heel star in the territory before they switched him babyface. The whole thing failed miserably. Even though I'd put Regan over in our feud leading up to my Japanese tour, the matches between Regan and Webster did not attract much interest from the fans, and I was moved back into the main events. Vancouver would continue to run solely on "Brute Power" for as long as I decided to stay there.

Gene told me to wrestle Regan, and to go "45 minutes, through." That meant we were going to do a 45-minute Broadway match without a conclusive winner. I told Sean, "For the first 15 minutes, all we're going to do is lock up."

Without exaggeration, we had the fans up out of their chairs, yelling and screaming, *just* from our lockup sequence. The fans believed everything we were doing was real because *we* treated it like it was real, so we didn't need to rely on highspots to get them excited.

For one trip to Victoria, I was on the ferry with Jerry Monte. Jerry brought his two young sons with him, so I started to joke around with the boys. Both of them were very familiar and comfortable with me because I regularly visited their home. Jerry's nine-year-old son was standing by the railing looking down into the water, so I thought it was a good opportunity to have some more fun with him. Sneaking up from behind him, I yanked the kid off the ground and yelled, "I'm going to throw you into the water!"

That was the *wrong* thing to do. The kid went crazy. He kicked, screamed, cried and scratched me up *so* badly, I had to set him right back down. He *really* thought I was doing to kill him! "Hey, hey, hey!" I pleaded. "I'm sorry! Forget it!"

For the remainder of the trip, the boy eyed me suspiciously and stayed more than an arm's length away from me at all times.

Sailor White, who later became Moondog King, was just a young guy working in the territory at the time. We were headed back to Vancouver in my 1972 Cadillac Coupe de Ville after a show in Vernon. As we drove through the Canadian Rockies, we reached a level of elevation about 6,000 feet above sea level. At the beginning of the drive, I'd stupidly begun drinking one of the two wine bottles I'd brought along with me. After finishing the first bottle, I looked over at Ed White who was drinking in the passenger seat.

"Hey, Ed, can you get me the other wine bottle?" I asked him.

"Haven't you had enough, Mike?" Ed asked. This was somewhat hypocritical, since Ed was slurring his words and had a can of beer in his own right hand. Then again, he *wasn't* driving.

"I don't even feeling anything," I laughed. "This stuff is weak!"

Ed obliged and passed the other bottle over to me, and I immediately began drinking it. Pretty soon, the wine was all gone, and Ed reclined his seat and fell asleep.

Soon, I started to feel *extremely* sleepy, and Ed wasn't awake to keep me alert. The combination of the two wine bottles and the encroaching darkness began to play games with my mind. I glanced off to the right and recognized the white mountaintop in the distance as a reference point, so I began to veer toward it. That's the last thing I remembered thinking before I lost consciousness.

Sure enough, we went right off that mountain. The car slid down the mountain for I don't know how long until it ran into a large tree lying on the ground. Almost as if it was a cartoon, the car bent the tree for a moment, and then the tree catapulted the car back into an upright position, which was the point at which I woke up. I sobered up *immediately*.

Ed and I scampered out of the car and started to evaluate our situation. We had no idea where we were relative to the road. To our surprise, there had been no real damage done to the car. There weren't even any obvious scratches or small dents. We climbed back into the car, which I managed to turn around, and we drove back up the mountainside and onto the road. From there we drove it all the way back to Vancouver.

"How in the *hell* are we still alive?" Ed asked in disbelief.

"We shouldn't be," I replied. "We definitely should've died just now."

That was the first time it dawned on me that God must have an obvious plan for my life, because we undoubtedly should have died in a fiery wreck on that mountainside.

Even the non-treacherous terrain of Canada could be made treacherous by the weather. One time we were in the eastern part of British Columbia, and we ran into a blizzard during our return trip along the highway to Vancouver. We were driving through the snowfall in June, which can be a downer for a guy from Indianapolis who is used to clear, sunny skies during the summer months. Out of nowhere, a Canadian mountie rolled up on me with his lights and siren on and pulled me over.

"Hey, officer, what did I do?" I asked him.

"Nothing," he replied.

"Well then why did you pull me over?" I asked, confused.

"Because I wanted to meet *The Brute*!" he responded, smiling.

When the Royal Canadian Mounted Police are stopping your vehicle during a blizzard just to meet you, that's when your know you're officially over. Our show out of Vancouver went all across Canada. A national survey was performed to determine who the most recognized television celebrities were. Jack Lord from the popular "Hawaii Five-0" television series was ranked number one in the poll, and I finished as the runner-up to him. Sandy Kovacs was the person who brought the results of the poll to my attention.

"Does this mean I get more money?" I asked, jokingly.

"Hell, no!" Sandy replied as he walked away.

Another cool thing that didn't result in me getting more money was the local Vancouver retailers selling t-shirts that said "Brute Power." To put things in perspective, I was the only wrestler with a t-shirt being sold in the Vancouver area, and I was a *heel*.

NOW ON SALE:—
BRUTE POWER T–SHIRTS — LIMITED SUPPLY

S – M – L – XL

ORDER NOW BEFORE THE CHRISTMAS RUSH

Send $3.95 plus 25c mailing charge to:—
SPECIALIZED PRODUCTS, 1008, 1011 Beach Avenue, Van., B.C. (add 5% sales tax if resident of B.C.)

Advertisement for the "Brute Power" t-shirts

Things got to a point where I was so recognizable that I would get followed by wrestling fans everywhere I went. I started taking steps to disguise myself in public because that level of attention gets old in a hurry. Plenty of the attention was negative, because tough guys on the street often attempted to impress their friends by fighting with wrestlers. Once world-famous-bear-suplexer Big Bad John came to Vancouver, we began going to bars and drinking regularly. I would alert John whenever I noticed guys in the bars who were looking in our direction with malice in their eyes.

"John, these guys over here, you'd better be prepared to fight them," I'd say. But nothing ever happened.

I also got hit on by more than a few ladies because I was The Brute. I even moved one of them in with me for a while. She was a singer and a stripper. Aside from her, there were also a few women I'd known from Oregon who would come up to Vancouver to visit with me.

I finally managed to get booked for a single shot for Verne Gagne's AWA while I was working in Vancouver. Nick Bockwinkel contacted Gene and got his approval to bring me into Winnipeg. At the time, Bockwinkel was being groomed to take over for Verne as the AWA World Heavyweight Champion. While in Winnipeg, I told Nick, "I'd like to come in and work for the AWA in the future."

"We'll have to see if we have a spot for you," Nick said. I shook his hand, walked away, and never heard from Nick again.

There was an English wrestler named Malcolm Kirk who came over and went by the ring name "Killer" Kirk. We traveled together and got along very well, and for some reason, he always called me "Ollie." After a match one night in eastern British Columbia, we went out to a club. Of course, we were recognizable to a lot of the people in there. Mal was a large man at 6'1" and well over 300 pounds. A couple of large guys at the club decided to pick a fight with The Brute, so I got up and prepared to confront them. Before I could do anything, Mal stormed over to intervene.

"Hey, Ollie, I'll take care of this!" Mal said.

Mal ran in and aggresively shoved both of the men to the floor. The two men got up and started tussling with Mal. While Mal was engaged with these two guys, another man came up behind Mal, and I could just barely make out some shiny object in his hand, which I was afraid might have been a knife.

This guy had long hair, which to me is a telltale sign that a person hasn't been in many real fights. If someone goes against me and has long hair, they're automatically going to lose, because the first thing I'm going for is the hair. Once I have control of your hair, I have control of your head. Once I have control of your head, the fight is *over*. I snatched this guy's hair, jerked his head back and slammed it into a metal chair. His freshly broken nose immediately began to spurt blood, and a few teeth fell out of his mouth and clattered onto the floor.

Now that we had an opening, Mal and I had to make sure we could get out of the club safely. Mal restrained his two guys by their hair, and I got up the stairs and through the door to the outside.

On another occasion in Victoria, Mal and I were standing outside by our car, and some guy got right in my face and made it known that he wasn't a fan of mine.

"You're the big, bad Brute, huh?" he snarled. "You ain't so fuckin' tough! I can kick your ass!"

His face was only inches from mine, and he was clearly on the verge of striking me, so I headbutted him right in the middle of his face. Sadly, my aim was off by a couple inches. While I managed to connect with the top of his head, my nose struck his forehead. A gash opened up on the bridge of my nose, and blood dripped down my face. Hurt and surprised, the guy turned and ran off.

Mal and I climbed into the car and tore off down the road. Along the way, the police whizzed past us headed in the opposite direction. I watched in the rearview mirror as they made a sharp U-turn, hit their lights, and accelerated until they were right behind us.

I pulled the car off to the side of the road and waited. Then, as the two officers walked up to the car, I rolled my window down to accommodate them.

"Step out of the car, gentlemen," one of the officers commanded us.

Mal and I did as we were told, and we got out and stood by the trunk of the car to face the music.

"We got a call from a gentleman who claims you headbutted him," the officer said, accusingly.

"I headbutted *him*?!" I said. "Look at *my* nose! He headbutted *me*!"

The officers both moved closer to examine my bloodly nose, glanced at each other, and then nodded.

"Yeah, that makes sense," the officer said. "Have a nice day, gentlemen."

With that, the officers turned us loose.

Despite my great success, I knew Vancouver was just a stop along the road for me. Even though I got along well with the promoters, the only way you were guaranteed to stay in a prominent position in a territory was to *be* the promoter. I was also leery of Kiniski's insistence on trying to push guys like Mike Webster and Guy Mitchell as the top heels in the company.

At Evel Knievel's Snake River jump with Lonnie Mayne

During one of my rare weekends off, I drove down to San Francisco to pick up Lonnie, and then we both drove over to Idaho to watch Evel Knievel jump the Snake River Canyon in a rocket. Evel was a legendary motorcycle stuntman who was famous for attempting death-defying, ramp-to-ramp motorcycle jumps over vast distances. In his career, he attempted 75 of these jumps; 20 jumps resulted in injuries, and he amassed well over 400 bone fractures before he retired. For his Snake River Canyon stunt, Knievel would attempt to traverse the one-mile gap while at the helm of his steampowered Skycycle X-2 rocket.

Lonnie and I were accompanied by an ex-midget wrestler who was working in Las Vegas as a blackjack dealer of all things. He hopped in the car with us when we briefly stopped in Reno, and then we continued onward to the Snake River.

When we arrived at the jump site, we started hearing people talking about the difficulties associated with Knievel's dangerous mile-long jump attempt.

We ultimately stumbled upon the place where they were hauling out all of the equipment required for the jump, and then we spotted the truck that was carrying the nose cone of the rocket. Since Lonnie and I were heels in real life, of course we *immediately* began conspiring to steal it. Had it not been for the abundance of people around and the high level of security, we definitely would've made an attempt.

Reports of the event led people to believe Knievel didn't successfully make the jump over the canyon, but I was there; he made it *way* over the canyon. When I say way over, I'm guessing he was at least a quarter of a mile past the bank on the other side. The problem was, the wind blew his parachute all the way back over, and he landed all the way back on the side of the river he started out on!

Other people close to us told us they thought it was a sure thing, and they were right. Had it not been for the wind, Evel absolutely would've made it. Some folks said they heard Evel screaming once the wind started blowing him back, because if he hit the water, he was guaranteed to drown in the river.

George Gordienko, who wrestled as "Flash Gordon," was brought into Vancouver around the age of 46. When he was younger, his physique was awesome. He had a well-earned reputation as a sadistic shoot wrestler. Surprisingly, outside of the wrestling ring, George was a tremendous artist whose paintings were even featured at art shows in London.

On top of all that, George was also a *card-carrying* member of the Communist Party. He'd been blackballed out of the U.S. territories because of his communist leanings. I have to admit that for a "Commie bastard," George had a terrific sense of humor. George wrestled a lot in Europe, and his exploits generated many mythical stories from his fellow European wrestlers which were so outlandish, you assumed they'd all been made up.

"One time I worked with George, and he threw me into the turnbuckle," one of them told me. "Except I never hit the turnbuckle because he did a cartwheel and got there well before I could reach it!"

"That's not possible," I replied. "*No one* is that fast. I don't believe you."

I'd also heard about how a promoter came into the dressing room one night to tell a wrestler he was working with George, only to have that wrestler collapse into a mess of tears.

"*Please* don't put me with George!" the man allegedly sobbed. "*Anyone* but George!"

I never believed that story until I saw it happen personally. George wasn't just any shooter; he was *the* shooter in wrestling. Reportedly, even Lou Thesz has attested to George's viability as a shooter. Still, I didn't believe any of it until I saw it in person.

We were working at a show on Galiano Island, which is about 100 miles from Victoria. George was scheduled to work with a Yugoslavian wrestler. Roy McClarity, the referee, came in and told the guy he was going to be working with George.

"No, no, no!" the man cried. "*Please*, no!"

The guy knew George didn't like him, and this grown man broke down in *real* tears in front of everyone. If George didn't like you, he would handle you. It made no difference to him how big you were or how skilled of a fighter you professed to be. Eventually, George got around to working in a championship match with me. I'd heard all of the stories about George, but I also knew I was 18 years younger than him and could bench press well over 500 pounds. For some reason, I was obsessed with the idea of finding out just how I measured up physically to the legendary George Gordienko.

When the bell rang for our main event match, I locked up with George, went behind him, locked my arms around him, hoisted him up and dropped him to the mat. I clamped down on the hold as hard as I could with no intention of ever letting go.

Just to make sure George was clear about my desire to challenge him, I leaned in and whispered into his ear, "*Now*... you son of a *bitch*... Let's see you get out of *this!*"

In less than two seconds, George had come out, up and over me, hooked my leg, then my arm, and then my head. I was left helplessly gasping for breath in the arms of this man who could easily have killed me if he'd felt like it.

"George," I sputtered. "Please! George! Stop! *Please*! I'll *never* do it again!"

George held onto the hold and simply chuckled. There wasn't a thing I could've done at that point if George didn't allow it to happen. It was as humbling an experience as I've ever had in a wrestling ring. Content that I'd learned my lesson, George relinquished his hold, and we went on with the bout as planned. After that, George and I became real friends; I made *sure* of it! This guy was the *ultimate* badass, and I *never* wanted to have an experience with him like that again!

George also had a run in with Sika from the Wild Samoans back when Sika was a much younger man. I was in the dressing room when Sika was made aware he was going to be wrestling George, and Sika wasn't thrilled about the assignment.

"I don't want to wrestle some old man!" Sika said. "The match won't be any good!"

I chuckled to myself, realizing what might happen to the Samoan powerhouse if George got wind of the fact that Sika wasn't thrilled to be paired with him that evening.

Once the match got in the ring, Sika tried to manhandle George right away, which was the *wrong* thing to do. I grinned from ear to ear as George put Sika through the ringer and did whatever he wanted with him. Not many men can say they rendered one of the "Wild Samoans" legitimately helpless.

Another European wrestler in Vancouver was a German named Eric Froelich. George didn't really care for Eric, which might have stemmed from a run in they had while working over in Europe.

Frankly, I didn't care for Eric very much, either. George was asked to wrestle Eric, and I made it a point to watch the match, knowing precisely what George was inclined to do when he worked with people he didn't care for.

Sure enough, in the middle of the match George hoisted Eric up into a slam position. Abruptly, he launched Eric three feet over his head and casually walked out from underneath him. Eric crashed to the mat in agony. I can't overstate how much you did *not* want to get on George's bad side.

During one of our fairy boat rides, my curiosity got the best of me. I asked George, "Hey, are you a communist?"

"Yeah, I am," he nodded.

I left it at that. I wasn't about to get into a contentious debate over political ideologies with a man who could so easily *murder* me with his bare hands.

Applying a stranglehold to NWA Champion Jack Brisco

As the top heel in Canada and the most popular star in the promotion, I worked with Jack Brisco in Vancouver for the NWA World Championship when his schedule brought him to British

Columbia. I'd wrestled him before in Florida in 1969, but the dynamic was quite a bit different then.

Undeniably, I was a legitimate superstar in Vancouver and the clear top heel on the roster, so there was no one else they could really put in the ring against Jack. I was carrying the territory on my back, and no one would tell you otherwise. The only other option might have been Gene Kiniski, but I'd supplanted Gene within his own territory and was honestly the far better draw. As I mentioned before, Jack was a fantastic worker who'd perfected his craft. He wasn't stiff, and he made everything look convincing.

Putting the squeeze on Don Kroffat

When I finally decided it was time for me to move back to the U.S., Kiniski brought in Guy Mitchell, who had once wrestled as Jerry Valiant, to replace me as a heel. They put a mask on him and renamed him "Mr. X." I think Kiniski also agreed it was time for me to move on, at least temporarily. If he was going to elevate someone else who would be there long term, it would be difficult to do it as long as I remained in Vancouver. I went back to San Francisco afterward to resume working for Roy Shire. I looked forward to having another chance to draw money in San Francisco and to perfect my craft with the great workers who were still wrestling in the Bay Area. I also wanted to see how my fame in Vancouver and my experience of consistently working in main-event matches might alter the perception of me and the treatment I'd receive in a major territory I'd previously performed in.

TEN – "We're going to call you 'McGraw'"

When I returned to San Francisco after my stint in Vancouver, I fully expected Roy Shire to roll out the red carpet and treat me like a star. To some degree, that's exactly what he did. Almost as soon as I arrived, Shire had me win the U.S. Heavyweight Championship from Peter Maivia on January 15th, 1975. I thought this would lead to big-money main events, but Shire would keep me off many of the spot show cards in order to make me seem more special, which was intended to draw even larger crowds inside the Cow Palace for the big shows. As a result, even though I was earning main-event money at the large shows, the relative lack of total appearances hurt my overall earnings, and my total pay wasn't what I would have expected as the top draw in San Francisco.

Upon my return to the San Jose locker room, Lonnie treated me to one of my favorite locker room ribs. One of the local guys was sitting on a chair at the far end of the locker room, and he was reading the daily newspaper which was completely opened up and obscuring his view of everything going on around him. Like the pyromaniac he was, Lonnie walked up with a lighter and set the bottom of the newspaper on fire. The whole thing burst into flames within half a second. The wrestler who'd been reading it dropped it to the floor.

As he watched the last embers of the paper burn themselves out, the guy looked up at Lonnie and said, "Wow! That was some *hot* news!"

By this time, Pepper Martin had begun helping Shire with booking. Pepper had also already appeared in a few feature films, including *Walking Tall* and *The Longest Yard*. His most famous role was probably as the truck driver in *Superman 2* who beat up Superman in a diner. I was also under consideration for a role in the movie *Farewell My Lovely* starring Robert Mitchum and directed by Dick Richards.

They wanted me to be the main bad guy in the film, and I sent them some 8x10 photos, but I later heard from Pepper that they didn't think I was tall enough for the role. Ultimately, they gave that role to "Irish" Jack O'Halloran, a guy who turned down the "Jaws" role in the James Bond series, but who later appeared as "Non," the enforcer for General Zod in both *Superman* and *Superman 2*.

When I was in Japan with Gorilla Monsoon, he kept prodding me to come to New York. The only things that held me back from making a move were Gorilla's demeanor, which I took to be condescending and rude, and also the fact that I had been having such tremendous success in Vancouver. Now, since the money as a main eventer for Shire wasn't what I'd envisioned it to be, there was nothing holding me back from seeing if pastures in New York would be greener. I called Monsoon and said, "Hey, Gorilla. I'd like to come to New York if there's any room for me out there."

"What's wrong?" Gorilla asked, sarcastically. "Are you *starving?*"

"No, not really," I replied. "I'm just looking to make a move."

Gorilla ran it by Vince McMahon Sr., who called up Shire to hash things out with him. The next time Shire saw me in the locker room, he seemed annoyed by my abrupt departure.

"Yeah, New York *probably* is a better fit for you," Roy uttered sarcastically. "Guys don't have to work very hard to get over with fans there. *You'll* fit right in."

Shire's comments couldn't sour my attitude toward him any further, because my opinion of him was already in the toilet. He was a rude, belligerent, annoying prick, and despite his payoffs generally being decent, the way he would toss paychecks to his wrestlers and act like he couldn't care less about us really rubbed me the wrong way. I was so frustrated and irritated with Shire, and so livid about working on top in the territory and not making the money that usually came with the main-event position, that I told Lonnie, "Man… I'm so pissed at Shire… I'm just gonna beat the *shit* out of him!"

"You've *got* to do it in San Jose," Lonne said, encouragingly. "That's the next night he'll be in the dressing room with us."

"You're right," I responded. "I'm gonna slap him right upside his head! The thing is, if I do this, you need to hold the other guys back in case they try to help."

"You got it!" Lonnie said. "I can handle those dicks!"

Usually, Shire would come to the shows in San Jose because it was a major city, but to my great disappointment, he didn't show up that night.

"It's probably for the best," Lonnie said after we realized Shire wouldn't be there. "If you kicked his ass, the NWA would blackball you for sure. There's *no way* McMahon would bring you to New York!"

Lonnie was right. Looking back, I think it was a blessing, because beating up a promoter probably would have been the surest way to put my wrestling career on a permanent hiatus. By the time I saw Shire again, my anger had subsided, so there was never a physical altercation between us. I said goodbye to San Francisco in July of 1975, spent about a week in Indiana, and started up with the World Wide Wrestling Federation at the end of that same month.

The World Wide Wrestling Federation's territory comprised all of the states of the Northeastern United States and the cities therein. Whereas most wrestling territories were fortunate to contain one or two heavily populated cities, the WWWF's territory arguably contained six: Boston, New York, Philadelphia, Baltimore, Pittsburgh and Washington.

I said "arguably" because a few of the southern cities were in territories for which the WWWF competed for supremacy against Jim Crockett Promotions, but having undeniable control over Boston and New York, as well as relative control over Washington and Philadelphia, made Vince McMahon's WWWF the only territory that contained four of the country's ten largest media markets. As a result, the WWWF was the richest wrestling territory in the nation, with access to more fans and more box office dollars than any other promotion.

While the WWWF officially formed in 1963 to separate itself from the National Wrestling Alliance and crown its own WWWF World Heavyweight Champion, it returned to the NWA in 1971 and dropped the word "world" from the name of its top championship. However, this was largely a distinction without a difference; "world" was the first word in the promotion's name. Moreover, the major events of the promotion took place in Madison Square Garden, the most famous arena in the world, in the number one media market in the country.

Therefore, if the champion who competed in the number one arena in the world, for the number one promotion in the world, which was headquartered in the number one city in the world, decided to declare himself to be a "world" champion, he *was* a world champion whether anyone liked it or not.

Structurally speaking, the World Wide Wrestling Federation Champion and the AWA World Heavyweight Champion both had inherent advantages over the champion of the National Wrestling Alliance. While the job of the NWA champion was to make the stars of every other member promotion look strong, which sometimes meant the NWA champion had to look exceedingly vulnerable against territorial champions, the job of the AWA and WWWF champions was to appear powerful within their designated territories so as to attract loyal, paying fans to their matches in every city in the territory, year after year.

To that end, the WWWF champion was usually made to look like a dominant world beater, and no champion in all of wrestling was booked to be more dominant than "The Living Legend" Bruno Sammartino.

For nearly two decades, the formula of the WWWF had been to bring in a new monster billed as standing at least 6'1" (usually taller) and weighing at least 270 pounds (usually heavier), and build that monster up over the course of one or two months. From there, the monster would be put in the ring with Bruno at Madison Square Garden, and then Bruno would reinforce his dominance over the wrestling world by beating that monster in the heart of New York City. Afterward, the monster would be shuffled down the card and eventually rotated out of the territory to make room for the next challenger to Bruno's throne.

Since I easily fit the mold forged by Bruno's other monthly nemeses, I pretty much understood what my role would be when I arrived in the WWWF in 1975. When I made it to the first television taping, I still assumed I would be going by the name I'd become famous under: "The Brute." Of course, Vince McMahon Sr. put an end to that idea almost immediately.

"Would you mind if we changed your name?" he gently asked me in the dressing room.

"Why?" I asked him.

"We just had another guy here who went by the name of Brute Bernard," McMahon said. "I don't want the fans to get confused."

To be honest, I was *totally* against changing my name; "The Brute" had been one of the most famous celebrities in all of Canada! But, I knew there was a lot of money to be made as a star WWWF wrestler if Vince liked me, and I wasn't about to upset the applecart on my very first day there.

"Sure," I told Vince. "I can do that. What do you want me to change it to?"

Anyone familiar with Vince McMahon knows he was extremely proud of his Irish heritage, and whenever he had an opportunity to plant a name on a big, strong wrestler, that wrestler typically wound up with an Irish surname. This happened most famously to Terry Eugene Bollea. McMahon allegedly took one look at that blonde, muscular giant and said, "You're going to be Hogan... *Hulk* Hogan."

"We're going to call you 'McGraw,'" Vince said to me. "*Buggsy* McGraw."

I'm sure McMahon was borrowing the name "Bugsy" from the notorious Jewish mobster, Benjamin "Bugsy" Siegel. Whenever I had any control over the spelling of the name, I always spelled it "Buggsy" with two "G's" to try to differentiate myself from everyone else.

I'd brought two pairs of wrestling trunks to New York with me, and one of them had "The Brute" stitched on the back; I now knew I wouldn't be wearing those again any time soon.

Along with the name change would come a slight change in the way I handled my interviews. However, my in-ring conduct remained virtually indistinguishable from that of my "Brute" persona. I was still a snug worker who liked to jump off the top turnbuckle and take big bumps. The first time I was working, they flew me to Madison Square Garden to work with Tony Garea. Just in case the significance of working at The Garden hadn't already occurred to me, there was a huge, flashing neon sign in front of the building that read, "The Most Famous Arena in the World" just to remind me. Tony put me over in the middle of the ring to set me up as the next monster heel to challenge for Bruno's belt.

As fate would have it, "The Mongolian Stomper" Archie Gouldie had been slotted for the main-event matcht with Bruno, but he canceled on Vince. Ironically, five years after he first said we should travel to New York as a package deal, I would be elevated to my first main event match at Madison Square Garden because Archie wasn't fulfilling his obligations.

When I worked with Garea, he knew his job was to put me over. Yet, as a worker who prided himself on entertainment value, I was insistent on leading the match, telling Tony what to do and when to do it, and selling for him when I probably shouldn't have been. Later on, Lou Albano told me McMahon and Monsoon were watching the match from the locker room, and McMahon turned to Monsoon and yelled, "*Who* told him to sell?!"

When my match with Bruno at The Garden rolled around, it was booked as a handicap match with my manager, "Captain" Lou Albano, as my tag-team partner. This was in September of 1975, which is a month when attendance levels for wrestling shows typically declined in every territory. Having kids back in school hurt in a couple different ways. First of all, the children were less likely to be free to see live wrestling matches. Second, families had to pay for books, clothes, and assorted education fees early in the school year. As a result, there were fewer fans available to attend shows, and many of the fans who wanted to attend those shows didn't have the spare cash left over to spend on tickets.

I'd heard stories about how strong Bruno Sammartino was, and the stories were *all* true. Not only was he a full-fledged Italian Superman who could bench press more than 500 pounds, but he was also rumored to have fantastic conditioning as well.

Before our match, Bruno, Lou and I had a brief conference with Vince and Monsoon in the restroom. This was the first time in my life I'd ever come across "The Living Legend" in person. Bruno really only worked the major shows, so he wasn't on the road at spot shows very often. It was rare to ever see Bruno at the television tapings, and he probably wasn't working in more than seven matches a month. During the meeting, there seemed to be some lingering tension between Bruno and Vince.

Posing with Captain Louis Albano

"Are there any questions?" Vince asked after the instructions had been given.

Bruno stared at me as if to say, "Say something, kid. Say something." I couldn't think of anything to say. I didn't want to be the annoying newcomer who complained or asked the wrong questions.

As Lou and I walked down to the ring at Madison Square Garden that night, I had a vision in my head of what I wanted to do in that match. I was trying to pump myself up, and saying, "I'm going to blow Bruno up," which meant I was going to challenge Bruno's purported conditioning level, and leave him sucking oxygen. I also planned to show him I was his physical superior, I was the boss, and I owned him. I was going to run right *over* Bruno.

I was *really* stupid.

As soon as the bell rang, I really took it to Bruno with everything I had. I did as many things as I could to make him move around and work. Bruno had obviously been the WWWF champion for years, but the heels typically called and led the matches, even against the champion. Bruno never objected once to anything I said in the ring, and he did everything I asked him to do. He did everything without hesitation, and his execution was flawless. We were both careening around the ring at a frenetic pace.

In the middle of this match that I'd been calling from start to finish, I was in one corner of the ring on my knees and sucking wind, and I looked up to see Bruno *dancing* in the opposite corner. He was *dancing!* I couldn't believe it! I'd called the entire match with the idea of breaking Bruno down and wearing him out, and now I was the one left on the canvas, staring up at him while he flaunted his conditioning in my face. It was *insulting!*

"You son of a *bitch!*" I said to him.

I got off the mat and charged the champion with every intention of running him ragged and upstaging him. I was determined to make him pay the price for embarrassing me. Yet, no matter how many times we slammed each other, or how many punches I asked him to throw, or how much running I made him do, Bruno simply refused to show any signs of petering out.

I'd been able to wear down just about any other wrestler I'd ever been in the ring with one way or another, either by challenging his conditioning or by asserting my strength. Bruno was the sole exception to the rule; he just kept going and going right up until the finish to the match.

When it came time for the finish, I told him, "I'm going to slam you three times. Then I'll come off the top. You move, and start your comeback."

In the past, I'd had plenty of guys who'd recoiled at the thought of taking three slams during a match, let alone in a *row*. "*Three* times?!" they'd ask, trembling. "*What for?!*"

Bruno seemed to *welcome* the physicality. The ending went exactly as planned, with me feeding into all of Bruno's offensive maneuvers as aggressively as I could. Some heels didn't like to sell hard for the babyfaces' comebacks because they felt it made them look weak, but match quality is the most important thing, and I always wanted to make the babyfaces look strong if my job was to put them over. When Bruno finished his comeback and took the pinfall on me, the crowd went berserk. Lou worked the crowd to perfection as well, so we all had reasons to be proud of our performances.

Undeniably, Bruno convinced me of his legendary status that night. Not only was he a great worker, but he was a *breeze* to perform with in the ring. Everything he did looked good, but you couldn't feel any of the supposed damage his moves were doing. That's the ultimate compliment you can pay to a fellow wrestler. Anyone who says Bruno wasn't a great worker was never in the ring with him, or they *flat out* don't know what they're talking about.

Would I consider Bruno the best worker I'd ever been in the ring with? No. But I consider him to be the *best* world champion of all time.

Behind the curtain, Vince McMahon and Gorilla Monsoon were watching our performance. When it was all over with, Vince turned to Gorilla and asked him, "Why don't any of our *other* wrestlers take bumps like him?"

Gorilla just shrugged in response. In the span of one month, I'd changed McMahon's tune from wondering why I sold so much of my opponents' offense to wondering why more heel wrestlers in the WWWF weren't selling like me.

Years later, I came across Davey O'Hannon at a wrestling convention. Davey was an Irish wrestler who worked in the New York territory for a long time, and who spoke with Bruno regularly. As we talked, the subject of "The Living Legend" came up.

"Do you know what Bruno said about you?" Davey probed.

"No... what did he say?" I asked.

"Bruno thinks you're one of the most professional guys he ever worked with," Davey said. "He said you were a credit to the business."

That's one of the best compliments I could ever get. That's why it pays to sell and bump big for the main babyface in a territory.

In Philadelphia the next week, Lou and I each received $1,750 as our payoff for the MSG show; Lou was irate that we hadn't received *more*. Between us, we assumed we'd each be making between $2,500 and $3,500, but it seemed like Vince decided to take the standard nightly wage for a heel main eventer at The Garden and divide it evenly between us.

I received my check while waiting to do my interview with Vince McMahon Jr., who everyone in the territory simply referred to as "Junior." We'd see him only once every three weeks when it was time to tape our interview segments at the Philadelphia Civic Center. I never once saw him at Madison Square Garden.

Lou was an insider in that territory, and he was very outspoken when he felt like he'd been wronged. After looking at the check, he began pacing the corridors of the Civic Center, spouting profanities. As Vince McMahon Jr. recorded interviews with wrestlers for the upcoming shows, Lou stormed through the halls screaming, "These fuckin' Irish pricks!" along with a host of other ethnically insensitive phrases. That was just one of the colorful statements I heard from the *opposite* end of the arena while I was trying to focus on conducting my interview with Vince Jr.

When Lou got to me, he asked me, "What did they give *you?*"

"$1,750," I told him, while holding up the check.

"They gave me the same fuckin' thing!" Lou said, in disbelief. "Fuckin' Irish *pricks!*"

Everybody could hear Lou's vulgarities, which was probably the point, but Vince Sr. just ignored him. If Lou hadn't told me to expect a larger sum, I would've been absolutely fine with that payoff. However, since Lou had raised my expectations to such a lofty level, I was left feeling somewhat disappointed.

According to Lou, Vince told him, "I'll be really happy to get 70 percent of a house for this show," and he was referring to our MSG match with Bruno. This wasn't owed to the fact that we weren't main-event draws. Rather, it was because our match was taking place during the notoriously bad September period when wrestling show attendance precipitously dropped every year, in every territory.

Much to McMahon's surprise and delight, the show was a sellout. Also, the theater underneath MSG, known as the Felt Forum, which holds roughly 5,000 people, was unmanned because McMahon hadn't expected strong attendance. As a result, roughly 5,000 people were turned away from the show who usually would have been able to see the action in the Garden's traditional overflow-seating area. If the Felt Forum had been open, we would've made significantly more money, so Lou was pretty perturbed about that.

After the match with Bruno, I started working matches with some of the other regulars in the territory, including Monsoon, Andre the Giant, Ivan Putski, Baron Scicluna and The Blackjacks. I was even involved in the Blackjacks' last match in the WWWF.

"Polish Power" Ivan Putski was a short, but great-looking, thickly-muscled powerhouse. Ivan once told me he got up to 595 pounds on the bench press, and I totally believe him. He was a living *ball* of muscle. On the flipside, Ivan was not a true worker. He typified the guys who refused to sell for their opponents in the ring because they were afraid to look weak.

We were at a television taping in Allentown, Pennsylvania, and the show management was being handled by Monsoon. He lumbered over to me while I was sitting down and said, "You're working with Putski tonight."

I threw a fit.

"No way, Gino!" I said. "You know this guy; he barely sells at house shows! If you put us in the ring on TV, he's *never* going to sell anything!"

"It's *you* and *Putski*," repeated Gorilla. "That's the match."

"If he doesn't sell for me, I'm going to make him look like *shit!*" I threatened. "I really don't want to work with him, Gino. Don't do this."

I kept riding Monsoon about it, until he finally got fed up and said, "Fine! I'll take care of it, Buggsy. *Trust* me."

"Sure you will," I said, sarcastically.

Gorilla left and took off through the door. About five minutes later, he walked back in.

"I took care of it," he stated, casually.

"You took care of *what?*" I said in disbelief. "How? How did you take care of it?"

"All I had to do was tell Putski that if he didn't sell for you, you'd kick him in the nuts!" Monsoon said.

"I hadn't thought of that!" I laughed. "That's pretty good. Thanks for that!"

When Ivan and I got in the ring, I told him point blank, "Listen to me, or you'll look like shit."

The match that followed was one of the best matches Ivan ever had, because I led, he followed, the crowd enjoyed it, and I made him look good. Once the other guys saw how I made someone like Putski look like he knew what he was doing, everyone was anxious to work with me even if it meant I would be getting my arm raised. I also never had a problem with Ivan Putski ever again, probably because he knew I would eventually make him look good, or because he was afraid of getting his balls kicked.

Working with "The Big Cat" Ernie Ladd in tag-team matches against Andre the Giant and Ivan Putski was always going to be brutal for me. Giants like Andre and Ernie never liked to leave their feet, and Ivan *wished* he was a giant and compensated for his lack of height by never selling anything. Guess who wound up doing *all* of the selling in those matches? Me, of course.

Within the structure of almost any match involving Andre, making the Giant do the selling for his team was the wrong thing to do. It made zero sense to build your heat on Andre by making him sell, and then to have him tag in someone half his size to make the comeback. Visually, it would look stupid. That meant we had to get the heat on Putski, which also meant staying on top of him and making him sell, which was a major chore. You couldn't give him room to breathe. At least Ernie seemed to enjoy working on the same side as me, because I was there to make the matches exciting.

We were filming TV in Philadelphia at the Civic Center, and Vince Sr. walked into the dressing room I'd been sleeping in. Once Vince stepped in, Andre came staggering in after him. We'd all gone out drinking the night before, so when I arrived, I found a spot in the corner to lie down in. Vince had come into the room thinking no one was in there, and then he ushered Andre in with him. I guess they'd been looking for some privacy to discuss a business matter, and since I appeared to be asleep, they figured I was unconscious and they could commence with their negotiations. To my surprise, they were haggling over Andre's weight. Since I'd first met him in Japan, Andre had gained well over 200 pounds.

"Andre, you've *got* to lose weight!" Vince said. "At *least* 50 pounds!"

"Okay, boss," Andre said. "I'll lose the weight."

Vince Sr. was so smooth, he seemed like he could talk anyone into anything.

I began to lose a little weight of my own because I'd modified my workout. I knew just doing excessive bench pressing wouldn't help me stay conditioned for in-ring activity, so I started doing more hanging cleans and presses while having myself on a timer. That helped me to maintain the integrity of my joints, lose weight, and improve my in-ring conditioning.

I worked several matches with Pete Sanchez, who put me over almost every time. Pete was notorious for hanging out with a well-known mafia hitman. Later, when the body of his hitman friend was found in a barrel in the Hudson River, Pete became pretty worried a similar fate might be awaiting him.

Working out in New York

One night, we were working at an arena in Queens called Sunnyside Gardens. Pete and I were sitting next to each other in the dressing room, joking around as we always did. Suddenly, three guys in suits burst into the room. Barging into our locker room area was a colossal violation of our policies; only wrestlers and other trusted industry workers were allowed into the dressing room. People couldn't simply waltz in any time they pleased, and doing so could be one of the quickest ways to get dismembered considering some of the monsters we had back there.

"What in the hell…" I started to say, rising to my feet.

"Uh-*uhhhh!*" Pete said, as his hand shot up to snag my arm and jerk me back to a seated position. "Nope. Don't even *think* about it."

The suited men passed right by us.

"Why in the hell did you grab me?!" I asked him. Then it dawned on me, these were mobsters Pete was familiar with.

"These guys *own* this place," Pete informed me, in a hushed tone. "They're *connected*. You *really* don't want any trouble with them."

"Got it," I whispered back. "Thank you!"

For all I know, Pete saved my life. At a minimum, he probably saved me from getting beaten up or pistol whipped.

Later on, Pete and I were working in Scranton, and Monsoon was handling the booking of the matches. As usual, I was leading the match, and Pete was doing everything I asked. Nothing of note happened as Pete put me over in a solid, 15-minute match, and I walked back through the curtain to the dressing room.

Monsoon was waiting for me as I entered, and he said, "That was nearly a perfect match."

Coming from Monsoon, that was unbelievably high praise, because he didn't throw compliments around freely. Also, Pete deserved his fair share of the praise, because he more than held up his end of the deal.

Even though Pete was a job guy - essentially a guy who gets paid to lose frequently - who I outweighed by around 80 pounds, and whom I probably could have squashed in the match to make myself look like a killer, I figured it would be better if I made him look competitive and *then* beat him. I was going over anyway, so why not make my friend look good in the process?

I found a semi-permanent place to stay in Woburn, Massachusetts, just outside of Boston. I was staying there at the Howard Johnson where the initial manager gave me a fantastic rate. When a new manager came in and took over, he took one look at what I was paying and said, "This is ridiculous!"

Once the rate was raised on my room at the Howard Johnson, I moved on to a different hotel in West Haven, Connecticut, which was run by a different manager whose family loved me. He also gave me a fantastic rate which he told me would be good for as long as I decided to stay there.

There weren't too many wrestlers who actually lived in New York City. Spiros Arion and I would travel together because he also lived close by, and he didn't even want us driving near New York City if we could help it. According to him, New York City gave him crippling anxiety.

The WWWF television program went northeast as far as Maine, west to Pittsburgh, and even made its way as far as northern Virginia. Filming for the TV tapings was done in Philadelphia, Allentown and Scranton, with nearly all of the interviews conducted in Philadelphia.

While I was in West Haven, I wondered why the company didn't run more shows in New Haven since it was a decently-sized town. The only time I ever remember wrestling there, the crowd was superb. Every wrestler there looked around at the crowd with a look of satisfaction, assuming our payoffs would be sizeable.

Typically, we would get the payoffs for the shows one week later. In the case of the New Haven show, five weeks passed with no check arriving. Finally, the check arrived in week six, and I was expecting a check for at least $500. When I stared at the $100 check they handed me, I went and asked Lou Albano what the deal was.

"Junior got into a bad deal with some shady guys," Albano said, referring to the younger Vince McMahon. "Junior came up and took all the money we made at the show because he needed to pay them off before something bad happened."

As a result, that check was at least $400 short of what it should have been. If anyone sees Vince McMahon Jr., let him know he owes me - including interest and inflation - about $3,000 for that show in New Haven.

Monsoon booked me in a few matches with Bobo Brazil in the WWWF, which meant I was working with him seven years after my first main-event match with him in Detroit. I'd improved greatly during the intervening years, but Bobo was now more than 50 years old. He was visibly older and slower than he'd been at Cobo Hall. Bobo was never a polished worker to begin with, and the passage of time had only slowed him down and made him more plodding.

In the middle of my program with Bobo, "Crusher" Jerry Blackwell came to me and said, "Bobo went to Vince and told him he wants to work a program with me instead of you."

I don't know what Bobo's reasoning was, but he didn't seem to want to work with me anymore. Perhaps he wasn't thrilled with our match quality either, but it would have taken a magician to make Bobo look youthful at that stage of his career.

"Crusher" Jerry Blackwell and I were partnered up a lot, and we were also frequent travel companions. At 400-plus pounds, Jerry certainly filled up a car. Despite his immense size, he could move around like a cat and get high enough off the ground to throw dropkicks where his feet would land in his opponent's face.

Jerry had an apartment in Connecticut, close to where I was renting a hotel room. There were two girls the two of us regularly hung out with. There was a skinny blonde girl who liked Jerry, which made for a very interesting image when the two of them got together given the size of Jerry's belly. The other one, who liked me, was Puerto Rican. She was a little on the heavy side, but she was cute and had beautiful skin.

During a TV taping in Pennsylvania, Jerry and I didn't have a ride, so the girls decided to drive us from Allentown to Scranton. As we were riding, with the two girls in front, and with Jerry and I crammed into the back seat, I leaned over and whispered to Jerry, "Hey... I saw a movie once where this guy sticks his dick through a hole in the bottom of a popcorn box and then his girl reaches in and grabs it."

"That's crazy," Jerry whispered back. "I don't think anyone could ever pull that off in real life."

"Watch me," I told him. "I'm gonna do it."

Once we stopped at a service station and I'd purchased some popcorn, I poked my dick through a hole I'd torn in the bottom of the popcorn box.

"Hey, honey," I prompted her. "Do you want some *popcorn?*"

"Oh, sure!" she said, and she gleefully began reaching into the back seat and eating her way closer to my exposed genitals.

After three or four handfuls of popcorn, she shrieked, "Oh my god! What's *that?!*"

Jerry and I exploded in laughter. That was *easily* one of the most juvenile things I'd ever done during a wrestling road trip.

A month or two after my match with Bruno, the champ sought me out inside the Philadelphia Civic Center and said, "You need to get out of here."

This was a huge surprise to me, because I'd only been there about three months.

Why? I asked him. "I *just* got here!"

"I asked Vince if I could work a long program with you, and he doesn't want to do it," Bruno said. "You should leave, come back later, and then work a program with me," Bruno continued. "I think I can send you to Charlotte to work for Jim Crockett."

The money in New York was pretty good, but it wasn't at the level I thought it would be. Frankly, I thought I was worth a *lot* more than I'd been receiving.

"If that's what you want me to do, I'll do it," I told Bruno. "I know if I work a program with you, I'll make *plenty* of money."

I knew it was a good idea to be on Bruno's good side, because the champ took care of the people he liked. For instance, Dominic Denucci seemed to wrestle for the WWWF forever, and he lived in Pittsburgh near Bruno as opposed to living closer to New York. Bruno loved Dominic and was able to use his influence in the company to keep him employed. It was common knowledge Denucci's job security was as stable as could be with Bruno looking out for him, so he was primarily used to groom people on the undercard to prepare them to wrestle against Bruno.

Bruno went off to Vince, told him I wanted to leave, and advised him to send me to Charlotte. According to Bruno's later report, Vince's response was, "*Hell* no! He *can't* leave!"

"Then make him some *money!*" Bruno told Vince.

At the time, the WWWF performers were essentially working on a salary, even if it was only in an unofficial sense. No matter how many times you worked or what the shows drew, the checks averaged out to around the same thing every week. For me, that figure was $800 a week. The week after Bruno spoke to Vince, my paychecks increased to $1,300 each week and stayed there for the rest of my time in the WWWF. When Bruno held Vince's feet to the fire, Vince decided he would rather increase my weekly pay by more than 50 percent than let me go off to Charlotte. I was always grateful to Bruno for that gesture. There aren't many guys in the business who would look out for their fellow performers like that.

Don't get me wrong; Vince Sr. was the furthest thing from a jerk. In fact, he was one of the nicest promoters I ever worked for. One time we were in Allentown, and Vince wanted to make sure everyone was healthy. To that end, he invited a doctor to the arena to make sure every wrestler on his roster received a flu shot.

Vince walked up to me and asked, "Buggsy, did you get a flu shot today?"

"No, sir," I replied, shaking my head. "I don't get flu shots. I've *never* gotten a flu shot. I don't trust them. I won't do it."

Vince just stared at me blankly, and then he calmly said, "Well… would you take a flu shot for *me?*"

I was now trapped between a rock and hard place. Arguably the most powerful wrestling promoter in the world was asking me if I would take a flu shot as a personal favor to him. How could I possibly say "no" to that?

"For you, Vince?" I said. "Okay."

With that, I dutifully marched straight to the doctor and received my first-ever flu shot. I don't think anyone else on *Earth* could have convinced me to get a flu shot with such ease.

The WWWF drew hot crowds all over the territory, and the rowdiness also extended to the small towns. We had a riot in Keene, New Hampshire, when Ivan Koloff and I were tagging against Tony Parisi and Jacques Rougeau. Up until this point, I'd been told if a fan tried to cut you with a razor blade, you wouldn't really feel the damage at first. Supposedly, it would feel like a normal scratch, and you'd have to look down at the cut before you realized you'd been sliced open.

During the match, I tagged in Ivan while I was on my knees near the corner. As he stepped into the ring to engage our adversaries, I felt a series of scratches on my right trapezius muscle. My initial thought was, "There's a guy behind me with a razor blade, and he's slicing the living hell out of me!"

Just like in the Cloverdale riot, my adrenaline surged. I took my right arm, threw it back over my head and grabbed my attacker by the head.

"You son of a bitch!" I yelled, as I flipped the assailant over and he crashed to the mat in front of me. It was a rather young-looking fan. Hearing the commotion, Ivan whirled around and drove three extremely hard kicks into the kid's head while I cheered him on. Incapacitated from the blows, the fan wearily rolled across the ring and out onto the floor.

What we later learned was the fan Ivan just finished punting in the head was a 16-year-old, mentally-retarded kid who already had a broken arm in a cast. Instead of a razor blade, he'd been hitting me with the edge of his hand. Unfortunately, my pent-up paranoia about getting slashed with razors resulted in this special needs kid getting publicly assaulted by two of the most dastardly, muscular heels on the WWWF roster.

Understandably, the people in the arena got more than a little upset with us. When the people saw the young man quivering on the floor, they rose as one and started moving toward the ring. Ivan and I wasted no time and bolted back to the locker room. Nowadays, this probably would have resulted in a major lawsuit. Back then, we didn't even consider such things. To this very day, it's hard for me to think of a better way to keep your heel heat than to beat up a mentally disabled kid in front of his family, friends and neighbors.

Being partnered with Ivan Koloff was a great position to be in. He had briefly been the WWWF World Heavyweight Champion after ending Bruno's first legendary championship reign, so his position as a major heel in the territory was etched in stone. He was also a fun travel companion, and we often went out drinking. After one night of matches at MSG, we were staying at the Edison Hotel, which is a couple blocks off of Broadway. Across the street was a bar, which Ivan and I frequented. By the time the bar closed at 3:00 a.m., we were both pretty hammered.

In 1975 in New York City, people would tell you, "Whatever you do, don't ride the subways after midnight, because you'll get robbed or killed by Puerto Ricans." Just about every New Yorker of that era seemed to live in perpetual fear of stumbling across a Puerto Rican in the subway under the wrong circumstances.

There are times I look back on my life and can easily recognize when God was watching over me and protecting me from the consequences of some really *stupid* decisions I'd made, and this was certainly one of those times.

When Ivan and I walked out of the bar, I turned to Ivan as we stood there on the dark streets, and I stupidly said, "Ivan... Let's go ride the subway and kick the *shit* out of some Puerto Ricans."

Ivan stared at me for a second before cracking a drunken smile, and then he said, "Yeah! Let's do it!"

So, like the two idiots that we were, we walked about a block and a half before finding a subway station. I managed to take one full step down the staircase to the station before a car pulled up, slammed on its brakes and came to a screeching halt on the road next to us. The doors on each side of the car swung open, and two police officers leapt out.

"What do you think you're doing?" one of the officers asked. "Where are you going?"

"What the hell is it to you?!" I replied, in drunken belligerence.

"Sir, if you go down there, they're gonna *kill* you," the officer stated, matter of factly.

I glanced over at Ivan, then I looked back at the cops. Even in my drunken state, I realized the officers probably wouldn't have been going to such great lengths to stop us from riding the subway if the threat wasn't so serious.

"Okay, *fine!*" I said, turning to leave.

Ivan followed me straight back to the hotel, and we turned in for the night. I weighed over 300 pounds, and Ivan was nearly 300 pounds in his own right, but neither one of us was strong enough to stop a bullet. If the police hadn't intervened, there's no question in my mind the two of us would have wound up seriously injured at a minimum, because we were definitely heading into the subway to pick fights with dangerous people.

Ken Chambers is a guy I used to hang out with in New York. Predictably, Vince Sr. changed Ken's name to Pat McGinnis, because he needed him to be Irish. He was a big, 260-pound man, and he was in great shape. Pat had a dark side to him, though, and it stemmed from his exploits as a loan shark. For protection, he always had a vicious Doberman Pinscher with him.

I went to visit Pat in his Boston-area apartment, which meant I had to walk up a flight of stairs and then walk down a 50-foot hallway to get to his residence. On this occasion, Pat's door was open, and he had a clear view of the hallways that approached his apartment. Once Pat saw me, that son of a bitch turned his dog loose on me thinking it would be funny.

As soon as Pat dropped the dog's chain, the massive Doberman broke into a full sprint right for me. Realizing I could never outrun the beast, I decided to try to trick it into considering me a friend. I bent over, patted my legs and yelled, "Here boy! Here boy!"

As he got closer, the dog's mouth opened, he extended his tongue, and he gently raised himself off the ground and began to lick my face. My plan had worked!

Whenever Pat and I drove to shows together, he always brought the dog along for the ride. During one trip, I was resting in the shotgun seat while Pat drove and the dog relaxed in the backseat. Without warning, Pat stopped the car alongside a man walking on the sidewalk, opened the door and screamed, "Get him!"

The dog sprang from the backseat, pounced on the unsuspecting man and began gnawing on his arm.

"Oh shit!" I yelled. "What was *that* for?!"

"The fucker owes me money!" Pat said as he climbed out.

As I watched from the car, Pat calmly walked over, jerked on the Doberman's chain and yanked him off the man who had probably soiled himself.

"That's a *warning!*" Pat informed the guy. "I want my fuckin' money!"

"I'll get it!" the man screamed, lifting himself from the pavement. "Please don't hurt me!"

"Don't make me come lookin' for you again!" Pat threatened, as he helped the dog back into the car.

Pat was not to be trifled with. He would fight anybody on the spot. He also carried a handgun everywhere he went.

"I need to get out of this business, Buggsy," Pat said. "At this rate, sooner or later, I'm going to get shot. There's no two ways about it."

That was one of the reasons Pat wanted to become a wrestler in the first place. He wanted to leave his loansharking days in the past.

We were headed to a spot-show town in Massachusetts, and I followed behind Pat's car in my own vehicle. Another group of wrestlers rode behind me, including Pete Sanchez and Pete Doherty, but I was completely unaware of their presence. They decided to play a prank on me when we were all waiting in line at the toll booth. The group of them ran up on my, car, opened my door, and began to pretend as if they were beating the crap out of me. Unfortunately for those wrestlers, Pat didn't recognize them, and he took their threat quite seriously. As I was being peppered with very light working punches, the next thing I heard was Pat screaming, "Move back! I'll shoot you sons of bitches!"

In his outstretched hand, Pat was aiming a 45-caliber handgun at the terrified set of wrestlers who had just seen their prank take a nightmarish turn for the worse.

"It's the boys! I screamed. "Pat! It's the boys! Don't shoot!"

"You *idiots*!" Pat said, lowering the pistol. "I almost *killed* you!"

"Sorry, Pat!" Sanchez said, before looking back at me. "You, too, Buggsy."

The very relieved wrestlers jogged back to their car and quickly climbed in. There isn't a doubt in my mind that Pat would have gleefully shot every one of those guys if there had been any further provocation.

Most pranks ended far more harmlessly. Davey O'Hannon and I were at a restaurant in the Boston area, and Lou Albano was eating in the same restaurant. When Davey and I finished up, we walked outside of the restaurant, and then I had an idea and told Davey, "Hold on a second."

In my front tooth, I have a plate. I decided to take my teeth out and crouch under the window, on the opposite side from where Lou was enjoying his meal. While obscuring myself, I reached up and tapped against the glass with only my teeth.

"Holy shit!" Lou said, before exploding into laughter.

I emerged from beneath the window to share in the laugh. Lou was half crazy himself, so he loved it.

When you're on the road as often as wrestlers were, those kinds of pranks were necessary in order to help us unwind.

As I was finishing up in the WWWF, I took a backdrop and wound up breaking my finger. I was wrestling Billy White Wolf at the time, and I slid off of his sweaty back in the middle of the move and landed crookedly. I had to tape my finger up for a while after that.

Billy's character came into existence because Joe Scarpa had gotten over so well as "Chief" Jay Strongbow, a Native American character. Billy was brought in to be Jay's partner in a Native American tag team. Outside of the ring, Jay's Native American portrayal was so convincing, he would actually get invited to tribal meetings around the Northeast, and he would drag Billy along with him once they began teaming together. The only issue was that the members of the tribe didn't believe Billy was actually Native American. Jay told me how an elder from one of the tribes approached him and said, "Don't bring *that* man with you anymore. We know you're one of us, but *he* isn't. *We* can tell!"

ELEVEN – "I *will* slap you in the face"

Right after finishing up in New York, I went home for the holidays. The options in front of me at the time involved going to Charlotte to work in the Mid-Atlantic territory, or going to New Brunswick to work for the Kay brothers. During my time off, I went to watch the local WWA matches because my friend Ivan Koloff had just started working for Dick the Bruiser. I met up with Ivan and accompanied him into the heel dressing room. Before long, Dick the Bruiser and Wilbur Snyder walked in and noticed me sitting there.

"Oh my God!" Dick said, playing up kayfabe. "We're in the wrong dressing room!"

Then he and Snyder abruptly whirled around to leave.

"It's okay!" Ivan called to them. "He's one of the boys!"

Dick and Snyder spun back around and resumed their activities inside the locker room. I was a little taken aback that they didn't seem to know who I was. I quickly found out it had all been a ruse, and the Bruiser soon approached me and asked, "Hey… do you want to come work for me?"

"Make me an offer!" I said to him.

I was actually intrigued by the idea of working for my hometown promotion and working with my childhood hero Dick the Bruiser. That would have been a dream come true. Instead, Dick shut all of my fantasizing down in a hurry.

"Ha… Keep on traveling, kid," Dick laughed, and then walked away.

"Okay, I will!" I shouted back.

When it was all said and done, I never wrestled in Indianapolis, nor did I ever wrestle Dick the Bruiser. Those are two of the greatest regrets of my wrestling career.

The Eastern Sports Association was founded in 1969 by Al Zinck and two of the brothers from the Cormier wrestling family, Rudy Kay and Bobby Kay. In addition to the aforementioned two, there were two other Cormiers who wrestled for the ESA, Leo Burke and The Beast, who I'd first met long ago while working for the Sheik as a rookie in Detroit.

Headquartered in Halifax, Nova Scotia, the ESA was ostensibly designed to give the Cormier brothers an opportunity to inflate their reputations within the professional wrestling world and provide them with a platform to work as top attractions. More often than not, the brothers held onto the top championships in the territory - the International Wrestling North American Heavyweight Championship, and the International Tag Team Championships, briefly sharing them with visiting stars and then beating those stars to reacquire their belts.

The ESA's territory was known as "The Maritimes" and it was supported by a series of small towns throughout Nova Scotia and New Brunswick. Some of the towns they ran consistent shows in were Halifax, Saint John and Moncton - which was where everyone in the territory lived. I spent my time living in a tiny apartment, which was about the size of a hotel room. They ran a lot of dates, but it often amounted to a lot of work for miniscule payoffs.

Even though I'd just finished a run in New York as Buggsy McGraw, the Kay brothers had me wrestle as The Brute since the fame I'd generated while wrestling under that name in Vancouver had spread all across Canada, even to the opposite coast. Had I not been promised a top position in New Brunswick, I never would've gone there. The Kays immediately put the North American Championship on me in May of 1976 after having me beat Tommy Gilbert, the father of "Hot Stuff" Eddie Gilbert and Doug Gilbert. Tommy was one of the Kays' favorites, but I didn't think his Tennessee style of wrestling jibed very well with the way I'd learned to work in all of the other territories.

In nearly all circumstances, the Cormiers came off as a group of arrogant pricks. They all seemed to believe they were collectively the best workers in the entire wrestling industry, and they also thought their tiny promotion in the Canadian Maritimes was the crown jewel of the wrestling world. They would make fun of *everyone*, and they were never friendly to anyone. On top of all of that, they would ridicule McMahon's WWWF promotion in New York, along with its staff and performers. The Cormier's were insane because they could clearly only *dream* of running a promotion like Vince's!

Getting tossed by "The Mongolian Stomper" Archie Gouldie

Al Zinck was no picnic either. He went out of his way to enforce rules that didn't even exist. I was outside the locker room eating a hot dog while watching matches with Davey O'Hannon. Both of us were heels at the time, but that didn't prevent Al Zinck from walking up and saying to us, "You gotta kayfabe."

160

I looked around; the only people there were Al, Davey and I, and *all* of us were heels.

"*Who* am I supposed to kayfabe?" I asked him. "The *hot dog?*"

Davey started his career in the Kansas City territory and had his second-ever match with the iconic Lou Thesz. As I mentioned before, Lou was highly respected as a real shooter in the business, which was one of the reasons he won the world championship in the first place. Davey knew he was going to have to put Lou over and was willing to do whatever the legend asked of him.

With Lou Thesz early in my career

Davey was an Irish-Italian boy from New Jersey and was raised in a very good home where strong family values were taught. I never met Davey's mother, but I did meet his father who impressed me as a man of character. Davey also played football at the University of Missouri and knew how to handle himself in a fight.

Lou began to explain to Davey what was going to happen in the match. Davey was as green as grass and knew that Lou was one of the ultimate icons in the business and wanted to show him respect as a legend and veteran, consistent with the way he was raised.

"Whatever you want to do is fine with me, Lou," said Davey, eagerly.

"Great!" Lou said. "The first thing I am going to do is back you into the corner and slap your face."

Davey's father had taught him that a slap in the face was a true insult that should never be tolerated. In response to Lou, Davey looked him square in the eyes and said, "If you slap me in the face, Mr. Thesz, I *will* slap *you* in the face."

Lou never did slap Davey, and the two of them had a good match. For a young, green kid in the wrestling business, Davey had some *huge* balls.

All in all, New Brunswick was a massive step down from working in New York. There was nothing likeable about it, and I decided to get out of there as quickly as I could. Truth be told, I could only blame myself. Vince had been willing to send me to Charlotte when I left New York, and that was a territory where there was a lot of money to be made. I always wanted to blaze my own trail and be independent, but joining the ESA had been a grave mistake.

If I'd gone to Charlotte in 1976, I could have been working in matches with Ric Flair, Wahoo McDaniel, Greg Valentine and Paul Jones, and making great money in the process. That would have been astronomically better than putting up with the Cormiers and making pennies!

The people I worked with the most were The Beast, Leo Burke, Rudy Kay and Archie Gouldie. Of the four, the only exceptional worker was Archie, which was no great surprise. Archie had the main-event experience and the pedigree, and he knew what he was doing. Mad Dog Martel and Frenchy Martin were also around, working in their tag team known as "The Mercenaries." If Mad Dog's brother Rick Martel had been around, then there definitely would have been a babyface worker around for me to tear the house down with, but I don't even know if that could have saved the territory from trending downward.

Choking out Eric Pomeroy

Instead of Rick Martel, I was stuck working with guys like Eric Pomeroy. Eric was a big-time alcoholic, and he had the terrible habit of working in matches *while* he was drunk, too. He'd get in the ring, stagger around with a glassy look in his eyes, and talk a *lot* of trash.

"You wanna try me, Brute?" he'd say through slurred speech. "I'll show you somethin'! Let's wrestle. You dumbass, you!"

In a real fight, I would have kicked Eric's ass in six seconds… especially given how inebriated he was. During one of our matches, I was supposed to drop a knee on him from the top turnbuckle. This drunken idiot crawled all the way into the corner, which made it impossible for me to drop the knee. Instead, I jumped off the top rope, turned around in the air, and stomped Eric.

Even Bobby Kay, who was a serial complainer and one of my top critics, took my side for once.

"What was that fool doing!?" he said, exasperated. "*Why* would he get himself stuck under the ropes like that!?"

"Because he's a drunk *asshole*!" I replied. "Talk to him about it!"

Even though he knew how dangerous Eric was, Bobby still came to me at another show and said, "How would you feel about letting Eric give you a piledriver out on the floor in your match?"

"Should I make my reservation for a hospital bed now or later?" I answered. "Absolutely not! I can't trust him. He's a *drunk*."

There's no way I was going to let Eric drop me on my head out on the concrete floor. Not only was he sloppy drunk half the time, but when he got drunk, he *thought* he was a shooter. Making myself physically vulnerable to this guy was far too risky. I'd be putting my life and career in his alcoholic hands.

When I was completely fed up with working for the Cormiers, I gave my notice, dropped the championship back to Tommy Gilbert, and drove home to Indiana to plan my next move.

Following my debacle in The Maritimes, I called Gorilla Monsoon, and he helped arrange for me to make my return to the Australian version of World Championship Wrestling. By that point, Larry O'Dea and Ron Miller were running the Aussie territory. Larry was a wrestler and an Australian who had worked there for essentially his entire career. It was widely rumored that Larry O'Dea used to provide sexual services to Jim Barnett, and that's how he procured control of the Australian wrestling promotion.

To say O'Dea wasn't the promoter Jim Barnett was would be a gross understatement. For one thing, O'Dea didn't attempt to run shows in nearly as many large venues as Barnett did. He was also far more of a penny pincher than Barnett, and often skimped when it came time to spend money on travel or accommodations.

In all fairness, some of the travel issues weren't entirely O'Dea's fault. Australia was in the midst of an air traffic controllers' strike, and no flights from anywhere in the world were allowed to land in the country. Well, theoretically they could, but no air traffic controllers would have been around to help them land at any of the airports. That dispute shut the country down for an entire week. There were also issues involved with train travel. The distance from Sydney to Melbourne was roughly 500 miles. If you took the train, they made you switch to a different locomotive once you crossed into Victoria, because the gauge of the track was different in each Australian state. It was insane to me!

Most guys aren't in Australia for that long. An average Australian tour for a wrestler was three to six months, so my one-year stints were downright lengthy by comparison.

Steve Rickard was running the New Zealand territory, and I also spent two months working there in cooperation with the Australia office. Malaysia and Singapore were part of his domain, so we also performed there. There were guys from several countries on that tour, including a few from Australia, several Europeans, about three Americans, and a handful of Japanese wrestlers.

Rickard told all of us we didn't need visas to get into Malaysia, which didn't sound right to me. Later, I learned that if you went into Malaysia and you were from *any* country other than the U.S., you were given preferential treatment. On the flipside, all Americans were *required* to have visas, which is something Rickard hadn't bothered to look into. I'd like to give him the benefit of the doubt that he simply didn't check on it. This was all happening toward the end of the Vietnam War, and Southeast Asians weren't very thrilled with Americans in that part of the world.

I went down to the U.S. Embassy, and they told me Malaysia would let you *into* the country with no problems at all, but if you tried to get *out* of Malaysia without showing them a valid visa, they'd slap you in handcuffs and throw you in jail. Believe me, nobody wanted to spend time in a Malaysian prison.

Compared to Malaysian prisons, America's worst prisons are like the Ritz-Carlton. Once I found out the risk we were taking, I went to Rickard and told him point blank, "I'm not going to Malaysia, because I'm *not* going to prison there. There's no chance of that happening. I just had a guy from the Malaysian immigration department tell me to my face, 'Yeah, you can get in, but you can't get out!'"

After that, I went to the U.S. Embassy for further clarification, and they confirmed my understanding of the situation. I wasn't anxious to go fooling around in a foreign country I wouldn't be able to get out of.

I told Rickard, "Either you get us visas, or I'm not going. I'm going to tell the other guys, too."

After I told the other American wrestlers about the situation with the visas, they weren't excited about the prospects of spending time in a Malaysian prison either.

"They'll let you in the country, no problem!" objected Rickard.

"That's *not* the problem," I clarified. "The problem is getting *out* again. If we don't have visas, they'll put us in jail."

After that, Rickard finally relented and forked over the money for the visas.

The first time I went to Malaysia in 1971, the headlines of the newspapers would show the position of the armed conflicts going on in the region. During this tour of the country, the newspapers showed the location of one of conflicts was only 20 miles outside of the town we'd be staying in.

Rickard was similar to Larry O'Dea inasmuch as he had a very difficult time filling Barnett's promotional shoes. For one thing, he had both faces and heels staying in the same hotel, which was both lazy on his part and damaging to the overall presentation of the business. Also, he was as bad as O'Dea when it came to the caliber of the hotels he booked us in.

During one of our Malaysia tours, I looked around at the room Rickard put us in and got royally pissed off. Everything was dirty and dilapidated. When I finally managed to get Rickard on the phone to complain about the accommodations, it was only after I'd been informed that he'd booked a much nicer hotel for himself and was staying there. He clearly knew he was booking the wrestlers into second-tier hotels, or he wouldn't have gone to the trouble of getting a room for himself elsewhere. And, it's not like he was simply the owner of the territory; Rickard was a wrestler just like us!

"This hotel is unacceptable, Steve" I told him. "Everything here is in horrible shape."

"Okay," he said. "I'll fix it."

Shortly thereafter, we were all moving into an upgraded hotel. For all of Jim Barnett's shortcomings, no one would argue that he didn't run WCW as a first-class operation, and his replacements just couldn't measure up.

No matter how poorly O'Dea and Rickard managed their promotions, working in Australia was still infinitely better than working for the Cormier family in Canada.

New Zealand seemed to be drawing decent crowds behind the efforts of Mark Lewin and King Curtis. The crowds weren't amazing, but they were solid for that part of the world. Lewin and Curtis knew how to position themselves to the point where they were essentially running the territory. In essence, they would ease themselves into assistant booking positions. They followed this same pattern in other territories, including Calgary.

Far from being upset by this, I thought Curtis and Mark did a great job. They took good care of their fellow Americans. Mark Lewin was extremely sharp and had a great head for the wrestling business, in addition to being a great worker in the ring. I'm sure his business savvy was one of the reasons Rickard invited him to Australia in the first place. Rickard *must* have known his product would suffer if he was the main person controlling it.

There were shows three times a week in New Zealand, which is actually where King Curtis was renting a house. There was plenty of beautiful countryside to enjoy. It wasn't much of a place to party, though. At 7:00 p.m., the country seemed to shut down entirely, so you couldn't find anything to do in the evenings. It was a very boring lifestyle for a wrestler, and I was more or less on my own. They brought me in as a heel, so I couldn't hang out with any of the babyfaces they were trying to push, like Rick Martel. Martel was establishing himself as a top, young babyface, and he was supremely energetic and always worked exceptionally hard to make his matches exciting.

Larry booked me to win the NWA Austra-Asian Tag Team Championships with two different partners - Butcher Brannigan and Mario Milano. Butcher was a regular in the territory who wound up spending the majority of his career in Australia and New Zealand.

I was doing a promotional interview one afternoon at a Melbourne television station, which wasn't far from a very nice apartment I was renting out there on Spring Street. Also at the TV station was Paul Hogan, better known as "Crocodile Dundee," who was there to promote his one-hour syndicated show which aired throughout the country.

Hogan sent one of his aides over to ask if I'd like to appear on his show, which he'd be recording in one hour. I readily agreed. As soon as the show opened, Paul went into his opening monologue and then brought out his special guest, Buggsy McGraw.

Paul was standing on a foot-high platform. I came out and said, "Paul, how ya doing? It's great to see you! You know, Paul, when I speak, it always helps me out to have the microphone in my own hand."

After I prompted him, Paul extended the handheld microphone to me. Once I had the microphone securely in my hand, I said to him, "Paul... you know what? I think we need to change the name of the show to *The Buggsy McGraw Show!*"

With that, I shoved Paul in his shoulder and he went flying off the platform and onto the floor. I turned to the camera and said, "Welcome to *The Buggsy McGraw Show*, everybody!"

I continued on this way even though I was truly concerned that I'd either injured Paul or seriously pissed him off. After I shoved him off the stage, he was sprawled out on the floor and never got up!

Once we cut to the commercial, I walked over to Paul and explained, "Hey, Paul... I hope you know I'm just working with you. I'm trying to be entertaining. I really wasn't trying to be a prick or an asshole out there."

"Are you kidding?!" Paul exclaimed. "I loved it! It was great!"

That was a relief. Paul was a big national celebrity and could have caused real trouble for me if I'd upset him, and I wouldn't really have been able to blame him if he'd been pissed at me. I wouldn't want someone shoving me off the stage of my own television show without any warning!

After the show aired, I saw Larry O'Dea before one of our wrestling events began, and I expected him to be over the moon about my appearance on *The Paul Hogan Show*. Instead, I got berated.

"What do you think you're doing going on *The Paul Hogan Show*?!" he asked, angrily. "*Who* told you that you could do that?!"

"What do you mean?" I responded. "Paul *asked* me to go on the show!"

"That's a *national* show!" Larry said. "I need to have a say in who goes on a national show representing my company!"

"You should be happy!" I told him. "This only helps wrestling!"

"That's not the point!" Larry replied. "You need to get *my* permission!"

That just blew me away. I'm sure if the people from *The Paul Hogan Show* had come to him, he would have gone on it himself, and I'll bet he wouldn't have brought any other wrestlers on the show to stand alongside him, either. Larry was just a royal asshole, and that was when I knew I just wouldn't be able to function in Australia for too much longer with him at the helm.

Even though Larry's dislike for me was obvious, he still came to me at the beginning of November and said, "If you want to come back next year, I'll bring you back."

"I'll think about it," I lied.

I was a little surprised Larry had offered to hold a spot open for me, even though I was drawing him money. Regardless, I had zero intentions of remaining there to work for him. I was *far* away from home in another country, and the promoter was constantly acting like an asshole. Larry was belligerent, loud and condescending, and his favorite way to communicate with the wrestlers was by raising his voice to us. If I stayed, I knew Larry and I would eventually get into a fight, and I'd go *out of my way* to kick his ass if that ever happened. Of course, I'd have been arrested if that ever happened, but it would have been worth it!

Larry's way of running a territory was backwards. The local guys were definitely paid less than the overseas stars, who received solid salaries. Yet, he screamed the loudest at the foreign talent, which meant he created a disincentive for anyone to want to travel all the way to Australia to put up with him. Most of the other foreign talent like myself, Bruiser Brody, Don Muraco and Butcher Brannigan, were all clearly socking away our money. Brody, in particular, tried to save every cent he could.

I wasn't around Brody much. I didn't like him, and the feeling was probably mutual. He was a very unpleasant person whenever I was around him, and he would always say things to cut down and belittle other wrestlers.

Brody got knifed and murdered by Jose "Invader 1" Gonzales in 1988, who I knew from working in Oregon, and who I actually always liked.

Of all people, Harley Race said, "Bruiser Brody was a bully," which in my experience was 100 percent true. It's probably what got him killed. For Harley to say this was noteworthy, because I never knew Harley to go out of his way to say a bad thing about anybody who didn't have it coming to them.

Harley was as hard a worker as there has ever been in the wrestling business. In my opinion, he's the *greatest* world champion in wrestling history. I rank Bruno Sammartino as the "best" champion because of the mystique he developed and how he carried himself as the champion of a major territory, including how he dressed and conducted himself in public, but Harley was the "greatest" because of how he performed and sacrificed himself to make other guys look great. Harley traveled all over the world and worked a physically taxing style for an hour every night in order to advance the business and make other wrestlers look like winners.

When I left Australia for the final time, I didn't have another territory lined up to work for. I was so sick of Larry O'Dea after 11 months that I just wanted out of there. I was also a little burnt out and was looking forward to some time off. I was at my parents' house in Indiana when, out of the blue, I got a call from Bill Watts, the owner and booker of the NWA Tri-State territory that ran shows in Oklahoma, Louisiana and Mississippi.

"You want to go to work?" Bill asked.

"Actually, Bill, I was hoping to take some time off," I said.

"Well, I've got a spot for you," Bill replied. "Just come on down and see how you like it."

Soon after that, I was driving down to work for Watts in the Deep South.

TWELVE – "You've done well for yourself"

Leroy McGuirk's NWA Tri-State territory extended from Louisiana and Mississippi to Oklahoma and Arkansas, and even included some towns in Missouri. Leroy was a star in the NWA as early as the 1930s, and held the NWA World Light Heavyweight Championship for more than ten consecutive years. Sadly, his career was cut short by a horrific car accident which left him blind.

With his in-ring career over, Leroy bravely turned to promoting, and in 1975 he turned the booking reigns of his territory over to "Cowboy" Bill Watts, a very popular wrestling star in the area.

Watts was a big Oklahoman who McGuirk once voted for to win the NWA championship during the annual meeting of the NWA's board of directors. He also challenged Bruno Sammartino for the WWWF title on several occasions, and was AWA kingpin Verne Gagne's protege in certain respects. Harley Race said Watts tried to emulate everything Verne did, which wasn't always a good thing. Race also referred to both Verne and Watts as "bullies." Thankfully, Watts never tried to bully me, and we got along fine.

Among the people working for Watts at the time were Pat Barrett, Bobby Jaggers, Steven Little Bear, "The Spoiler" Don Jardine, Paul Orndorff, Skandar Akbar, Ernie Ladd, Cowboy Bob Ellis and my old friend "The Assassin" Jody Hamilton, who was also assisting Watts with the booking from time to time.

I'd grown up watching Cowboy Ellis wrestle Dick the Bruiser in front of huge Indianapolis crowds, so I was thrilled to finally have an opportunity to meet and work with him. Boy, was I ever *disappointed!* After finally working with Ellis, I was forced to lump Ellis in the same category with all of the old timers who had a format for their matches which they refused to deviate from. If you didn't work the way Ellis wanted to work, then the match could never be good. Even after two decades in the business, he lacked any ability to improvise. Every time I suggested something different to

Ellis outside of his comfort zone, he would just flat out tell me, "No!"

This may be hard to believe, but Paul Orndorff was really green when I got to NWA Tri State. Despite his lack of experience, Orndorff had a phenomenal - or dare I say "Wonderful" - look to him, including a well-sculpted physique. Paul also had the internal engine of an athlete. Watts obviously saw all of the potential Orndorff possessed, and he told me point blank, "Buggsy, I want Paul to learn how to work, so I'm putting him in the ring with you."

ORNDORFF VS. BRUTE MOST BITTER FEUD

ORNDORFF   BRUTE

Promotional poster for a match with Paul Orndorff

After that conversation, Orndorff and I worked together every night for seven straight weeks, except for a lone night off, and there were a few nights we nearly engaged in legitimate fisticuffs simply because Paul was so stubborn.

"Do a knee lift!" I'd tell Paul.

Instead of throwing a knee lift, Paul would do something else entirely, as if I'd been speaking a foreign language. So I'd grab him, herd him into the corner, lift him over to the turnbuckle and say, "*Listen! This* is what we're going to do now!"

I understood Orndorff was young and inexperienced, but I was trying to get him to learn to do things the right way and listen to the crowd. Despite Paul's hardheadedness, he improved by leaps and bounds over the course of our run together. Every night, he got incrementally better.

I got along very well with Watts, but there were some things I didn't like about the way he ran his territory. Like many other promoters, Bill would invite locals who ran their mouths about how fake and easy wrestling was to come to the shows early. When they arrived, Watts would offer them a chance to climb into the ring.

Once those locals were in the ring and ready to work up a sweat, a few of the guys from the roster would put them through a strenuous workout. After the local tough guys were thoroughly exhausted, Watts would climb into the ring and entertain himself by smacking the *shit* out of them.

I can totally understand the idea of protecting the reputation of our business, but if you're going to whip someone's ass, you should do it fairly, when they're fresh, and while they can still defend themselves. Don't wait until someone else has turned the guys into limp rags before you climb in and start beating them up.

We were driving from Little Rock over to Oklahoma City, which was easily a 300-mile trip. There were at least three of us in the car. Along the way, the car broke down. We needed to make sure we would be arriving at the town that night because the show was the same night. We called all of the airlines, and there were no flights. Then we checked the train station, but there were no trains. We called a cab company, and none of the companies were willing to drive us all the way to Oklahoma City.

"You're crazy!" they told us. "That's too far!"

I called Bill Watts directly, because I had the highest position on the card of all the people in the car, and they felt I would be the safest from the wrath of Watts if he opted to explode.

"We're stuck, Bill," I explained to him. "There are no planes, trains or cabs that can get us there."

"Just get to the airport," growled Watts. "I'll meet you there myself."

Watts actually got on his plane and flew from Oklahoma City to Little Rock to pick us up and bring us back. When I saw Watts waiting by his plane at the airport, I went up to him and said, "Bill... I'm *so* glad you didn't have anything else to do today!"

In response, Bill simply grumbled something under his breath. I'm sure he wasn't in a joking mood after that unplanned trip.

When I worked in NWA Tri State, I didn't have a regular apartment or house. I took whatever lodgings I could find in whatever town we were working in. In that territory, we were constantly on the move, so there wasn't much time to get settled in one place.

The Deep South crowds could get worked up in a hurry. I never experienced a full-scale riot there, but we were close on more than one occasion. At the Fayetteville Civic Center, we had police protection around the ring, and the head of the city's police force was there as the man in charge of the arena security. Even though he was friendly, I got the sense that this guy would create real trouble for anyone who crossed him.

Before I ever worked in this town, the boys told stories about the police chief. He was the kind of guy who could tell the fans to sit down, and they would do it instantly. If they didn't, he would crack them with a nightstick on the spot. This guy was always standing at ringside while the matches were underway. During my match, there was a row full of fans who stood up as if they were ready to charge the ring. The policeman casually sauntered over and snarled, "Sit down!"

Immediately, they complied and took their seats. Never before or since have I ever seen an entire row rise to its feet as one and then sit right back down in unison immediately like that. The police chief's aura was more than enough to attain their compliance.

While we were in Lafayette, I wrestled Erik The Red one night. Jody was in the heel dressing room before things got started, but he came out in the middle of the match to watch. It was a back-and-forth match, and I bladed and got juice. Jody was sitting outside the door watching the matches, and when I walked past him, he told me, "That was one of the best matches I've ever seen." Again, it was one of those matches I called in the ring and led the other wrestler through. This was high praise coming from someone I respected as highly as Jody.

I was able to get home to see my parents in Indianapolis for a few days before I had to catch a flight back to Tulsa. When I got to the airport, I saw a familiar face while I was waiting for my plane. It just so happened that Dick the Bruiser was on the same flight as me, except he would be getting off in Memphis to wrestle there, while I would be changing planes and continuing on to Oklahoma. True to form, I waited until everyone else was on the plane before I walked on. As I headed over to the plane, I saw Bruiser standing outside the gate, staring at me menacingly. I continued right past him, got on the plane and sat in my seat, all without saying a single word to him.

When we arrived in Memphis, I was one of the last to deplane. Once I walked off the flight, I looked up and saw the Bruiser standing opposite the gate, watching me. As soon as he saw me enter the terminal, he turned and walked off into the hall. He thought I was working in Memphis. He didn't realize I would be getting on another plane bound for Tulsa.

Gary Hart used to go up to St. Louis, and he said he'd see the Bruiser there every so often. The first time he tried to shake the Bruiser's hand, he stuck his hand out, but the Bruiser wouldn't shake it. Rather than withdraw his hand, he held it out there and *made* the Bruiser shake it.

It was as Ivan Koloff had once told me, "Bruiser is not exactly a nice guy."

Watts wanted to get a feud going between myself and Steven Little Bear, and we started working a revenge angle in Shreveport after I'd beaten him senseless. The fans expected him to be out for my blood after we'd worked our angle, and so was I! I was waiting for Little Bear to come to the ring to try to extract violent retribution at my expense. Instead, he got in the ring, casually took off his headdress, and then stood around signing autographs for the fans at ringside while I stood there waiting for an assault that never came.

"You dumb son of a bitch!" I thought to myself. "You should be *attacking* me!"

We'd set the whole angle up, and we could have drawn money if he'd acted like he was even remotely upset with me. Instead, he wasted the whole setup.

"Bill, please… we worked this angle so that Little Bear should be hitting that ring like a wild Comanche because he's pissed at me!" I explained to Watts afterwards.

"Yeah, you're right," Watts said.

The next week, Watts talked to Little Bear right in front of me, and said, "Listen… you're *supposed* to be excited. You're supposed to be *pissed off*. You're supposed to be *angry*. Try that this time instead of just *standing* there and waiting for the fans to shove photos in your face for you to sign!"

I just got the feeling Little Bear wasn't excited to be working with me in particular. If you set up an angle properly, you could ride the heat from that angle for months. The babyface should be acting like a pissed-off asskicker every time he sees you!

My saddest moment while in New Orleans working for Watts was when I found out about my friend Lonnie Mayne's death from "The Outlaw" Ron Bass. Lonnie had died in a car accident in Los Angeles, and word had finally trickled over to Ron from one of his friends out west.

"What?!" I replied. "*No!*"

I grabbed my head and dipped it toward the ground. It was quite a huge shock to hear about the death of such a great friend. It was obviously unexpected.

"Oh, no!" I said. "*Damn… Lonnie…*"

177

By the time Ron found out about it, the funeral had already taken place. Lonnie had been working for NWA Hollywood Wrestling and was holding their top championship, the NWA Americas Heavyweight Championship, at the time of his death. I felt especially sorry for Lonnie's son, Nathan. I've heard all kinds of theories related to Lonnie's death, including the theory that it may have been a suicide. I have no way of knowing anything about it; I'm sure the pain of a divorce, mixed with depression and alcohol, is a perilous combination.

In April of 1978, NWA Tri State held its biggest event of the year, The Superdome Extravaganza. We drew over 30,000 people for the event, which Watts was thrilled about. I wrestled Paul Orndorff on the undercard, and the two main events were Andre the Giant against Ernie Ladd, and Harley Race against Dusty Rhodes. This was the only Superdome show I was ever part of while working for Watts.

They closed off the majority of the building and filled the reserved seating sections all the way to the top. Even with 30,000 people present in the arena, it was only one-third of a full house, so it didn't look nearly as impressive as a sold-out Madison Square Garden.

At the time of Dusty's appearance at the Superdome show, I still hadn't hung out with him much. In fact, the only time I could remember seeing him socially before that is when I got together with Dusty and his wife at Baron Von Raschke's house back when I worked in Detroit.

Dusty was clearly a great worker, but you kept hearing rumors swirling about how he had a large ego. I hadn't been around him enough to have an opinion about that, and human nature being what it is, most of the wrestlers talking about him were probably jealous of Dusty's success in the business. If Dusty had a huge ego, he'd earned the right to have one, because he was a true national superstar in the industry.

During one of the later shows in Louisiana, Dusty crossed over into the heel dressing room just to see me, which was genuinely unheard of for a babyface to do. Watts liked to fine people for doing just about anything out of line, and walking into the wrong dressing room was definitely fine-worthy behavior.

"Hey, Mike," Dusty said. "They told me you were in here, so I wanted to come over and see you. You've come a long way since we worked together in Detroit. I heard about the business you did up in New York with Bruno."

"Thanks, Dusty," I replied. "Yeah working with Bruno was fun. I made some decent money working with him, too."

"Well, if you ever want to make some more money, just come down to Florida," Dusty said. "I'm sure Eddie would love to have you back."

With that, Dusty turned and headed back to the babyface dressing room.

While I was still working for Watts, Vince McMahon Sr. got me on a tour of Japan called the Madison Square Garden Series. It started toward the end of April and continued until the beginning of June. This time, I would be working for New Japan Pro Wrestling, the company Antonio Inoki founded after leaving the Japan Pro Wrestling Association for the second and final time.

Nikolai Volkoff, Jay Strongbow, Baron Scicluna, and Bruno's son David Sammartino were there with me to fill out some of the undercard spots, while Andre the Giant, Antonio Inoki and Bob Backlund worked as the headliners. Along with providing us a spot on the tour, McMahon also got Strongbow and I involved in an advertising shoot for Suntory Whisky. One of the Japanese wrestlers held me in a headlock while the photographers took photos for the magazine ads.

Over the course of the next month and a half, I worked with Antonio Inoki and three of his young proteges who would soon leave an indelible mark on the landscape of puroresu: Yoshiaki Fujiwara, Riki Choshu and Tatsumi Fujinami.

Yoshiaki Fujiwara was the first graduate of the NJPW dojo, and he went on to solidify himself as one of the kings of worked-shoot matches, where the bouts looked hyper realistic and could only end in a knockout or a submission. In the '80s and '90s, Fujiwara played a role in the founding of two different promotions involved

Brute Power: The Autobiography of Buggsy McGraw

in the furtherance of this style: The Universal Wrestling Federation and Pro Wrestling Fujiwara Gumi.

Tatsumi Fujinami and Riki Choshu's careers intertwined considerably as they were clearly the two wrestlers poised to take the reins from Inoki whenever the NJPW founder decided to take a step back from in-ring competition. Fujinami was the ultimate ring technician, and Choshu was the charismatic power wrestler. In the early '80s, the two would feud over the World Wrestling Federation International Championship, which was defended in New Japan.

Disappointed at being left out of Inoki's first IWGP Heavyweight Championship tournament, Choshu formed his own company within a company, Japan Pro Wrestling. This developed into a real-life situation when all of the members of Choshu's JPW "company" formed a *real* promotion named JPW and defected to Giant Baba's All Japan Pro Wrestling! Choshu even won the PWF Heavyweight Championship in 1986, which for many years had been the top title in AJPW. After nearly a full year with the PWF belt, Choshu forfeited the title, abruptly returned to NJPW and began his feud with Fujinami all over again.

I've already written in glowing terms about what a wonderful worker Antonio Inoki was, and I experienced it firsthand during our MSG Series matches. His kicks *looked* vicious, but they really weren't stiff at all. All he cared about was making money, so he didn't mind selling for me either.

The Sheik requested that I travel north to appear on a show for him in Detroit. Coming back to the place where my wrestling career began was bittersweet. I was a far bigger deal in the business than I'd been as a rookie, but the Sheik didn't have much of a territory left, and all of the duct tape and crazy glue in the world couldn't have held things together for him in Detroit. When I flew in, I took the shuttle bus to the hotel inside of the Renaissance Center. This meant we had to travel through several parts of Downtown Detroit.

It was a very disheartening journey. Granted, it was the wintertime, but I only saw a *single person* on the street as we ventured into the downtown area. Also, the once luxurious hotel I'd stayed in

180

ten years prior, the Sheraton Cadillac, had been boarded up with plywood. The sight of that beloved hotel in such a deteriorated state nearly had me in tears.

"You've done well for yourself, boy," the Sheik said when he saw me. "I was right to get you started in the business."

The Sheik had me split the difference between my two names; he had me billed as "Brute McGraw" during the show, and I worked with Ox Baker yet again. Just like in years past, I had to come up with ways to work around Ox to make him look good, because if someone wanted to make Ox look bad, it wouldn't take a whole lot of effort. And, Ox knew that, too!

Unlike Ox, I really prided myself on my ability to work a match and control the crowd once we'd drawn them to the arena. Before our match I approached Ox and said, "Okay, Ox... here's the deal: If you want to have a great match, you listen to everything I tell you, because if you don't, I *will* make you look like shit."

"Yeah, okay!" Ox replied, not anxious to be made a fool of.

"Just stay in the middle of the ring and do what I tell you," I told him, and he nodded to show me he understood.

In the middle of our match, I knocked Ox down, and he said, "Mike! Don't leave! I can't get up!"

Ox was literally stuck there on the mat, helpless. This guy was so stiff and uncoordinated that he truly couldn't get to his feet. Once he was flat on his back, he was reminiscent of a turtle with its legs flailing helplessly in the air as it tried to roll back onto its stomach.

There were very few wrestlers with such a total lack of agility that they couldn't even get off the mat once they'd been knocked down, so in that respect, Ox was truly one of a kind. I helped Ox to his feet, ostensibly for the purpose of inflicting more damage to him, and then I refrained from knocking him down ever again. There was no point in creating extra work for myself.

"Just *stand* in the center of the ring!" I commanded him. "Do what I tell you! All you have to do is *listen* and we'll have a great match!"

Ox was the truest example of the proverbial broomstick, when high-level ring workers are forced to carry a hopeless, relatively immobile opponent to a good match.

Choking Ox Baker with a camera cable

Watts sent me to Georgia Championship Wrestling once I was done working for him in Louisiana. Jim Barnett was now the owner of GCW, and Ole Anderson was the booker waiting for me when I got there. If you know anything at all about Ole Anderson's reputation, it probably won't surprise you to learn that I didn't care for Ole Anderson very much.

Ole's real name is Alan Rogowski, and he worked under the name "Rock" Rogowski when he wrestled for Verne Gagne in the AWA in the '60s. Then he moved to the Mid-Atlantic territory and lucked his way into an established act - "The Minnesota Wrecking Crew," which was originally a tag team comprising Lars and Gene Anderson. Lars' real surname was Heiniemi, so Gene was the only true Anderson in the group.

After Ole replaced Lars, he and Gene captured nearly every major tag-team championship in the Carolinas and Georgia. Along the way, Ole offered his services to Barnett as a booker after Harley Race was finished with his attempt to book the territory, and Barnett agreed.

Ole brought me in as a babyface with a truck driving gimmick, which I thought was one of the *dumbest* decisions imaginable. I'd been the top main event heel in three different territories, and I'd even main evented in Madison Square Garden as a heel. I couldn't understand why the hell Ole would take an established heel worker like me and saddle him with a truck-driving babyface gimmick. It was highly limiting and made no sense at all!

"I need you to get a trucker hat and an airhorn," Ole said, explaining the gimmick to me. "You're going to work babyface as truck driver. You also need to start working in blue jeans."

"Excuse me?" I asked. "Babyface? Truck driver?"

"Did I stutter?" Ole said sarcastically. "A babyface truck driver. Go buy the stuff."

Ole probably could have warmed me up to the idea of becoming a babyface if he'd approached it properly, but arbitrarily telling a seasoned heel to make an instant transition to a babyface trucking gimmick was a poor way to broach the subject. Since I knew I could make money simply by working the way I always had, with the same gimmick I was accustomed to using, I just wasn't interested in Ole's wacky ideas.

Maybe things would have worked out better if I'd given it my all, but I honestly had no interest in running around as a truck driver in blue jeans while setting off an airhorn.

As a truck driver in Georgia

Early on in my Georgia run, we were working in a spot
show town, and a guy from the crowd hopped over the rail, and then
he jumped in the ring to try to attack Ole. However, the police were
able to corale the guy before he reached his target. After the guy was
held down and handcuffed, only then was Ole finally brave enough
to approach the guy and punch him in his unprotected face.

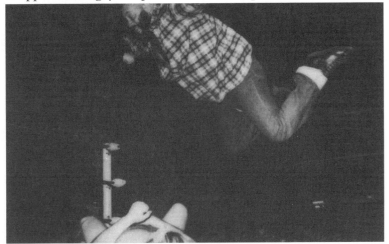

Hitting the big splash

To me, that was pure cowardice. The *real* badasses in our
business are able to face whatever comes at them head on. They
don't wait for the police to subdue an attacker before they take a
cheapshot at him. Once I'd seen that episode, there was no chance
Ole was ever going to earn my respect as a man.

That incident aside, Ole constantly made biting remarks
about wrestlers and their performances. On a couple occasions, I
pushed the envelope with my responses to him after he'd annoyed
me.

"Hey, you fuckin' Polak!" I said to him in front of the boys,
who were all aware of Ole's real surname and his Polish descent.

"Shut up!" some of the guys around me whispered. "What
are you doing?"

Really, I just wanted to see if I could goad Ole into a fight so
I could kick his ass, but he never took the bait.

Despite Ole never fighting me, there were other combustible elements in our locker room. I was fortunate to be in Georgia when Angelo Mosca got into his fight with Gordon Nelson. Like me, Gordon already had one divorce on his resume, and he'd been frequently seeing a very attractive lady in Atlanta. Angelo took note of Gordon's new flame, and waited for Gordon to be within earshot in the dressing room before saying, "That girl Gordon's with... she's *definitely* a cockholster!"

Mosca may have been a big, strong ex Canadian Football League All-Star, but Gordon had a reputation as a legit shooter. I didn't have a great view of the fight, but a lot of the boys intervened before things got too far out of hand.

Despite being saddled with the truck driving gimmick, I still managed to get over as a babyface with plenty of fans. One night after the matches, I was at a nightclub in Atlanta. Mosca was also there, but he'd been working as a heel. Sticking with kayfabe protocol, the two of us didn't get close to each other.

There was a group of fans at a table, and a fan who was wearing a sport coat came up to me, introduced himself as "Mr. Lucky," and invited me over to the table for a drink. I graciously accepted his offer, and before long I was drinking and joking with Mr. Lucky and his friends. Eventually, Mosca walked past us. Thinking he needed to say something to maintain kayfabe, the heel Mosca made some wiseass comment to me and kept walking.

Mosca was underestimating just how loyal and crazy the wrestling fans in Georgia could be. As Mosca walked away, Mr. Lucky stood up, walked over to me, and pulled a nickel-plated .45-caliber handgun from his fancy sport coat. Gesturing over at Mosca's retreating figure, Mr. Lucky whispered, "If you want me to *kill* that son of a bitch, I will! Just say the word."

At first I thought it was a joke, so I almost said, "Yeah! Shoot the son of a bitch!" Then I saw the look in Mr. Lucky's eyes and I realized he was *dead serious.*

"No, no, no, no, no!" I responded, quickly. "You don't have to do that!"

Almost looking disappointed, Mr. Lucky concealed his revolver and returned to his seat. The next day, I told Mosca about his close shave with Mr. Lucky's handgun from the previous evening, and he said, "Maybe I *should* watch my mouth a little more."

Teaming with Rufus Jones

Ole partnered me with Rufus Jones, who was a large African-American wrestler that got over huge with everyone, but expecially the black fans. I was familiar with his work in the Carolinas where he'd made a lot of money working with Blackjack Mulligan.

By no means was Rufus a great worker, but he was a downhome, black, southern wrestler with a sizeable fan following of both blacks and whites. He built this following by being highly charismatic and entertaining in the ring.

Perhaps the best thing about Rufus was how he would address the boys backstage. Often, he would forget people's names, or simply wouldn't bother to learn them, so he would just call everyone "Horse Cock" instead.

"Hey, Horse Cock!" he'd say when you entered the room. "How's it hangin'?"

I've yet to meet a man who would ever object to being called "Horse Cock."

As nice as it was being called "Horse Cock" all the time, three months in Georgia saddled with a truck-driving gimmick was about all I could handle, no matter how massive my horse cock was.

THIRTEEN – "I want that alligator"

I finally called Dusty to take him up on the offer he'd made me back in that Louisiana dressing room. I was sick of portraying a truck driver and wanted to work in my preferred heelish capacity.

Georgia had a hierarchy, and I couldn't see myself getting a main-event role there no matter what I did. On the babyface side, they were loaded with talented, popular guys, including Mr. Wrestling #2 and Rick Martel. However, the number one guy was future world champion "Wildfire" Tommy Rich, who was hot as a *firecracker*. I don't know that I've ever seen a wrestler who was more over with female wrestling fans than he was in those days. There was absolutely no room for anyone else to crack into a top, money-making position as a babyface, and certainly not a truck driver.

Dusty may have gotten me my job in Florida, but he wouldn't be booking me… at least not right away. That responsibility fell to the former NWA World Heavyweight Champion *and* the first ever WWWF World Heavyweight Champion, "Nature Boy" Buddy Rogers. Rogers had been one of wrestling's top attractions from the late 1940s right up until the early 1960s. In many ways, he was the prototype for every cocky, strutting and muscular bad guy who ever graced a wrestling ring. He practically *invented* the heel wrestling interview. The big problem Rogers had was that nobody in the industry liked him very much. He had a reputation for screwing people over, which led to plenty of wrestlers and promoters coming up with ways to preemptively screw Rogers out of self preservation.

Bruno told me to my face about the title change between himself and Rogers in New York that resulted in him wearing the WWWF World Heavyweight Championship for the first time. According to Bruno, Vince Sr. told Bruno he was winning the belt, but no one wanted to tell Buddy he was supposed to be losing it. Vince was concerned about Rogers' health after he'd had a heart attack, which was one of the reasons they wanted to get the championship off of Rogers' waist, but Rogers had no desire to lose the WWWF title and the main-event money that came with it.

Bruno said Vince and Toots Mondt - one of the other WWWF owners - approached him and said, "Can you *take* the fall on Rogers?" The way they said it implied they didn't think Rogers would lose the belt willingly. Early in his career, Bruno was probably 40 muscular pounds heavier than he was when I worked with him, so very few wrestlers would have been able to overcome his power unless it was a highly trained shooter. Rogers was *no* shooter.

Almost as soon as the match between the two started, Bruno called for his backbreaker finishing hold, which Rogers probably assumed Bruno would be letting him escape from, so he gleefully fed into the move. Once Bruno had Rogers up over his shoulder in the backbreaker, Bruno simply cinched the hold in and told Rogers he needed to clearly, vocally and openly give up, or his back would be broken. Rogers soon complied, and Bruno began his record-setting reign as WWWF champion.

When I first showed up in Florida, Sonny King approached me in the dressing room.

"I hear you're looking for a place to stay," he said.

"Yeah, I haven't got a place yet," I told him.

"Well, you can stay with me if you want," Sonny said. "All I'd need from you is five dollars a day."

Both of us were heels, so if the two of us were seen together, or were known to be living together, it wouldn't insult the wrestling fans' sensibilities. I stayed with Sonny for the next three months, and we also traveled together to nearly all of the shows. Sonny's wife was back at their home in Louisiana, and he was *constantly* screwing around with the local white women. He was usually involved with more than one girl at a time. There were occasions when Sonny would be in his room with one girl, and another girl would be banging on the door and hollering for him.

"*Don't* let her in!" Sonny yelled to me. "Keep her *outside!*"

Of course, being the friend that I was, I walked right over to the door and opened it up to see this petite lady standing there, fuming.

"I want to see Sonny, *now!*" she screamed at me. "I *know* he's here! Tell him to get out here!"

"No chance," I said, while closing the door on her. "You should get out of here. He *doesn't* want to see you."

Instead of leaving, the girl walked around to the window and tried pry it open. All the while, Sonny was in bed with his other lady friend, waiting for the ruckus to subside. To say Sonny had no difficulty wooing women would be an understatement. He could secure any race of woman he wanted, but for some reason, I only ever saw him out in public with the local white girls.

As soon as I got to Florida, I dumped the truck driver gimmick, but I also felt I needed to give my prior heel routine an update. I knew Eddie and Buddy didn't have any real plans for me, nor did they foresee me progressing past the middle of the card. To counter this, I watched as many matches from our shows as I could so that I could figure out who my real competition on the roster was, and then I figured out what I needed to do to overcome them. I took to wearing colorful headbands, and an assortment of t-shirts with different catchphrases on them.

Once I won a championship, I came to the ring wearing the title belt, while wearing a shirt emblazoned with a photo in which I was wearing the exact same outfit *and* wearing the very same title belt. It was fun to be obnoxious and get under the skins of the fans. Standing by my side to help me elicit rage from the audience was my manager, the evil Sir Oliver Humperdink.

In the ring, I was working my butt off. There is *nothing* in the world that can draw money in the wrestling business quite like a vicious heel. I used to kick the *crap* out of the babyfaces, and the fans would think I was killing them. One of the things I started doing as a heel in Florida would be to climb into the ring and then pace back and forth between the ropes. I'd never stop moving, nor would I even acknowledge my opponent's presence. Then, when the bell rang, I would come to a sudden stop, pound my chest, and then charge after my adversary. Before long, I'd captured the attention of the people, and I also had the attention of Eddie and Mike Graham. They could see I was a kickass heel who knew how to work the crowd into a frenzy.

We were at the office at 106 North Albany in Tampa, which was where we did the TV tapings. I was there on a Wednesday when the checks were being handed out. As I was looking at my check, Mike Graham walked by just as I said, "Awww crap! Look at *this!*" Mike paused and looked at me for a moment before whirling around and walking straight back into the office. Immediately after that, the amount of money on my checks increased. That's when I knew for certain that Mike and his father saw value in me.

Interview segment with the great Gordon Solie

Mike was a small guy relative to most pro wrestlers in the industry, but he could work and was *very* strong. He also had balls, and wouldn't hesitate to fight you. There were guys who'd complain about not wanting to sell for Mike in the ring because he was small, or because he was the promoter's son. However, Mike was a guy you could have a tremendous match with, and the crowd would be totally into it. If you could steal the show and win the favor of the owner by having a great match with his son, why *wouldn't* you want to sell for him? If selling for Mike was going to make me money, then why kill the goose who was laying the golden eggs? Besides, in a business replete with promoters' sons who sucked in the ring, Mike was one of the standouts who could actually wrestle.

Dusty put me in a tag team with the big Korean wrestler Pak Song, and in March we won the NWA Florida Tag Team Championships in West Palm Beach from Mike Graham and Steve Keirn, only to drop the belts right back to them one week later. Then they immediately put me in best-of-three-falls matches with the NWA Florida Heavyweight Champion, Jimmy Garvin. I saw all of this as a test to see if I could get over in main event tag team matches and singles matches, and it appears as if I passed those tests.

A different type of sign that I was getting over came in the form of imitation. Sweet Brown Sugar, a popular black babyface who wore a mask, began to copy my chest-pounding and charging move almost immediately, which I didn't appreciate at all. Dusty eventually had to tell Sugar, "Knock it off and come up with your own shit!"

During that heel run, I was driving in the car with "The Viking" Scott Irwin beside me, and with Pak in the backseat. We were traveling along a two-lane country road at around 70 miles an hour. Along the way, a car came right up behind us. Through the rearview mirror, I could see the trailing vehicle was filled with four young men in their 20s. Since they were riding our bumper, I decided to slow down to 50 miles an hour to make it easy for them to pass us. Instead, they slowed down and remained glued to our bumper.

Since that tactic didn't work, I decided to try outrunning them. I gunned the car to 90 miles an hour, but the men reacted by matching my speed and staying as close as they could to the rear of our vehicle. Obviously, they were itching for a conflict. When we arrived at the nearest small town, I pulled our car into a convenience store parking lot. While Song and Scott walked into the store to grab some chips and Coke, I lingered inside our car and kept my eyes on the road. The car containing the four men made a U-turn, and then pulled into the parking lot right behind us.

As the four men climbed out of their car, I walked around to the trunk of my car, popped it open, and pulled out a club. Seeing

193

this, the driver of the other car popped open his trunk and retrieved a *shotgun*. After taking a few steps from behind his car to move closer to me, the man leveled the shotgun at my chest. I looked at his shotgun, then to my club, then back to his shotgun, and then back to my club. Realizing the hopelessness of my predicament, I quickly tossed the club into the trunk of my car and slammed it shut. If bringing a knife to a gunfight is stupid, bringing a *club* to a gunfight is even more idiotic. The last thing I wanted to do was give this fool an excuse to shoot me.

"You think you're so big and tough on TV, don't you?" the man asked. "But you guys are nothing special in person!"

Scott Irwin poked his head out of the convenience store's door to observe the scene as the man kept berating me. I just stood there, patiently waiting for the guy to finish his diatribe. When he was satisfied that he'd made his point, he climbed back into his car, and his friends followed suit. As they drove away, I walked into the convenience store and used their phone to call the police. Babyface wrestlers had their fair share of conflicts out on the road, but heels almost always got it worse. Frankly, I'm surprised there aren't a bunch of stories of heel wrestlers getting shot dead by fans as they walked around in public.

One of my wildest nights in wrestling occurred when we were in Hollywood, Florida, at the Sportatorium. That place was huge and could hold about 20,000 people. At the time, we were only using half of the arena, so a 100-foot-long black curtain was drawn to cut us off from the empty space, and it extended 50 feet in the air to obstruct the view of the unused part of the building. There were 7,000 people in the crowd, which was a sizeable group of fans for that part of the state.

Sonny and I were at the ringside area standing right next to the huge black curtain, observing the action taking place in the ring. Out of nowhere, some guy in the uppermost row of the bleachers bellowed out, "*Heyyyy nigger!*" It goes without saying that he was referring to Sonny King with that racial slur and not to me. Even under the best circumstances, Sonny was a hothead who took no shit from anyone at any time. If a racist fan thought he was safe from

194

Sonny King simply because he was in the top row of a huge arena, with thousands of people separating them from one another, he was in for a very rude awakening!

Taking note of where the heckler was sitting, Sonny charged into the stands and started running up the steps.

"What are you doing, Sonny?" I said to myself.

Even though Sonny was running, it seemed to take forever for him to make it to the top of the arena. In the meantime, the heckler just stood there in stunned surprise that the wrestler he'd insulted was headed straight for him. When Sonny arrived at the top of the stairs, he worked his way over to the fan for what I assumed would be an intense argument. Instead, Sonny simply socked the man squarely in the jaw and dropped him right back in his chair.

Satisfied that he'd exacted a measure of justice, Sonny then turned and ran all the way back down the aisle to join me at ringside. By the time he made it back down the aisle, the rednecks in attendance were already starting to move angrily toward the front of the arena. Sonny's back was to the crowd, but I could plainly see just how upset that were, and how big of a problem we might potentially be facing in just a moment or two.

"Sonny…" I said quietly, as I slowly started backing my way toward the dressing room.

"Yeah, I know," Sonny replied, and he followed my lead.

All of a sudden, a huge section of the black curtain started to come apart, and we realized there were about 200 people trying to get through it to get to Sonny. In response, the two of us dove to the floor to find some weapons. I grabbed a two-by-four, Sonny found a lead pipe, and the two of us started swinging at whichever rioters got close to us as we backed our way toward the dressing room door. It was clear that if this mob ever managed to pull us down to the floor and hold us in place, we would both be *dead*.

Finally, when we were close enough to the dressing room, we sprinted inside, slammed the big metal door behind us, and bolted it shut. In the meantime, the security team was having a horrific experience inside the arena, and several officers were injured trying to restore order to the Sportatorium.

"Are you okay, man?" Sonny asked me after we got back through the door. "*Shit*! I'm sorry about that!"

"What are you sorry for?" I replied. "That guy was an *asshole*! He had it coming."

Even outside of the arenas, Sonny was constantly getting into fights. One time, we were driving to a building, and some driver made an unflattering comment to Sonny while we were sitting at an intersection. Rather than let it go, Sonny emerged from our car brandishing a .45-caliber handgun, and the guy's tires squealed as he tore through the red light to avoid catching a bullet from a crazed wrestler.

On a different trip, Sonny was behind the wheel as we were driving to Naples. We came across a young, four-foot-long alligator which was slowly making its way across the street. We had to swerve a little to avoid it, and we still probably would have hit it if it hadn't skittered backwards off of the street.

Sonny slammed on the breaks, pulled the car off to the side of the road and looked over at me with purpose in his eyes.

"I *want* that alligator," he said.

"Let's go get him then!" I responded.

Sonny reached into his glove compartment, extracted his .45-caliber handgun, and handed me a towel from the gym bag he kept in his backseat. Then the two of us climbed out of the car and chased the alligator down.

"Throw the towel over his head!" Sonny yelled.

I obliged, and then Sonny handed me the .45, grabbed the alligator by the tail and began wrestling with it. I leveled Sonny's handgun at the reptile while Sonny struggled to hold it in place.

"Don't shoot *me*!" Sonny screamed. "Just shoot *him*!"

"I ain't gonna shoot you!" I yelled back.

For a few more moments, Sonny struggled to gain control of the alligator. Suddenly, he decided he'd had enough.

"Oh, the hell with this!" Sonny said, relinquishing his hold on the critter's tail. The two of us then returned to the car.

"Why did you let him go?" I asked him.

"I was afraid you were going to shoot me!" Sonny said.

"I wasn't going to shoot you!" I responded, somewhat insulted. "I was going to shoot him in the *head!* How was I going to shoot *you?* You're at the tail and I'm at the head!"

"It wasn't worth the risk," Sonny said as we pulled off.

When I wasn't riding with Sonny, I would ride from town to town in a van with Jos Leduc. Because there was plenty of room, other wrestlers would pile into the van with us. During one of the trips, Bill Dromo took it upon himself to make fun of my speech impediment in front of Jos. As soon as the ride was over and we stepped out of the van, Jos looked Bill directly in the eyes and said, "You are no longer welcome to ride in my van, Bill."

Jos made that declaration as payback for Bill making fun of my speech impediment. I *never* forgot the way Jos took up for me like that. He was a *great* friend.

Everyone from Danny Miller to Bruno Sammartino had warned me that Buddy Rogers was a guy you couldn't trust. In fact, Miller told me the story about how his brother Bill got into a fight with Rogers in the locker room and broke Rogers' arm. As a booker, Rogers was crap. Right off the bat, he lied to everyone and said, "I will *not* be working in any matches. Eddie Graham didn't hire me to get in the ring, so I'm not getting in the ring. I'm the *booker* and that's it."

The moratorium on Rogers wrestling didn't last very long at all. One evening when Sonny King and I were sitting around the apartment conspiring, Sonny said, "I'm going to get Rogers to work."

"How are you going to do that?" I asked Sonny. "He's not allowed to work."

"You watch," he said. "I'll get that son of a bitch in the ring again. It won't be hard to do."

"No way," I laughed. "Rogers *can't* get in the ring."

Sure enough, Sonny had Rogers back in the ring within a week, and he was right that it didn't take much effort at all. Sonny played Rogers like a puppet just about any time they interacted. By either insulting Rogers or catering to his ego, he could manipulate Rogers into making a fool of himself. In fact, while we were in St.

Petersburg at the Bayfront, Rogers inserted himself into no less than *three* matches.

A short time later, we were in Melbourne, Florida, and Rogers made it clear didn't think much of me. For the finish to the match we would be having, Rogers told me, "I'm gonna put you in the figure four. It won't be legal because I won't tag in, but the ref will still call for the bell and give me the win."

Rogers' reputation was as a guy who would routinely hurt other wrestlers. In the pre-television era, Rogers could legitimately hurt a wrestler's leg with the figure four, and the newspapers would print stories about it. Publicity would spread, and Rogers would be an even hotter heel attraction everywhere he went because of the *real* injuries he was dishing out to other wrestlers. As you might imagine, I wasn't excited about spending three months on crutches because Rogers wanted to rebuild his reputation. I let Rogers put me in the figure four, but I adjusted my leg so that he couldn't put much pressure on my ankle or my knee when he cinced in the hold.

When we all went out to a convenience store after the matches, Sonny goaded Rogers about his physique, and in a matter of seconds, Rogers was walking through the store with his shirt off. He just *had* to prove to everyone that he still looked great, even though he was pushing 60 years old at this point. Rogers' ego wouldn't allow him to let an insult to his physique slide.

The next time we did a television taping, I watched as Eddie Graham stormed into the studio with a pissed-off expression on his face.

"I thought I told you not to work!" Graham yelled at Rogers.

The two of them walked off and began a heated exchange out of earshot from the other wrestlers. A little while later, Rogers was walking out of the studio for the final time. He'd taken Sonny's bait, and now he was done as the CWF booker.

In my opinion, Rogers was an unmitigated disaster who didn't know how to effectively book a wrestling territory unless he was the star. At age 60, that was an impossible feat to pull off. His plans were all outdated. In his prime, he was exceptional, but his strategies were designed for an era where there was no television. He made massive amounts of money in his prime, but as we approached the 1980s the business had passed Rogers up completely.

Dusty replaced Rogers in the booking role, and Dusty appeared to have a far less selfish approach to how he treated talent. Like me, Dusty also built his early career reputation as a big heel who moved a lot in the ring and took a lot of bumps, so I'm sure he appreciated seeing another big heel who liked to move and bump for the babyfaces. As soon as Dusty had booking control, he made me the top heel in Florida almost overnight.

I was supposed to lose a match to Rhodes in Orlando, but right in the middle of the match he changed the finish and had *me* go over on *him*. That was shockingly unselfish coming from a star wrestler who was also the booker. Rogers *never* would have done something like that.

"Why did you do *that*?" I asked Dusty afterwards.

"Cuz you're gonna make us some *money*," he said.

Dusty wasn't lying. Not only did the promotion start making more money, but I also saw a corresponding increase in my own paychecks. I moved out of the apartment I shared with Sonny King and got a very nice apartment in Tampa. Shortly thereafter, Sonny left the territory altogether. I hated to see him go, because he was a fantastic friend.

I don't know if there was a wrestling territory anywhere in the country that ever had the type of year Florida had in 1979 with Dusty in charge. Everything he touched turned to gold during that period. For the entire year, we performed in front of packed houses all across the state. This held true even during the month of September, which is always *impossible* to maintain momentum through, but somehow Dusty's magic allowed us to do it.

Nikolai Volkoff and Leroy Brown were brought in to join Scott and I. The four of us were all heels, and we became great friends on the road. We traveled together every night and had a lot of fun in the process. Leroy was the rookie of the group, so the rest of us would watch him work and then huddle up after his matches to advise him of the things he could do to improve his performances.

He had a positive attitude, was receptive to feedback, and made rapid improvements. Before long, the four of us - including Leroy - unquestionably controlled the heel side of the locker room.

Walking to the ring in Florida

Nikolai was the quiet man of the group. He was incredibly strong, and had a good look although he wasn't great at selling, nor did he take a lot of bumps. If we were teamed together, I had to be the one to take the bumps and compensate for Nikolai's lack of bump-taking prowess. As "Thor the Viking," Scott Irwin was a large, agile wrestler who wasn't all that great on the interviews, but he made up for it by taking big bumps and selling hard for the babyfaces the same way I would.

No matter who I was partnered with from our group, I took it upon myself to be the guy making the matches exciting. Every time Eddie received a report back in Tampa of how things were going on the road, I did all I could to make sure he always received a great report about my match performances.

Finally, in September, they had me defeat Buzz Sawyer for the vacant NWA Florida Television Championship. I've heard several stories over the years about guys who've had run-ins with Buzz, but fortunately I'm not one of them. Buzz would get in that ring and go to *work*. He obviously wanted to be one of the top hands in the business, and he aggresively demonstrated that desire in the ring. It was equally obvious that Buzz would fight absolutely anyone who rubbed him the wrong way. In addition, Buzz had a knack for coming up with good finishes, which was probably owed to the fact that he was so vocal. If he thought a finish was stupid or didn't make any sense, he'd tell you about it and make you change it on the spot.

There were constant rumors of Buzz taking pills and other drugs. During one road trip, he started throwing up and passed out in the car. If the people riding with him hadn't jerked his head upright, he probably would've choked to death on his own vomit.

For the sake of being different, I began to wear the TV championship belt around my neck so that it would hang down onto my chest. I assumed anything that helped me stand out from the pack was a good idea, but some of the guys in the company thought it looked a little too weird.

"Buggsy, would you *please* quit wearin' that belt around your neck?" Dusty finally pleaded. "Wear it around your waist like everyone else!"

Dusty was the boss, so I did what he told me.

Our heel squad didn't have room for anyone else in the car with us, and we didn't *want* anyone else in the car with us. All of our available seats were filled with likeable people who enjoyed each other's company, and we didn't need any negative energy infiltrating our space. On the other hand, compared to my trips with Sonny King, riding with any of these other guys was downright *boring*!

All of us were right around the 300 pound mark, with Leroy being close to 320 pounds, and we all operated under a feed-the-babyface philosophy… except for Nikolai. As the two big bumpers, Scott and I would look at Nikolai and say, "Nik, you've got to *sell*! When they make their comeback, sell the *shit* out of it!"

For Nikolai, selling the shit out of something meant he would gingerly fall down to the mat. Leroy was an average bumptaker, but Scott and I were the feeders when it came to taking the majority of the bumps. Dusty really liked the two of us together, so he made Scott and I the NWA Florida Tag Team Champions. Unlike Rogers, Dusty used the talent around him appropriately. He had an eye for what worked, and he knew what would make money.

With the Florida Television Championship Belt

In December, Bobo Brazil showed up in Florida. Once he arrived in our locker room, I asked him, "Hey, I heard you were supposed to be here a long time ago. What took you so long?"

"Ha! Rogers," Bobo said. "I'd *never* have worked for that guy. I don't trust him."

I worked with Bobo in a few matches, including a singles match in Jacksonville. Bobo was now well into his mid 50s and put far less effort into selling damage during our matches than he used to. After one of my matches with Bobo, Dusty said, "Hey, Bobo dropped down to *one* knee for you during your match tonight. He must *really* like you! He usually won't even sell *that* much!"

During one of my matches with Dusty at the Civic Center in Lakeland, the people once again decided to come after me. The Civic Center could easily hold more than 5,000 people. When the riot started and the fans stormed the ringside area, I stayed in the ring and watched as the rioters encircled the ring and began taunting me.

"Come on down here, Buggsy!" I heard one of them say. "I'll *kick* your ass!"

When I heard that, I decided to call that fan's bluff. I climbed through the ropes and hopped down to the floor. Then I pounded my chest and screamed just like I would at the beginning of my matches. The fans scattered like roaches when someone turns a light on. As tough as some wrestlers might pretend to be, I played my heel role as a crazy person so convincingly that no one in Lakeland on that night truly wanted to mess with me.

Just to drive the point home that getting involved in my matches was a bad idea, I began marching around the outside of the ring, chasing away any fans who were standing in my path. Meanwhile, Dusty Rhodes was standing in the corner of the ring watching my rampage with an amused look on his face.

"You love it!" he called out to me. "Don't you?!"

"Oh, yes I do!" I yelled back without breaking stride.

If a riot lasts too long, it will not only ruin the match you're involved in, but it also has a strong chance of spoiling future shows, because some of the fans will be too afraid of their personal well being to ever show up again.

FOURTEEN – "Do you believe in *Jesus?*"

The achievements of 1979 would be tough for the CWF roster to match in 1980, but we managed to come pretty close. We just kept rolling from show to show, putting on great matches, attracting fans and making money.

We had some new names on the roster in 1980, like Dick Slater, Dick Murdoch and my friend Ivan Koloff. Ivan was routinely paired up with Nikolai to create a Russian tag team. Stan Lane also showed up in 1980 as "Nature Boy" Stanley Lane. Eventually, he would join up with Steve Keirn as "The Fabulous Ones," and they would be a featured act in Memphis.

In March of 1980, they had me drop the TV title to Steve Keirn in order to begin the process of turning me into a babyface. Nikolai and I worked the angle that resulted in my defining babyface turn. We were engaged in a tag-team match against Dusty Rhodes and Manny Fernandez. As the match progressed, Nik and I found ourselves involved in a disagreement that escalated into a brawl.

I got the upper hand and chased Nikolai back to the dressing room, which meant he had to run up the stairs to the second floor at the Tampa Armory. When I reached the top of the stairs, I turned to face the audience and went out to the railing. As I waved my arms in the air to egg them on, the crowd began chanting "U-S-A! U-S-A!" at me. This was in the midst of the Cold War with the Soviet Union, and also when the Iran Hostage Crisis was in full swing. When I turned on Nikolai to become an American hero, it really resonated with the audience.

My feud with Nikolai turned into a big hit at the box office. In fact, we wound up setting a record in Key West with our outdoor match, which drew the largest crowd for any event ever to take place in Key West. As things progressed, Nikolai and I occasionally found ourselves bound together in Russian Chain matches. Going into those matches, we knew we were obligated to get juice and bleed all over the ring. The chain was rather thick and could seriously hurt you. There are wrestlers who are masters at chain matches. Sadly,

Nikolai was not one of them. Still, our angle was over so well that the quality of our chain matches didn't have to be phenomenal in order for us to hold the fans' interest. We also worked together in steel cage matches and lumberjack matches.

Even when I was a heel, I had very unusual interviews. I liked to play the role of the heel who was trying to play psychological games with the babyface, all while degrading the wrestling fans who supported them. I would say things like, "Your wife is fat and wears a *moo moo*! *You're* fat, and you need to cover up that tire tube around your waist. You're probably wondering if your kids are retarded, just like you are."

American Hero

After I became a babyface, Gordon Solie told me my interviews were so well liked that I was under consideration for a local Emmy award due to their content. Gordon later told how Eddie Graham decided to put the kibosh on my Emmy nomination, but he never told me why.

Patriotism became a major part of my gimmick. "Buggsy 'U.S.A.' McGraw" was how I signed my autographs during that time. Part of my ring attire consisted of what I called a "flight cap," which was really just a camouflage helmet liner. The cap was just another thing I could wear to separate myself from the crowd of other wrestlers. My general mindset was to have the fans talking about me during their drives home from matches once the shows concluded. The Florida fans took an undeniable liking to me after my babyface turn. Once I got in the ring, I didn't care how big the crowd was. The crowd became one, and I had to remain in control of the crowd and never let the crowd control me.

Following my turn into a fan favorite, I could no longer hang out with my established crew of heels. Instead, I started traveling with different babyfaces, like "Mr. Florida" Paul Jones, Barry Windham, and referee Bill Alfonso.

I also hung out with Dusty a few times at the Junkyard Lounge, which was a club that featured a lot of live rock and roll bands. The Dream and I went there after our matches one night, and the place was completely packed. As we sat there enjoying the music, two fairly large men approached us. One was about my size, and the other was the size of Dusty.

The guy who was Dusty's size stepped forward and got in our faces.

"You guys are two of those phony-ass wrestlers, right?" he snarled. "You guys are such fakes. We could kick your asses without breakin' a sweat!"

Obviously, these guys were looking to build a reputation for themselves at our expense. At that moment, I'd have preferred to have a wrestler other than Dusty with me. The Dream was no true fighter, which meant I would probably end up with the two of them pounding on me if things got physical. I decided to try to defuse things before any physicality occurred.

I looked the man right in the eye, then I snatched his collar in a vice grip with both of my hands and pulled his face right in front of mine.

"Do *you* believe in *Jesus*?!" I screamed into his face.

The man's eyes went from confident to terrified.

"Do *you* believe in *Jesus*?!" I repeated.

"Yeah…. We *do*!" the visibly shaken man assured me.

I released my grip of his collar, and the two men tore away as quickly as they could. Sometimes if you can convince people you're insane, that can be the simplest way to defuse a situation and ensure that no one will ever mess with you.

I didn't travel with Dusty all that often. The only times I really recall being with him would be when we were aboard Lester Welch's private plane. There were times we'd fly to Jacksonville or Miami. TV tapings were held on Wednesday, and then we'd cut all of our interviews afterwards. By the time we were finished with everything, we would have had plenty of difficulty making it to some of the shows if we didn't have a plane standing by to transport us. If Dusty and I were the only two on the plane, that was the only time he would really open up.

In general, I didn't care for Manny Fernandez, who I worked with in several matches when he carried the NWA Florida Heavyweight Championship. The company put a lot of stock in him because he was of hispanic descent, which meant a great deal to a select group of fans in Florida. Behind the scenes, he simply couldn't be trusted. He always wanted to come across as a tough guy, and to that end, he used to tell everyone that he was a Navy Seal. There is plenty of evidence contradicting these claims.

One of the guys Manny used to hang out with was Barry Windham. One time, Windham went on a vacation for two weeks, which was probably to Charlotte to see his father, Blackjack Mulligan. While Barry was gone, Manny took Barry's Corvette and sold it right out from under him without permission! That's just *one* example of how shady a character Manny was.

We were in a six-man tag match one Sunday night in Orlando, involving Steve Keirn, Manny Fernandez and I against Scott Irwin, Nikolai and Leroy. Keirn, Jimmy Garvin and Manny used to travel together, and they all made it clear they didn't care for Nikolai because he refused to sell or bump for them as much as the rest of us would.

In Nikolai's defense, I don't know if he didn't want to sell, or he just lacked the agility to sell the way Scott and I did. Whatever the reason was, Keirn, Garvin and Manny decided it would be a good idea to teach Nikolai a lesson by striking him with stiff potato shots during their matches with him. As you might suspect, Nikolai did *not* take kindly to the disrespect.

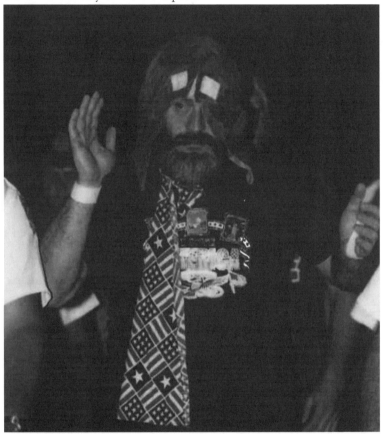

Heading into the arena

Outside the ring, Keirn, Garvin and Manny also wouldn't talk to Nikolai whenever we shared a dressing room. Of the three, Manny was definitely the *most* disrespectful toward Nikolai, and also the guy who would hit him with the stiffest punches in the ring.

Finally, we had our six-man tag match, and Manny had ball bearings in his hand and was using them to hit Nikolai in the jaw. Obviously, that hurt a lot, and Nikolai got justifiably pissed off.

"Manny, stop it!" Nikolai said to him.

A little more time elapsed, and the stiff punches continued. "Manny, *don't* do that anymore!" Nikolai warned him again. To the surprise of no one, Manny paid no heed to the warnings and continued to bully Nikolai with the ball bearings in his hand. What Manny didn't know is that Nikolai had once trained to be a professional fighter, and he knew how to throw a punch with lethal precision. That knowledge, combined with his powerlifting background, gave Nikolai's punches the knockout force of a heavyweight boxer.

For weeks, I'd overheard these guys talking in the dressing room about what an uncoordinated coward Nikolai was, but I knew better. Nikolai wasn't a coward; he was forgiving and patient. Well, his patience had just run out. Nikolai rose out of the corner, and struck a fighting stance, as if to give fair warning to Manny that he was about to be involved in a real fight, and he wanted his adversary to be prepared. Manny obliged and raised his own hands - albeit with the ball bearings still in them - in a reciprocal gesture to indicate that he knew what he was in for.

For ten seconds, the two exchanged stiff blows, and after Nikolai connected with a *rocket* of a left hook, Manny found himself face down on the mat, lying half outside of the ring, with saliva oozing out of his mouth. He struggled to speak, and as his mouth tried to form words, the movement of his lips resembled the breathing actions of a fish.

I was struggling to contain my excitement, because I didn't care for Manny to begin with, and I didn't like the unjust treatment Nikolai had been subjected to. Unfortunately, we now had a different issue to contend with. Nikolai and Manny were the legal men in the ring, and Manny was lying there, drooling, and mostly motionless. If the match went to hell, word of the episode might get back to the office and affect our pay. As much as I enjoyed seeing Manny receive his comeuppance, it wasn't worth losing money over.

Answering the call to action, I leaped into the ring to take over for Manny, and I faced off with Nikolai, whose eyes were still filled with bloodlust. Even though we were friends, he looked like he was ready to continue his knockout streak, and I was the next victim in his sights. For a moment, I wondered what I'd gotten myself into, because I really was not eager to have a shoot fight with a pissed off Yugoslavian strongman.

We stood there with our eyes locked onto one another for what seemed like minutes, even though I'm sure it was only a matter of around ten seconds. Finally, out of a desire to save the match, mixed with a hint of self preservation, I charged Nikolai as fast as I could, wrapped my arms around him, and corralled him into the corner.

"Nikolai!" I yelled, as he struggled to break free. "It's a work! It's a work! It's a work! Don't hit me! Calm down!"

To my great relief, Nikolai relaxed, clearly understanding that I meant him no harm. It's a good thing I was the one who hopped in to save the match, because I was Nikolai's trusted friend. Steve Keirn seemed deathly afraid to get in the ring, and rightfully so. Nikolai would have eaten Keirn alive.

After the match, Manny was hunched over on a chair in the dressing room trying to recover. I decided to pull up a chair directly in front of him and needle him now that Nikolai had embarrassed him so thoroughly and publicly.

"I guess we discovered that Nikolai actually *would* fight," I taunted him.

"Yeah, well… we found out that I'd fight, *too*!" Manny insisted.

"Yeah, but you didn't last too long!" I laughed.

The following Tuesday, we were all in the Tampa office on the second floor. There was no segregating the heels and babyfaces there. I was sitting right next to Nikolai when Garvin and Keirn entered the room. As soon as they saw Nikolai, they gave him the warmest greeting you could imagine.

"Oh, Nikolai!" Keirn gushed. "Niki… It's so good to see you!"

Keirn extended his hand, and an amused Nikolai clasped it.

"Yeah, Niki, how are you?" Garvin joined in, also offering his hand.

Before then, they'd only ever called him "Volkoff," but now he was suddenly "Niki"? It was *comical*.

"You should come over and have dinner with me at my house sometime!" Keirn said, concluding his greeting.

As Garvin and Keirn turned and walked away, I leaned over and said to Nikolai, "Hey… they seem to *like* you now. I can't imagine why!" Nikolai *exploded* laughing.

To his credit, Manny did stand toe to toe with Nikolai in the ring that night, even though he definitely got the worse end of the exchange. I certainly hope he's in good spirits these days. Similarly, Steve Keirn is now a great friend of mine, and he's a great Christian man who I'm very proud to know.

Jerry Prater was the writer of *The Grapevine*, which was the official program of the CWF. While writing content for the programs, he decided to give me the official name of Herman E. "Buggsy" McGraw. As far as I know, that's the only place where my "full" wrestling name was ever established. The "Herman" supposedly came from the large, black snake who lived under my fictional home while I was growing up. By this account, I was an insane child who fed the snake and named it "Herman," and then I liked the name so much that I adopted it as my own.

Jerry also had a featured segment in *The Grapevine* called "Uncle Buggsy's Fables." Fans even approached me and asked me about them. At the time these articles were printed, I was over as much as Dusty Rhodes, and Dusty began to use his booking control to make sure he stayed over everyone, including me.

On May 20th, 1980, Dusty finally booked me to win the NWA Florida Heavyweight Championship from Don Muraco in Tampa after I chased him for a short while. We then wrestled each other throughout the summer. I dropped the championship back to him in June, then won it from him a second time in August. Having or challenging for that title meant I was near the top of the Florida cards, and it also meant I was making some great money.

A lot of guys really loved to wear the title belts, but the belts could be a hassle. There were a few times I actually forgot to bring the belt to our events. They are nice accessories, but if they don't translate into more money, it's more of an annoyance. It's much better to be a main eventer without a championship than an undercarder with a belt to carry around. The main eventer is always going to make more money whether he's a champion or not.

The belts we wore were all made by Reggie Parks. He was lean and had a great physique, which was a result of him having the highest metabolism I'd ever seen. He could easily outeat anyone on the roster. Whenever we'd go to a lunch buffet, Reggie would come in late with a newspaper in tow. After enjoying the selection at the lunch buffet for a while, Reggie liked to relax and read his paper, and then resume eating once the staff had swapped out the lunch items with the dinner options. He certainly got his money's worth!

"The American Dream" & Buggsy "USA" McGraw

Dusty and I were tag-team partners for a short time. Because he was a booker, I always did the selling during the matches, and then I tagged Dusty in to make the comeback and give our team the victory. I always recommended that pattern to him, because I didn't want to outshine the booker. I already had enough fans coming up to me telling me they liked me more than Dusty, so if I upstaged him, he would gladly have moved me down the card.

Dusty selected me as his partner to win the 1980 U.S. Cup Challenge Tournament in July. We beat Nikolai Volkoff and Ivan Koloff, followed by Masa Saito and Dick Slater, and finished it off by beating Dory Jr. and Terry Funk. Sadly, we did *not* get to split the advertised $50,000 prize. Even though Dusty was making the comebacks and getting the glory during every match, Scott Irwin told me, "I don't know if you've noticed, but you're more over than Dusty right now!"

We had regular talent meetings at the CWF office in Tampa. Before one of the meetings, I waited outside in the parking lot for a little while just so that I could be intentionally late. Then, I donned a full gorilla costume, casually walked into the building and took a seat in the bleachers alongside the rest of the wrestlers. All of the boys started cracking up as I sat there like it was no big deal.

"Who the hell are *you* supposed to be?" Dusty laughed.

At that point, I took the mask off to the applause of the wrestlers, and then Dusty continued with the meeting.

During that summer, I also participated in a softball game in which the wrestlers competed against members of the Tampa Bay Buccaneers football team. The game was held at Al Lopez Field, which was right across from the old Tampa Stadium. Thankfully I was a babyface at the time, because I don't think they would have used heels for the event, which was fairly well attended. We won the game, but only because Jerry Brisco rigged it so that the game was called off as soon as we took the lead from the Buccaneers.

I never thought very highly of the football players. Many NFL veterans would tell me they wanted to get into wrestling, and I'd usually tell them, "This isn't football. There's no time outs, and there are no huddles." Because wrestling requires constant movement, I always thought of myself as being in better shape than most of the guys in the NFL... especially for my size.

There were two different lounges in Tampa that were very popular with the CWF wrestlers. One was the aforementioned Junkyard Lounge, which was known as the hangout for rock and roll aficionados, and the other was the Imperial Lounge, which catered to fans of country music. Since I was into rock and roll, I seldom went to the Imperial Lounge.

During one of my trips to the Junkyard Lounge, I was hanging out with Mike Graham. A little while earlier, Mike had arrived with Barry Windham, but Barry had absconded to the back seat of Mike's limousine with a young lady fan. That left Mike and I leaning up against the wall and drinking at the far end of the bar. As we talked and drank, Mike lit up a big cigar.

After a little while, a man who was considerably larger than Mike slid in along Mike's left-hand side and said, "I've seen you guys on TV! You're two of those wrestlers!"

"Yeah, we are," Mike said, taking a big puff from his cigar.

"You guys act tough, but it's all bullshit," the guy continued. "*Everything* you do is *phony*!"

Obviously, this was the *wrong* thing to say to the son of a famous wrestling promoter.

"*Phony?!*" yelled Mike.

Before the man could react, Mike repeatedly and aggressively stabbed him in the chest with the lit end of the cigar. Holes appeared in the man's shirt, and the acrid scent of burning flesh filled the air around us.

"Is *that* phony, you son of a *bitch?!*" asked Mike.

The man ran away toward the exit, clutching his chest. Mike watched the door for a moment just in case the man came back looking to escalate the situation. Without a doubt, Mike didn't mind protecting the wrestling business and standing up for himself physically if the situation mandated it.

About half an hour later, some people came up to us and told Mike the man had come back with a handgun. However, instead of coming back inside, he'd opted to fire four bullets into Mike's limo. The two of us ran outside, primarily concerned that Barry Windham and his lady friend might still have been in the back seat of the limo at the time of the shooting, but they were long gone.

As Mike and I stood there surveying the four bullet holes in the car's windshield, Mike turned to me and said, "You know that guy who did this? I wouldn't expect to see him again anytime soon. I think he might just *disappear*."

Mike had guts, and you didn't want to mess with a member of the Graham family, especially not in Tampa.

In September, I got a disqualification victory over NWA World Heavyweight Champion Harley Race in Tampa. Facing a heel NWA champion was usually a right reserved for a territory's top babyface. Not only was it an honor, but it was affirmation that I was right at the top of the heap in Florida, alongside Dusty Rhodes.

Two days after facing Harley, I partnered with Bobo Brazil to win the NWA Florida Tag Team Championships from Nikolai Volkoff and Ivan Koloff. This very brief championship reign was my only babyface run with the tag-team titles. Bobo would never have been my first choice for a partner because of how limited he was. If he was involved, the match quality could only be so good, and he needed someone else to do the selling for him in order for things to be exciting. No matter how slow and plodding he appeared to be, Bobo was still a solid draw among the local black wrestling fans, and I also added to the package as the the down-to-earth American hero.

Of course, when I tagged with Bobo, I also frequently traveled with him. He was very laid back at this stage of his life, taking everything in stride, and understanding his role as an elder statesman in the wrestling business.

Perhaps the most shocking evidence of my surging popularity in Florida came in the form of a letter I received from Howard Marc Baum, from the desk of his father, Howard Burt Baum. The letter informed me that Howard decided to run *me* for the position of student body president of Highland Oaks Junior High School in the Miami-Dade School District… and I *won* after receiving more than half of the votes. I'm pretty sure this makes me the only wrestler in history to be simultaneously recognized as a champion in a NWA territory *and* as the student body president of a junior high school.

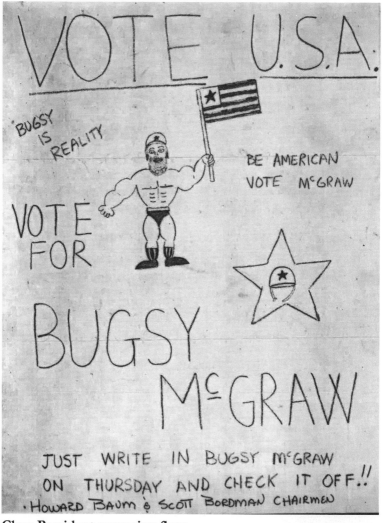

Class President campaign flyer

The very next month after I worked with Harley and won the tag titles with Bobo, Dusty booked me to work with Bobby Jaggers. First he asked me to do an angle with Bobby that required me to get juice and bleed. *Then* he asked me to drop the Florida championship to him! *None* of this made sense to me given where I had been positioned as as main-event babyface while Bobby was positioned as a lower-card heel. I had to confront Dusty about it.

Tag Champs with Bobo Brazil

"Hey, Dusty, why are you putting me with Bobby Jaggers *and* having him beat me for the title?" I asked. "He's not over."

"I need you to build Bobby up," Dusty answered. "You can help to *get* him over."

"Why don't *you* help to get him over?" I retorted. "You should be able to get him over just as easily as I can!"

"You'll just have to trust me on this one, kid," Dusty laughed.

There were times I felt like I was being held back by Dusty, and this was definitely one of those occasions. It was obvious to him that I was getting over very well, and he did what he could to contain it. Under no circumstances would Dusty have ever shared the ring with a lower-card wrestler like Bobby Jaggers simply for the sake of giving him "the rub."

From my perspective, Dusty was clearly holding me back because he wanted to remain the top guy at all times, and having me work with Jaggers and drop the title to him was a clear way of lowering my stock in the eyes of the fans. Meanwhile, Dusty would keep working with the top heels himself, and eliminate any potential threat to his role as the number-one babyface in the territory.

Even though I wasn't carrying around a championship belt anymore, I still challenged NWA World Heavyweight Champion Harley Race for the title at the Jacksonville Coliseum on November 11th of that year.

Paul Boesch asked Eddie Graham if I could come into Houston once in a while, and Eddie agreed, so I flew into Houston from Tampa for a few shows. I didn't interact with Paul very much, although he seemed like a very nice man. During one of my trips to Houston, I challenged Bruiser Brody for his Brass Knuckles Championship. Boesch came to me and proclaimed how Brody had been instructed to put me over cleanly that night.

"Yeah, *right*," I said. "I'll believe it when I see it happen."

I went out to the ring first, and then Brody came out, stomping around and acting crazy. Throughout the match, he was overly physical with me, and it became clear he had zero intentions of cooperating or putting me over as Paul had suggested. Instead, Brody held the both of us outside of the ring and got us counted out.

"Wasn't I supposed to win the match tonight?" I asked Brody afterward.

"I didn't like the finish Paul came up with, so I came up with a *better* one," Brody laughed.

BRODY RISKS BRASS KNUCKS BELT!

Bruiser Brody defends his highly regarded Brass Knucks belt against the wild and rugged Bugsy McGraw in one of three title tilts on tonight's card. These same two power-houses collided head on several weeks ago in a savage scrap that still has fans talking. Bugsy has made a stormy debut to Texas Wrestling and wrestling officials fear that the worse is yet to come. McGraw is as big as he is unique. It has been a long time since a star as unusual as Bugsy has made an appearance here and the question still remains—Is Houston ready for Bugsy? We know Brody will be tonight!

Promotional article for a match against Bruiser Brody

I wasn't about to get into a fight with Brody over the finish to a match in a Houston-area town. It's not like Houston was my home territory, and I would be getting right back on a plane and going back to work for Eddie in Florida. That wasn't a battle I was prepared to fight. Still, it was a typical Bruiser Brody stunt. He was always a selfish, unprofessional worker who made himself exceedingly difficult for many of the other wrestlers to like, and I certainly didn't care for him in the least.

A far more pleasant experience in Houston involved Don Diamond. I'd worked with Don in Florida when he was booked in the openers and in the mid-card matches. However, when Paul put me in the ring with Don, I quickly found out how skilled he really was. Once the bell rang, the two of us began a game where we would circle, move in, move out, stall, point fingers, interact with the referee, and talk trash. We did all of this while avoiding even touching each other for *ten* full minutes. The entire time, the fans were up out of their chairs, screaming at us.

The two of us had complete control of the crowd. Don knew how to work and quickly grasped what I was attempting to create in that moment, and I consider it an achievement on both of our parts that a Houston newcomer and an opening-match wrestler were able to elicit that kind of reaction from the local audience.

Once we got down to the business of wrestling, we had a solid match, and Don put me over in the middle of the ring.

"Hey, kid… you know what you're doing!" I said to him afterwards. "That was a *great* match!"

"Thanks, Buggsy!" Don said, clearly unphased by the fact he had to put me over. "It was fun!"

That same night, I flew back to Tampa and arrived around midnight. From there, I drove straight to Robiconti's, which was a very nice club where a lot of the wrestlers hung out because the owner treated us very well. Everything about it was high end, and there was often live music. To this day, I carry a handheld wallet with me, and I certainly had one with me on that night in 1980. It held the payoff from my Houston shows, which was $700 in cash.

Before long, this guy named Bill arrived at Robiconti's. He was only an inch shorter than me, and he weighed around 265 pounds. Around Tampa, Bill was known as a street fighter who had been trained in karate. Although I'd never met or laid eyes on Bill before in my life, he still came over and said something to me. Over the music, I couldn't make out anything he was saying to me. To accommodate him, I turned my head and lowered my ear to see what

Bill wanted. Apparently, what Bill wanted was a *fight*. Without warning, he punched me in the side of the jaw.

The force of the blow spun me completely around. I turned back to face Bill, only to be met with another thundering shot which dazed me.

"Son of a *bitch!*" I said.

Finally, Bill caught me with a third consecutive punch to the lower-left part of my jaw, and I realized I needed to stop him *immediately* or I would be in considerable trouble. Despite the barrage of punches, I'd still managed to hold onto my wallet. My first thought was to throw the wallet down and tear into Bill, but I truly didn't want to throw $700 onto the ground of a packed nightclub. Instead of dropping the wallet, I reached out and grabbed Bill by his long hair and jerked his head down toward my waist. It was a reflex from years of working in the ring; you can control a guy's movements very well if you can manage to get ahold of his hair. When wrestlers get into fights against guys with long, exposed hair, the result is usually going to be an easy win for the wrestler.

Bill flailed away with both his arms and legs, but he failed to do any real damage from such an awkward fighting position. In a matter of seconds, I recovered from Bill's punches and shoved his head into a stained-glass window. Then, in an effort to bring the fight to a hasty conclusion, I reached into his face with my fingers and jerked out Bill's eye. *That* stopped him cold.

As Bill fell to the ground and clutched at his face, I walked over and leaned against the bar to finish recovering. That was when I realized Bill had a friend with him in the form of a 6'6", 350-pound monster. When this gargantuan man reached out and grabbed my arm, I reared back and luckily caught him flush in the jaw with an upward swing of my elbow. Honestly, I wasn't even trying to hit him, but the force of the blow knocked the guy spark out. His body quickly plummeted and crashed to the floor like an oak tree.

Bill had a reputation around town as a bully who would pick fights with guys he knew he could whip. Then he would physically take advantage of them. Well, I'd just managed to simultaneously take out the schoolyard bully *and* his colossal best friend.

Brute Power: The Autobiography of Buggsy McGraw

It seemed as if the entire city of Tampa heard news of the fight within three days. Someone had even written a poem about the fight which made its way all over Tampa. Some of it also made its way into a local paper, and was recited on some of the radio stations. After Eddie got his hands on the poem, he approached me and said, "Hey, I heard what happened in the club, and I think there's a way we can make some money with this. Will you fight this guy for me?"

"Fight him where?" I asked.

"In the ring," Eddie said. "If I bring him down to the studio and put him in the ring, would you fight him?"

I knew any altercation I had with this guy would be a complete shoot, but I didn't want to turn Eddie down.

"Yes!" I shouted. "And the other guy, too! I'll kick *both* of their asses again!"

"Okay!" Eddie said, gleefully. "I'll set it up!"

With that, Eddie set out trying to make this fight happen on his terms. In Eddie's mind, If I could beat Bill in a televised fight, it would be great for business since one of his top stars would look like a true badass. Ron Slinker actually found Bill and warned him, "If you go down to the office at Albany, you'll be making a big mistake! One way or the other, they'll make sure you lose."

I'm sure Ron was right. If things went badly, Eddie would have been sacrificing the credibility of one of his top two babyface attractions. I suppose he could simply not have aired the footage from the fight if I'd lost, but word certainly would have trickled out to the public regarding the outcome.

Not only was Ron connected to the Tampa police force, but he was a karate champion in his own right, and he was familiar with Bill's level of martial arts training.

"Bill said to me, 'I got a little worried when I hit him the third time and he still didn't go down!'" Ron informed me.

Bill had a girlfriend who worked for the Hertz rental car company at the Tampa airport. She broke up with him shortly after the fight, so he was completely distraught. Somehow, he made his way to the roof of the airport building Hertz was based in, and he took a suicide leap, landing right in front of the doorway to the

222

Hertz building. Coincidentally, his ex-girlfriend had taken the day off of work, so his suicidal act was all for naught.

True to form, Dusty couldn't stand to see me getting that amount of *real* respect from either the boys or the community thanks to a real-life incident. Dusty liked to think he was tough even though all the boys knew he wasn't, and I think he was self conscious about people getting over who were also physically superior to him. One time in Tallahassee, Dusty walked up to me out of the blue while I was minding my own business and began berating me.

"You're not as tough as you think you are, you understand?!" said Dusty. "You think *I* can't kick your ass?!"

I don't know what got Dusty so worked up. If I'd leapt up and actually kicked Dusty's ass the way I wanted to, Eddie would have fired me immediately. Instead, I looked at Dusty and said, "Dusty, you don't even know what you're saying."

Dusty walked away after that, but I vowed to pay him back one day when he would be forced to fight for himself and wouldn't have the office protecting him.

Florida's top belt - the Southen championship - still elluded me. Plenty of different wrestlers held the Southern title from time to time, including gimmick wrestlers. Honestly, Dusty was more of a gimmick wrestler than anything, so there's no reason why they couldn't have put it on me, even if it had only been for a month.

Once again, I got to challenge Race for his NWA title on March of 1981. This time, a slew of Japanese photographers were on hand to take photos. My guess is that Giant Baba wanted me to have some momentum going into April's forthcoming All Japan tour, and having me challenge for the championship again was a way to raise my notoriety in the eyes of Japanese wrestling fans.

As if working with a Japanese wrestler would somehow prepare me for the All Japan tour, I worked in a ton of matches with Mr. Pogo on my way out of Florida. Although his name was Tetsuo Sekigawa, Pogo told me he was actually Korean. We worked in several main event matches, which usually had some sort of gimmick attached to them. They were either "Lights Out" matches with no holds barred, or they were lumberjack matches with other wrestlers surrounding the ring to keep us inside of it. Finally, I lost a "Loser Leaves Town" match to Pogo to explain my absence to the Florida fans while I toured Japan with Baba's company.

Soaring onto Harley Race

By the time my grandest run in Florida was over with, I'd still never held the top championship in the company, the NWA Southern Heavyweight Championship. Of all the championships I never won, not winning the Southern title bothered me the most, because I thoroughly believed I was worthy of it and had earned it. Getting that belt might have cemented me as the top man in the company, though, so Dusty was never going to let me touch it.

Each territory's promoter had a mindset about what type of wrestler should hold his company's major championship. For example, when the WWWF put its belt on Bob Backlund, several wrestlers, including myself, felt that wasn't a smart decision by Vince McMahon. As a goodie-two-shoes babyface with a strong amateur wrestling background, Backlund seemed more suitable to be the champion of Verne Gagne's AWA, since Verne really prized amateur wrestlers.

In New York, Backlund didn't seem to be much of an attraction, nor was he a great fit for the wrestling style of the Northeastern United States, but Vince insisted on running with him as the champion. They even took out a huge advertisement in the newspaper to welcome Backland to New York after he won the championship. The brawling ethnic champions had always done well in the New York market, and Backlund didn't fit the mold developed by guys like Antonino Rocca, Bruno Sammartino and Pedro Morales.

In my opinion, Don Muraco would have been a vast improvement over Backland as the world champion in New York during that era. He had the size, talent and physique to thrive in that environment, and it's a shame Vince didn't give him an opportunity with the main belt.

FIFTEEN – "There nothing to be scared about"

In May of 1981, I returned to Japan to finally work for Giant Baba's All Japan Pro Wrestling promotion. After founding AJPW, Baba joined the National Wrestling Alliance almost immediately. This gave him a distinct advantage over Antonio Inoki inasmuch as Baba had unfettered access to nearly all of the most popular American professional wrestling stars, and he could pay all of them a lot of money to fly to Japan and lose to him.

Inoki may have passed the eyeball test as the more exciting wrestler, but Baba had the larger bodycount on his resume for having slain the most American giants. If you were a major world champion between 1973 and 1981, you probably lost a match to Giant Baba in Tokyo. Baba even won and lost the NWA World Heavyweight Championship in Japan on three different occasions, including one exchange with Jack Brisco, and two with Harley Race.

Dory Funk Jr. was helping out in the office for All Japan Pro Wrestling during that time period. I was all set to go to AJPW for $2,500 a week, but Dory came to me and said, "You're only going to get $2,000."

"My price is $2,500," I reiterated to him.

"Well, there's a $500-per-week fee attached to Americans wrestling in Japan that the All Japan office has to pay," said Funk. "So you'll be getting $2,000."

It was funny that I'd never heard of this fee before. When I thought it all over, it dawned on me what was transpiring.

"That son of a bitch!" I thought to myself. "He's trying to *screw* me!"

Dory was responsible for booking the American wrestlers and handling their payoffs, so he was *pocketing* money off of each talent he booked! To this day, I'm *convinced* this is what he was doing. In the end, I did receive my full $2,500 after I spoke directly to Baba.

I suppose Dory didn't care for me, which is fair, because I *never* cared for his work at all. At best, Dory was an *average* worker, and even *that* is taking it to an extreme! There are certain individuals

Dory looked good with, like Jack Brisco for instance. But, as far as I'm concerned, if those matches were good, the credit for them should be laid squarely at the feet of Jack Brisco. Any time I worked with Dory, I never ranked the matches very highly, because his working style slowed everything down and killed any excitement.

Obviously, Dory was a former NWA World Champion, and people overestimated him because of that credential. On the contrary, I didn't look up to him at all. He had *zero* personality to speak of.

It's one thing to take a hold and work the hold, and I knew how to take a hold and make it exciting. Funk would take a hold, maintain it forever, and do nothing special with it. He just didn't excel in any aspect of presentation that would make a match exciting.

I just didn't understand why anyone would objectively evaluate Dory and want to make him the world champion. That's why I'm sure his father pulling political strings and getting him appointed as the world champion had something to do with him getting the belt in the first place, and then he coasted on that world title claim forever even though the quality of his work never lived up to his unearned reputation. He was *never* a great champion.

Once I arrived in Tokyo, Baba booked me to tag up with the Sheik a few times during the tour. When I saw the Sheik at the hotel, I said, "Hey, I heard you were working for Inoki's office over at New Japan."

"I was," said Sheik. "I switched back. Inoki's backers weren't happy about it either. They tried to *kill* me in Tokyo. As you can see, it didn't work."

I knew better than to ask him any more questions about it. The Sheik was a true free agent by then. His NWA territory in Detroit had closed down the prior year. Certainly, the hard financial times in Southeast Michigan had plenty to do with it. Outside of Michigan, the Sheik was still a tremendous draw everywhere he went, and he was still wildly popular in Japan.

When you worked on the Sheik's team, the best thing you could do was stay out of his way and let him do his thing. He was the real fan attraction, and he definitely wasn't about to change his style now that he was working well into his 50s. Gorilla Monsoon always spoke about fans "literally hanging from the rafters" when an arena was packed, even though he meant to say they were "*figuratively* hanging from the rafters." Well, after one of our matches in Japan, the bloodied Sheik *literally* climbed to the top of the *literal* rafters and stared down menacingly at the fans below. I guess since the Sheik could no longer work very aggressively in the ring or take many bumps, he had to come up with other ways to make the fans feel as if they'd gotten their money's worth.

Getting choked by Giant Baba

Possibly as a means of honoring the promoter who had offered him his biggest paydays outside of his home territory, the Sheik booked Giant Baba and Jumbo Tsuruta as the final team to win NWA Detroit's World Tag Team Championships before the company closed down. Jumbo was clearly being groomed to take Baba's place as the "ace" of All Japan, and he had all of the in-ring tools to do it. Jumbo was tall, strong, agile and resilient.

Baba had a way of using championship belts as a means of marking certain wrestlers he wished to feature. The PWF

Championship was *his* belt, but Baba resurrected the NWA United National Championship and made it a near-permanent fixture around Jumbo's waist for the better part of *six* years. When it was time to elevate Jumbo to a higher championship plane, the fans would already be warm to that idea.

Karl Kox told me about how great a kid Jumbo was when he was younger. Whenever they flew on a commercial flight, Jumbo would carry a ceremonial sword in order to live up to American expectations of his gimmick. Kox would help Tsuruta out because his English wasn't that great. Jumbo would also commonly dress himself in ceremonial Japanese robes.

During one of their flights, Jumbo picked up the ceremonial sword, slammed it against the floor of the plane and yelled, "Hijack!" Obviously, that didn't go over well with the airline personnel working on the flight. Kox said he spent a long while smoothing things over with the airline employees and passengers, and then he had to admonish Jumbo that no one found his joke funny.

Stan Hansen had recently jumped to All Japan as well after a few years of headlining for NJPW. He was such a massive star in Japan at the time that you couldn't escape it no matter where you went. Even if you went to the book store, you'd find full-color books on the shelves that were entirely devoted to Stan.

Stan told me Inoki's backers were so anxious to keep him in New Japan, they even offered to buy him his own *island* in order to keep him there, but it wasn't enough to get him to stay. I can't imagine what Baba offered Stan to come over if a private island couldn't get the job done for Inoki.

After roughly three years working in Florida, Eddie and Dusty told me it was about time for me to leave the territory and work elsewhere for a while. They framed it as a chance for me to go away for a while so that the fans would be even more excited when I finally made a return.

"I can send you to New York," Dusty said. "I know Vince wants you."

"Don't do that," I said, shaking my head. "When I go back to New York, I'm going to go through Bruno."

229

In my mind, getting booked in New York through Bruno was the smart thing to do, because Bruno had been the one who went to bat for me in the WWWF years earlier. He'd gotten me job security and a weekly pay raise, so I figured if I called Bruno to set up my return to New York, whenever it took place, he would have the leverage to secure a sweetheart deal for me.

In the end, that wound up being a huge mistake. When I initially called Bruno, it seemed like everything was fine for me to return to New York as an upper-card heel. However, Bruno called back a short time later with some bad news.

"Vince says he has to cancel the deal," Bruno said.

"Cancel?!" I asked, stunned. "Why?!"

"A lot of the New York fans can see the programming from Florida up here," Bruno explained. "Everyone can see you're a popular babyface. You coming up here to work as a heel right now wouldn't work."

So, rather than going to New York after I returned from Japan, I spent the next three months in Memphis working as a heel for Jerry Jarrett and Jerry Lawler. It's hard to think of a wrestler more synonymous with a single state than Jerry "The King" Lawler is with Tennessee. Lawler was the top attraction in Jarrett's Continental Wrestling Association, and in many ways he was the Mid-American version of Bruno Sammartino.

Different top stars would find their way to Memphis to challenge "The King," and Lawler would often lose his championships to those stars and then regain them shortly thereafter. In the process, it was reinforced to every wrestling fan in the region that Lawler was as good as the very best wrestlers outside of Memphis at a minimum, and potentially even better. In the ring, the King showed tremendous ring generalship.

The territory consisted of Memphis and Nashville in Tennessee, Louisville in Kentucky, and West Memphis in Arkansas. From time to time, we also went to places like Tupelo, Mississippi, which was the site of their infamous concession stand brawl in 1979. After Lawler and Bill Dundee were screwed out of the tag titles by Wayne Ferris and Larry Latham, they had what appeared to be an impromptu brawl all over the arena. During the brawl, they used all sorts of inanimate objects as weapons, including a 10-gallon mustard jug which shattered against the wall after Lawler threw it at Latham. It was a promotional ploy dreamed up by the booker at the time, Robert Fuller, and it worked to *perfection*.

When I arrived, Jarrett put me with manager Jimmy Hart, who walked out for an interview on crutches and introduced me as "The Killer" Buggsy McGraw, the newest member of his "First Family" stable of wrestlers, along with Chick Donovan and "The Nightmares" - Danny Davis and Ted Allen.

Jarrett immediately booked me to win the Tennessee Division Tournament, and I beat my friend Steve Keirn in the final. In tag-team matches, I teamed with the Dream Machine and feuded with Lawler and Jimmy Valiant. The very next month, Jarrett had me win the NWA Mid-America Heavyweight Championship from Keirn at the Mid-South Coliseum. Even with this success, I didn't feel like I really belonged in Memphis. I got along great with Jarrett and Lawler, but the territory was very cliquish. Guys like Jarrett, Lawler, Eddie Gilbert, Bill Dundee and Jimmy Hart were mainstays of the area who had been around forever, and it didn't seem like it was an easy crew to settle in with or feel genuine camaraderie with.

Behind the scenes, Bill Dundee was a little Australian *prick*. He definitely had a Napoleon complex, which made him abrasive and made him reek of insecurity. He sucker punched me on the ear during an interview segment, and then he did the same thing *again* during our actual match, so I went after him with shoot punches to try to take him out. One thing I can give him credit for is he *definitely* knew how to duck. I was swinging like crazy, fully intent on hurting him, but he ducked every one of the haymakers I threw.

Jarrett seemed to be working with a different co-promoter in each of the territory's towns. In Nashville, there was a woman who would stand out by the dressing room door. I was late, and this lady, who was probably a member of the Welch family, said to me, "You're late! Why are you late?!"

I just glanced at her and said, "I *left* late." Then I kept walking. I wasn't about to blame it on traffic like some of the other guys would, and I didn't feel the need to explain myself to her.

All in all, Memphis was an okay place to work, but there were a lot of politics involved there. *No one* was going to get over Lawler, and hardly anyone was going to get over Dundee or Dutch Mantell for a top heel position. By the time I got there, those three guys had held the Southern Championship - the top title in the company - for something like 50 different title reigns between them! Jimmy Valiant seemed to have the smartest method for working in Memphis, which was to come in for a week or two, and then go to another territory on a longer-term basis.

One of the nice things about being in Memphis was seeing Jos Leduc again. He'd been my friend since my very first visit to Canada, and he'd also been with me on my first trip to Japan. There wasn't a lot of ego where Jos was concerned. However, Jos being around wasn't enough to keep me in Memphis for very long. I gave my notice to Jarrett and Lawler in September, dropped the Mid-America title back to Keirn, and came straight back to Florida.

In my absence, Dusty had won the NWA World Heavyweight Championship from Harley Race in June, which meant he was off in other territories defending the championship quite a bit and was less concerned with booking Florida. That responsibility fell to Jody Hamilton. With Jody handling the booking, I never felt like we were missing Dusty. Jody was far less concerned with which star was drawing the money, as long as money was being drawn.

I worked a series of matches with Jody after I returned to Florida. I lost a hair vs. mask match to him on October 31st, 1981 in St. Petersburg at the Bayfront, which meant I was obligated to shave my hair off. They brought a lady who was a professional barber into the ring after the match to cut my hair, but this lady looked *terrified* of me. As nervous as she looked, I didn't want her anywhere near my head with a sharp object, so I asked her to hand me the clippers so I could do it myself. She shook her head, "No."

"There's nothing to be scared about," I assured her. "Just hand me the clippers!"

"No... no... no!" She screamed.

"Will you just hand me the *fuckin'* clippers?!" I yelled, losing my patience.

With that, she quickly handed the clippers over to me and bolted from the ring. To the sullen sounds of lamenting fans, I walked around the ring and sadly shaved my head. Was I *actually* sad? Not *one* bit! I'd do *anything* to draw money. Besides, it helped set the table for me to get my ultimate revenge on Jody by beating him in *two* "Loser Leaves Town" steel cage matches in early November.

I'm pretty sure one of the reasons Jody was booked to "leave town" was because Dusty had returned by then after dropping the NWA championship in September to one of the most dynamic champions of all time, "Nature Boy" Ric Flair. Compared to Dusty, Flair was far better suited to take up the mantle of Harley Race as a champion who could make all of the other NWA wrestlers look amazing, without losing any heat of his own.

I started looking for my own options outside of CWF, and was made an attractive offer by Fritz Von Erich in Dallas. Unfortunately, I was about to learn that the Von Erich family in Texas was just as sensitive as Dusty when it came to making sure the right person was drawing the money *and* attracting the attention.

SIXTEEN – "We're professional athletes"

Fritz Von Erich brought me into Dallas as a heel in December of 1982, and he had me beat the enigmatic Great Kabuki to win the NWA American Heavyweight Championship almost immediately. Kabuki had the gimmick of a painted-up Japanese heel who would blow green mist from his mouth; that stuff was a *mess*. It would get all over your body and your tights, and it was a *huge* pain to wash off.

By this point, I was confident in my ability to comfortably transition back and forth between heel and babyface. I knew what needed to be done in order to make a match spectacular no matter which role I was asked to play. Still, I preferred working as a heel simply because heels had more freedom and could perform a broader range of actions because bad guys didn't have to be liked. As long as you're hated in the end, and you make the fans love the babyface more, heels have *carte blanche* to do whatever they feel like doing. The other thing was, with the three main Von Erich brothers working as the eternal babyfaces in Dallas, the only way to really make any headway or money in Dallas was to work opposite them as a heel.

Fritz had been a big wrestling star using a borderline Nazi gimmick during the 1950s and 1960s. He'd also won the AWA World Heavyweight Championship, *and* popularized the infamous "Iron Claw" as a devastating submission hold. After setting up shop as the owner of the NWA promotion in Dallas, he eventually built it around his three most athletic sons, David, Kevin and Kerry. Fritz's two youngest sons, Michael and Chris, were also ostensibly in the pipeline, even though neither of them could match the athleticism of the three brothers who were already established stars. In that regard, Fritz's promotion was a marked departure from other family-run wrestling companies.

While Verne Gagne was still booking himself for occasional runs as a world champion or tag team champion well into his 50s, and the majority of his established stars were also in their 40s, Fritz was able to build the Dallas territory around his 20-year-old sons.

This brought a livelier dynamic to Dallas wrestling compared with other companies, and also filled the Dallas Sportatorium with *young* female fans who were all *obsessed* with the Von Erich boys.

David Von Erich was probably the most complete worker of all the young Von Erichs, so he was being justifiably groomed for bigger things within the NWA. He left for Florida to further his reputation. In fact, you might say the two of us had been part of talent exchange; I arrived in Dallas at the same time David arrived in Florida.

Spitting water on a Von Erich

235

Brute Power: The Autobiography of Buggsy McGraw

After letting me carry the American championship for a few months, Fritz asked me to drop the belt to his son Kerry at the Coliseum in Ft. Worth. Kerry had a fantastic physique and could work effectively when he was motivated, but when I tried to lead him, he seemed to have difficulty following instructions. Therefore, our match wasn't great, and Fritz demoted me immediately afterward. Fritz refused to fault his sons for *anything* they did wrong, and Kerry was the golden boy even amongst the Von Erichs. If a match with Kerry went south, it was *always* the other guy's fault.

Instead of letting me work on top, Fritz had me defeat Jose Lothario in Ft. Worth for the NWA Brass Knuckles Championship. That way, I was relegated to hardcore matches, and away from Fritz's sons. Being booked in Brass Knuckles matches was the kiss of death in many ways. In all of the years they wrestled, no Von Erich boy *ever* won the Brass Knuckles title, because it wasn't the main-event style that Fritz wanted his sons associated with.

All of the Von Erich kids seemed to be taking *serious* drugs. Whenever I spoke to them, they all seemed to have slurred speech and far-away looks in their eyes. They took no efforts to conceal their drug use, either. It was one of the worst kept secrets of the territory. In the case of Chris, it seemed like his brothers' mission was to get him high on as many drugs as they possibly could, and I honestly think it played a role in stunting his growth.

If you look at the Von Erichs, they were all fairly sizeable individuals with the sole exception of Chris. Mike Von Erich wasn't built very well, but at least he was tall. The maximum height Chris ever achieved was reported as 5'4", but I'm pretty sure he was even shorter than that.

One time, Kerry and Kevin got Chris so high on drugs that he passed out on the floor right in front of the concession stand after he placed an order for some hot dogs. His brothers had to pick him up off the floor and carry him to the top of the bleachers so he could sleep off his buzz during the matches. Another time, we were at the Sportatorium, and Chris came walking into the dressing room wearing a golf cap. Since this was his daddy's company, it was customary for Chris to walk into the dressing room like he owned the place. His face was so pale, he looked ghostly.

After standing next to me with a blank stare in his eyes, Chris looked around exhaustedly at the wrestlers in the room before announcing, "Man… I'm *so* sick and tired of blow jobs!"

"*What?!*" I asked him in disbelief.

"These women, man…" Chris continued. "I'm just sick of them giving me blowjobs."

The rest of the wrestlers in the room were laughing at *me* because my jaw had dropped in shock. By now, they were used to the fact that Chris was getting regular sexual favors from the female fans who frequented the shows, and at a rate exceeding that of most of the wrestling stars on the roster.

Having a fanbase made of 50 percent young girls sounds like a dream scenario to a young wrestler, but Chris Von Erich was living proof that those sorts of indulgences can destroy you from the inside out. He was only a twelve-year-old kid, and he was being corrupted beyond all measure! Later, when Chris turned 13, he had all of his friends of similar ages join him at the arena. That evening, he admitted one of his brothers' groupies to his birthday party, and she proceeded to dole blowjobs out to *all* of his young friends.

Whenever I drove around with the VonErichs on the way to matches, they had this mantra they'd often repeat, which went, "Don't forget… you're a Von Erich!" I'm sure they meant it to instill a sense of family pride in each of them, but what it amounted to was, "Everyone else is beneath us, and we're owed all of the best things in life." To that end, they seemed to want to include Chris in as many of the trappings of their success as they could.

While not as big as Kerry, Kevin Von Erich also had an incredible physique, and he was the most natural athlete of the Von Erich clan. He had the raw athleticism to do *anything* he wanted, even as a heavyweight. He's the only guy I've ever seen deliver a *seamless* spinning sunset flip off the top rope to a man standing dead in the center of the ring. It's one of the most impressive things I was ever an eyewitness to in my wrestling career. Sadly, Kevin was also high all the time. I spoke with him in the dressing room once while he was talking about working for Sam Muchnick in St. Louis.

"I went to drop an elbow on this guy, and I was so high up, I landed on his *face*," Kevin lamented. "I really fucked his face up. He had to get surgery."

"That sucks!" I said. "What did Muchnick say?"

"He went to Fritz and complained about it," Kevin said. "It wasn't my fault, though. Somebody opened one of the doors just as I came off the top rope. The wind rushed in, and it blew me right over on top of the guy! It was an accident!"

"The *wind*?" I responded. "The *wind* knocked you off course? Okay, Kevin. *Whatever*..."

I couldn't believe what I was hearing. This was actually the excuse he'd fed his father, and his father swallowed it and tried to sell it right back to Sam Muchnick. With Fritz supporting them, these kids could literally have gotten away with *murder*!

Outside the ring, Kerry and Kevin acted like they were the coolest guys around. Even though Kevin was the brother who would wrestle barefoot, Kerry would walk around barefoot in the parking lot during the *wintertime*. He thought he was the *coolest* thing because he could walk through the gravel with his bare feet. Again, I chalked it up to the drugs having numbed his senses.

There was a spot show that started at 8:00 p.m. that I was running late for. I eventually arrived around 7:40 p.m., which was still 20 minutes before the bell time for the opening match. I walked in, and Kerry was sitting by the door in a folding chair wearing his standard, glazed-over expression on his face.

I expected him to make some smartass comment about the fact that I was late. Instead, as I walked into the building with my suitcase, Kerry said, "Hey man... Who did you work with?" I stopped dead in my tracks.

"*What* did you say?" I asked.

After about five seconds, a hint of recognition hit Kerry's face.

"Oh *yeah*!" he exclaimed. "That's right! You haven't worked yet!"

238

I was dumbfounded. Not only had I not worked that night, *no one* had worked that night, because the matches wouldn't even be underway for another 20 minutes!

In 1982, Fritz's *World Class Championship Wrestling* was in the process of becoming one of the most-watched wrestling programs in the country. To help Marc Lowrance with the announcing duties during the syndicated broadcasts of WCCW, Fritz brought in Jay Saldi, the captain of the Dallas Cowboys special teams, to handle the color commentary. Jay seemed to be very taken with my gimmick, because he would use his time on the microphone to promote me rather aggressively, and he didn't seem to exalt the Von Erichs nearly as much as he did me. It wasn't even like Jay and I were friends; we never once hung out. He just liked the character I was portraying.

I heard rumors that Fritz wasn't happy with Jay's commentary due to the lack of praise his sons were being given. Assuming that getting rid of Jay would be a simple task, Fritz had Gary Hart call Jay into the office, and Gary said, "Unfortunately, we can't afford to pay you anymore, Jay. I'm really sorry about this."

"That's okay; I'll do it for *free!*" Jay said, to Gary's great surprise and Fritz's chagrin. Jay continued on for free after that.

Fritz paired me up with the massive King Kong Bundy back when he was still in his first year of active wrestling. In April, we won the WCCW American Tag Teams Championships from Al Mandril and Kerry.

"With your size and the way you move, you're going to make a *lot* of money," I told Bundy. "There's no two ways about it."

I used to slap Bundy behind the head all the time, though, because he was *constantly* being distracted and not doing the right things in the ring, and not being focused on getting the matches over. Bundy would go to convenience stores and buy a *ton* of food. He'd say, "Why go out and spend a bunch of money when I can go to a convenience store, spend five dollars, and eat *really* well?"

Bundy wasn't concerned about food quality; it was all about the maximum quantity of food he could acquire for the cheapest price. I couldn't really argue with his logic, because at his size he had to eat a lot of food every day to maintain his 400-pound body.

King Kong Bundy

Bugsy McGraw

King Kong Bundy and Buggsy McGraw – American Champs

In June, the promotion held a major show at Texas Stadium, the home of the Dallas Cowboys football team. On the undercard, I wrestled Andre the Giant in a match which he won by disqualification. Then I worked in a $10,000 Bodyslam Roulette match which featured eight different wrestlers, including Bundy and Andre.

I wound up as one of the finalists, but then Andre slammed me with ease and "won" the $10,000. In the main event, Bundy dropped the American championship to Fritz Von Erich in a falls-count-anywhere match. The final pinfall occurred in the endzone of the stadium, and the match was billed as Fritz's swansong from wrestling.

During one of our trips to Amarillo, I found myself in a rare situation where I had my car all to myself. I decided to have a great time on the way back to Fort Worth, so I turned up the rock and roll, lit up a joint, and threw down a six pack of beer over the course of my five-hour road trip. There was no interstate between my starting point and my destination; I was driving solely on State roads. Every so often, I would pass through a small town.

Given how late in the evening it was, most of the streets in these small towns were empty, so I decided to gun the accelerator and race right through the towns without slowing down at all. As I got to the other side of one of the towns, I noticed red-and-blue flashing lights in my rearview mirror. The local Sheriff had been lying in wait for an offender just like me, and as I looked at all of the empty beer cans in the car, I knew I was in very hot water.

Following protocol, I climbed out of the car to prove I was no threat to the Sheriff. I stood right behind the trunk of my car to face him, but it suddenly dawned on me that something was amiss. I'd tried to lean up against my vehicle, but it was retreating from me. I immediately realized I'd forgotten to put the car in park, and it was now rolling down the street on its own!

In a panic, I ran as hard as I could to catch up to the car, latched onto the open door and launched myself into the front seat. As my legs dangled through the door, I reached for the parking brake and then cranked it until the car screeched to a halt.

"Well… this is it," I thought to myself.

As if nothing had happened, I sheepishly walked over to the trunk of my car and said, "Hi, Sheriff! What can I do for you?"

I don't know if the Sheriff was a wrestling fan or not, but he and his deputy decided to let me go. How I managed to get out of that, I have no idea. Between the alcohol, the marijuana and the obvious lack of control I demonstrated over my vehicle, I was certain I would end up in jail that night.

On a different night, I was driving in the opposite direction toward Amarillo, except this time I had "Wild" Bill Irwin riding in the shotgun seat. Along the way, we spotted a cop on the other side of the road who was occupied with handing a ticket to some unfortunate individual who must have been exceeding the 55 mile-per-hour speed limit. Seeing this, and stupidly assuming the cop was too engaged with his first victim to bother with me, I accelerated right past him at 70 miles an hour.

Without hesitation, the officer ran back to his car, turned his lights on and bolted after me. In seconds, he was right up to my bumper, and I pulled off to the side of the road.

"Shit…" Bill said. "I think we're in trouble."

The two of us had been sharing a joint, and the car reeked of marijuana. Not wanting to alert the officer to any wrongdoing on our part, we climbed out of the car and walked over to the trunk in order to establish our willingness to cooperate with the authorities.

"Hey, officer," Bill greeted him. "How are you doing today?"

"I'll ask the questions," the officer said.

After sizing us up, the officer ushered me over to his squad car and had me climb into the passenger seat. Once he'd gotten in and closed the doors to the car, the officer became aware of the scent of weed emanating from me and began sniffing the air.

"I smell marijuana!" the officer said. "You were smoking pot!"

"Officer, we don't do things like that," I scolded him. "We're *professional* athletes! How dare you!"

Unconvinced by my lies, the officer leaned back and sniffed me some more. In the process, he noticed my handheld wallet, which I'd brought with me under the assumption that I'd need to show him my drivers license. There were five different compartments to my wallet, all of which opened with zippers, and one of which contained my remaining supply of weed.

"I *definitely* smell marijuana," the officer insisted. "Unzip that part. Now that one. Mmmhmmm... now *that* one..."

After going through the first four compartments, I knew the next unzipping of the wallet would unveil the metal case which held my joints. I was *finished*.

"Open up your trunk!" the officer said in frustration. "I want to see your trunk!"

"Yes, sir!" I said, quickly jumping out of the car and practically *running* over to my trunk.

I knew there was *nothing* in the trunk, but if the officer had asked me to open that one final compartment on my wallet, Bill and I would undeniably have been on our way to jail. After failing to find anything in the trunk of my car, the officer reluctantly let us leave.

Gary Hart could see I had the ability to work, and he knew all about my successful babyface run in Florida, so he switched me to a babyface role right after Bundy and I dropped the belts to Kerry and Kevin in July. Afterward, he had me shoot some lifestyle video segments all over Dallas. The babyface character I played had the sensibilities of a child, which Bill Mercer referred to as "The Manchild" during interviews. Gary wanted me to film some of the lifestyle segments at a local waterslide park. When we got there, the park manager said, "It's going to be hard for you to film what you want because we have all these people here."

Gary looked around and said, "Well, can we just rent out the whole park for as long as we need to shoot?"

"Sure!" said the surprised manager. "That will *definitely* solve the problem."

For the remainder of the day, I spent time riding all of the slides and splashing around in the water until Gary and the cameraman decided they had the footage they needed. It was a fun and productive way to spend a workday.

During my babyface run, I suggested that I could dress in a gorilla costume and smash a whipped-cream pie in Gary Hart's face.

We went through with it, and it was one of my most memorable moments in Dallas.

Everyone could see I was starting to get over huge with the fans while working as a top babyface. My finisher, a splash off the top turnbuckle, was also a favorite of the fans. Gary even had me win the WCCW Television Championship from Bill Irwin. The reception I received in Dallas was nearly at the level things reached during my peak in Florida. As things were going so undeniably well, I was sitting in the locker room with "The Spoiler" Don Jardine, and he leaned over and said, "You see how well you're getting over?"

"Yeah, it's going pretty well right now!" I conceded.

"Once you outdraw the Kerry and Kevin, you'll be back in the middle of the card in three weeks," warned Don.

"Why three weeks?" I asked.

"That will be the point when all of the advertised shows have run their course, and then they can switch up the matches and move you down," he said. "Mark my words; it's going to happen."

Don couldn't have been more right. Three weeks later, they had me drop the TV title back to Bill Irwin. I had absolutely nothing against Bill, who I considered a great hand in the ring. The two of us had some very good matches, and he sold wonderfully. I was offended by the principle of being demoted for doing my job well. I was relegated to being the Brass Knuckles Champion yet again, and I was no longer booked to work in any main events in WCCW... *ever!*

There was an independent film group in Texas working with Fritz on a film about WCCW. The guy in charge of it had a few film productions under his belt already, and Fritz thought whatever project this film crew was working on would help WCCW to become a bonafide national promotion. To Fritz's great consternation, the producer became a big fan of mine, and he wanted to mold some of what I was doing into his vision for the film and his plans to help WCCW enhance its national presence.

"Hey, Buggsy, we should do something in the ring together," he said. "I'll come out in a clown costume after you win your match, and we can dance together in the ring. I think the kids will eat that up!"

"Sure!" I said. "I've got no problem with that!"

After my match that day, the guy did exactly as he'd proposed. He got in the ring while wearing a clown outfit, and the two of us danced around to the applause of the fans.

"This is totally *ridiculous!*" Fritz said when we got back. "Now *you* look like a clown!"

It wasn't my idea; it was the *producer's* idea. He thought it would set me apart and help me garner attention, so I was all for it. I couldn't tell if Fritz was truly upset about me doing something silly in the ring, or if he was upset that someone other than one of his sons was being favored by the production team. No matter what the motivation behind it was, that was the last time the production team ever got involved in any matches or segments with me in them.

I heard Fritz complain about what was happening in the territory on more than one occasion, and I understood it to mean he specifically wasn't happy with the way Gary Hart was handling his boys. Meanwhile, Gary was clearly frustrated by having Fritz hovering over his shoulder all the time and second guessing his booking decisions. A few months later, Gary left the promotion after a dispute with Fritz. Without Gary around to offer me a small amount of protection, Fritz quickly booked the Great Kabuki to take the Brass Knuckles Championship from me.

I was pretty annoyed with the political landscape of WCCW. Clearly, I wasn't being used the way I should have been, but there was no way to convince the owner of the territory that I deserved to be pushed harder than his own sons. Fritz was determined to build the promotion around his boys, and that wouldn't work if any other wrestlers were featured in a role where they could steal glory from Kevin and Kerry.

Before I left Dallas, I became pretty good friends with The Fabulous Freebirds - Michael "P.S." Hayes and Terry "Bam Bam" Gordy. During a car trip with the aforementioned Freebirds, we were riding into a small town that had a sign on the side of the road which said, "Bob Is Back; Flats Are Fixed." I don't know why, but all of us thought this was *hilarious*, and we laughed hysterically at the idea that Bob was the *only* one who could fix flat tires. To this day, if Michael

Hayes and I see each other in person, we'll greet each other by saying, "Bob is back; flats are fixed."

Flying off the top turnbuckle

Even though I was determined to leave Dallas, I definitely wasn't heading back to Florida. When I'd left Florida, Eddie reasoned it was time for me to leave before my act got too stale after my successful three-year run there. I don't think he ever imagined Dusty Rhodes would *also* leave Florida within a year of my departure.

In 1983, CWF sank as a result of losing its two top babyfaces in short order. Fortunately for me, Gary Hart got a job as booker for Jim Crockett Promotions in the Mid-Atlantic territory, and he called to ask me if I'd like to join him there. Very quickly, Kabuki and I were whisked out of Dallas and added to the JCP talent roster. I appreciated Gary providing me with work and getting me away from Fritz, but I knew pushing Kabuki as a star was going to be his top priority in Charlotte.

The Mid-Atlantic operation was already huge when I entered the territory. They were running three to four shows every single night, which meant we were driving all over the place. Bruno and Vince both had prior conversations with Jim Crockett about bringing me to Charlotte, but I'd never actually spoken to Jim Crockett directly until I'd signed to his company.

Terry Funk said to me, "Crockett *better* be making money here, because when you're running this many shows and you're not making money, you'll be in the hole *fast*."

Gary made the decision to pair me up with Jimmy Valiant in a tag team since we were both playful babyface gimmick wrestlers who could get the fans out of their seats, dancing and physically involved. I was okay with the decision, but I quickly discovered Jimmy was only out for Jimmy. He was also a *horrendous* seller, so our working styles didn't mesh all that well even though we both played colorful characters.

During his early career, Jimmy was seriously hurt by Moose Cholak. Moose did this move where he'd jump in the air and drop his ass on you; when he hit Jimmy with this move, it broke several of Jimmy's ribs. He was out for three to four months recovering from the rib injury, and it may have contributed to Jimmy's lack of selling later on.

I decided to modify my finishing move to a running body splash when I got to the Mid Atlantic. After pounding my chest, I would hit both ropes very hard while hopping over my opponent, and then I would deliver the big splash. I think it got a bit more exciting for the fans when I performed this version of the move as opposed to coming off the top turnbuckle. I would still get six feet into the air with the leap, and all the movement that preceded the splash helped to build the anticipation for it.

Plenty of wrestlers have told me they were afraid to hit the ropes as hard as I did. It's *not* as easy as it looks. Some young talent have even hit the ropes hard and wound up in the emergency room with broken ribs!

As teammates, Jimmy and I traveled together frequently, and Jimmy would stoop to any level or invoke every imaginable excuse to make sure his travel companions handled 100 percent of the driving duties.

"I know I'm supposed to drive, Daddy, but my back hurts," Jimmy would say one night. The next night, he might say, "I know I'm supposed to drive, Daddy, but I carried most of the last match, and I'm dead tired."

Remember, if Jimmy said he carried a match, it simply means he spent a lot of time getting his offense in. It's not like he *ever* did much bumping or selling, and he burned most of his energy by dancing. He always had an excuse as to why *you* had to be the one to put miles on your own car instead of him putting miles on his.

During a recent fanfest, I was talking to "The Honky Tonk Man" Wayne Ferris. When Honkytonk noticed Jimmy, he told the story about how he'd been riding with Jimmy and started feeling sick, so he asked if he could pull the car over and let Jimmy drive.

"Hey, Daddy," Jimmy said. "I can't drive, Daddy. My hands don't fit the steering wheel."

Apparently, a one-size-fits-all steering wheel was a fit for everyone's hands *except* Jimmy Valiant's. He also couldn't be bothered to go out of his way to help *anyone*. Crockett flew me into the territory a few times to see if they could get me over before they decided to bring me in permanently. During that stint, I flew to Charlotte and called Jimmy Valiant after I'd arrived at the airport.

"Hey, Jimmy," I said, "It's Buggsy. Can you pick me up from the airport?"

"No, I can't," replied Jimmy, roughly.

I was calling pretty early in the afternoon, and I wondered if Jimmy thought I wanted him to pick me up *and* bring me back over to his house. I honestly just wanted him to swing by the airport so I could hop in his car on the way to the TV tapings. Either way, he refused to come get me.

During my wrestling career, I was hardly in church at all. I always had a belief in God and perceived there was a higher power in the universe, but I didn't make any effort to get close to Him at all. There was a man who lived in St. Augustine, Florida, named Paul Lentz. He was a big fan of mine, and a big fan of wrestling in general. He was also a Christian, and we often spoke on the telephone even when I was in Dallas and Charlotte.

Paul would regularly encourage me to accept Christ as my savior and believe in Him, but I had myriad reasons for rejecting Christianity at that time.

"I'm not sure if I can believe this, Paul," I told him. "I just don't see how all of this stuff can be true."

One time, Paul and I were on the phone, and he got me to pray the "Sinner's Prayer."

"Buggsy, you're saved now!" Paul said. "Glory to God! You're now a child of God!"

Of course, that wasn't true, and I knew it. Just because someone says the "Sinner's Prayer," that doesn't make them a Christian... especially when they *don't* believe it when they say it. At the time I prayed that prayer, I certainly fell into the "disbelief" category.

Paul even got up in front of his church and announced to them that he led Buggsy McGraw to Christ. Since I was a relatively well known celebrity in Florida, I'm sure that impressed some people at his local church back in St. Augustine, but it simply wasn't true.

SEVENTEEN – "You're just a clown in the ring"

I'm sure a few guys on the Mid-Atlantic roster were worried about their job security when the Great Kabuki came in alongside Gary Hart. It was no secret Gary had every intention of pushing the talent he brought with him. Unsurprisingly, Kabuki was pushed very hard as a heel in Charlotte, and Gary handled all of his interviews for him.

I worked a lot of matches with the colossal One Man Gang, and he could be truly selective about which moves he opted to sell. During one of our matches in Richmond, Virginia, I was in the midst of making a comeback against the Gang, and he continued his pattern of not selling any of my offense. As *soon* as I tagged in my partner, Ricky Steamboat, Gang started taking *all kinds* of bumps for him. He seemed to be selectively selling for the guy he thought was the most over.

Steamboat was over *huge* with the crowds, and he was one of the main guys for Crockett in the Mid-Atlantic territory. He was athletic, sharp, did everything the right way, and he didn't have his head up his ass like a lot of the other guys.

One night I was sitting in the dressing room in Charleston with Barry Horowitz, and Barry had his eyes on the very nice sport coat which was hanging in the corner of the dressing room.

"Hey, is this your coat?" asked Barry.

I knew for a fact it belonged to Dory Funk Jr., who had wrestled earlier and left it behind accidentally.

"Yeah, it's my coat," I lied. "It's nice isn't it?"

"That's a *really* nice coat!" said Barry. "It's *beautiful!*"

"I can always get another one," I explained. "Why don't you buy it off me?"

Barry shook his head.

"I don't really think I can afford it," he lamented.

"Hey, for you… I can let it go for $65," I told him.

"Seriously?! That would be *great!*" Barry exclaimed, and he began searching for the bills to pay me with. Soon, he was holding his newly purchased sport coat aloft, and smiling at it with pride. The next time I saw Barry, he was looking quite snazzy in the sport coat, which he'd had tailored specifically to fit him. Within a few weeks, Dory noticed the coat on Barry and said, "Hey! That's *my* coat!"

"No it's not!" Barry said, defensively. "It was *Buggsy's*, and he sold it to me!"

I thought the whole thing was hilarious. Dory was not one of my favorite people, but I still realized it wasn't the right thing to do. I found Dory after that incident and said, "Yeah, I sold your coat to Barry, and I feel kind of bad about it. If you want me to pay for it, I'd be glad to."

"Don't worry about it," said Dory to my astonishment. "We're good."

To his credit, Dory seemed to think the rib was funny, too, and since no one got hurt, what I'd done had fallen within the boundaries of a well-executed wrestling rib. I wasn't much of a ribber, though. Wrestling ribs have a tendency to escalate and become too serious, and that's when people's feelings get hurt, and ultimately, it can lead to violence.

Mid Atlantic had a solid roster *full* of true workers, like Greg Valentine, Ricky Steamboat and Ric Flair. While it might seem like this meant Jim Crockett had a thing for high-quality workers on his shows, you have to keep in mind they were running up to four shows *every* day. This means they had to have a lot of wrestlers in the company, *period*. The fact that Mid Atlantic had so many top workers was primarily due to the sheer size of the roster they'd assembled.

I would usually only see "Nature Boy" Ric Flair in the dressing room when we were booked on the same card, or on the very rare occasions when we were in the same car headed to a show. Only once did we ever work a match together, and that's a shame, because it was *impossible* to have a bad match with Flair.

Even though there were so many stars in the Mid-Atlantic territory, Flair was clearly *the guy*, and I can say that without hesitation. He was unquestionably number one, and probably number one in the entire wrestling business. He had a ton of stamina both inside the ring and outside of it in social settings. I recall the time we were scheduled to do interviews, and Flair had been out all night with Roddy Piper and gotten the kilted wrestler drunk. Over the course of the evening, Flair had somehow convinced Piper to purchase the $10,000 Rolex watch right off of Flair's wrist.

As they came in to do their interviews, Piper was clearly hungover and agitated. While we waited, he marched over to Flair with the Rolex outstretched in his hand and growled, "Take this *damn* Rolex back! I am *not* going to pay for it!"

"You bought it, Piper!" laughed Flair. "That's *your* Rolex now! It looks good on you, too!"

"I'm *not* buying this!" yelled Piper. "You take this back *right now!*"

Eventually, Flair relented, and the Rolex adorned his wrist once again by the time the interviews were finished.

Piper's substance abuse was the stuff of legend, but that locker room had more than one wrestler in it who liked to binge on illegal drugs.

"Last year, I spent *$25,000* on cocaine!" Piper bragged to us in the locker room.

"That's nothin' kid," piped in Wahoo McDaniel. "I spent *$35,000* on cocaine last year, *easily.*"

These sorts of sparring sessions over which wrestler could out-snort the other would take place out in the open, in front of every wrestler in the company. It seemed as if no Mid Atlantic wrestlers were ever ashamed enough of their extracurricular activities to have kept them a secret from the other men in the dressing room.

Every so often, Piper would ride with Jimmy and I. As well as anybody, he understood the benefits of selling and then letting the crowd make the comeback with him. Just when it looked like he couldn't take any more punishment, he would start screaming, "Come on! More! Hit me again!" The crowd would eat it up! He fully understood the abundance of selling he did made him look even more heroic and superhuman in the long run.

It's not like Piper was a big guy, either. I once teased him during a car trip, telling him, "Roddy, you don't *really* look like a wrestler. You look more like a swimmer!"

Roddy just shrugged and didn't say much. His performance did the talking. Regardless of his size, Piper was one of the smartest wrestlers I've ever seen. He knew how to get over better than just about anyone. His later run in New York with Vince McMahon Jr. is one of the greatest examples in wrestling history of how to use every tool in your arsenal to get over when it counts in front of a national audience.

While some wrestlers were bragging about how much money they could blow on *blow*, I was in a financial bind. I'd been having major problems in my life for quite some time. It seemed like just as soon as one of the problems was beginning to subside, another problem would materialize, and then the process would repeat itself. It was quite overwhelming.

One of my problems was an engine failure with my car. I'd had to fork over a ton of money to have the engine replaced. Granted, I'd been in more than 20 car wrecks in my wrestling career; seven of those wrecks resulted in cars being totaled. This particular breakdown just happened to occur at a very bad time.

For years after I'd first injured my knee in Vancouver, I either wrapped it, or I would wear a brace to hold my knee in place so that the cartilage wouldn't slip. Well, the cartilage finally did slip, and my knee locked up to the point where I couldn't even bend it a little bit. It required an expensive surgery that I had to pay for. Then the IRS contacted me and said I owed them $60,000 in back taxes from a prior year. As it turned out, during the year in question, I'd *only* made about $50,000. It was a damaging sum of money to have to produce on short notice with the IRS breathing down my neck.

Fortunately, I knew someone who used to work for the IRS, and I stayed in close contact with him until we worked the situation out. Thanks to his involvement, I managed to negotiate the settlement fee down to $7,000. It was nothing compared with the $60,000 I'd been asked to pay, but it *still* hurt.

Finally, I'd purchased a large amount of stock, and the value of the stock I'd purchased *plummeted*. I was left with a small fraction of my original investment. All in all, I had about seven *major* life setbacks over a short timespan. They left me feeling drained and defeated.

I'd been told before by several people over the course of my life, "The Lord has His hand on you, Michael."

In response to that, I'd usually shrug awkwardly and say, "Okay… well… that's alright I guess." I didn't understand what they meant, so I just gave very non-committal answers.

A group of us were on our way back to Charlotte from Greenville, South Carolina, which was a town the Crocketts ran shows in quite often. Senior referee Tommy Young was driving the car, and I was riding behind him in the back seat.

After a year's worth of major problems, I was dwelling on everything that had happened to me while sitting in the back of that car during that ride home while holding a quart of beer between my legs. I was at my wit's end. My plan was to go back to Florida, take the remaining money I'd saved up, buy a small house in Brandon and spend my free time riding around on a bicycle. I was fed up, and I wanted nothing more to do with wrestling, or life in general for that matter. I didn't want anything to do with society. I wanted to get away from everyone and everything, and my bike would permit me to ride over to the grocery store and buy whatever I needed to live on. In short, I wanted to drop out of society… *period*.

Everything hit my head at once, and I said to myself, "Oh my God… I can't take it anymore!" I laid my head back on the seat, and I started screaming at the top of my voice. I was screaming so loud that my jaw locked open. I just let loose for about 30 seconds. After that, I raised myself up and looked around, and I realized no one was looking at me, or even acknowledging that I'd been making any noise at all. Instead, they were carrying on, drinking beer and having a good time as if nothing out of the ordinary had happened.

That's when I realized I'd had a silent scream, like one you might see in a motion picture. Until that point, I'd always wanted to accept Jesus Christ on my own terms, which isn't how it works. He's the King of Kings and the Lord of Lords, and you can't dictate any special terms to Him; you have to accept Him on *His* terms. In that moment, I said, "Jesus, I will accept You on Your terms right now."

Then, there came a bright light out from the front of the car, and it pierced right through me. The first thing that came to my mind was that I'd somehow cracked through to the foundation of the world, and Jesus Christ *is* the foundation of the world. As the scripture says in John 1:1 with respect to Christ, "In the beginning was the Word, and the Word was with God, and the Word was God. He was in the beginning with God. All things were made through Him, and without Him was not any thing made that was made."

I accepted Christ right then and there, and my life has changed ever since then. The first 15 years of my career, I really enjoyed wrestling, and it was all I ever wanted to do. I'd even passed up some fantastic career opportunities in California along the way in order to continue my pursuit of wrestling success. After I accepted Christ, it wasn't the same anymore. I just didn't find wrestling as fulfilling or exciting as it had been in the past.

At the very first Starrcade, in 1983, Rufus R. Jones and I worked a match against The Assassins - Jody Hamilton and Hercules Hernandez. I assume Jody was helping out in the office at this point. He was so sharp, they would have been stupid not to use him in a booking role. Hercules was one of the most well built, heavily muscled guys I've ever seen in the business, and he had a very trim waist. Unfortunately, the Assassin outfit required him to cover everything up. It created quite a contrast, because Jody was much heavier and far pudgier than Hercules. When the two of them stood side by side, It was quite simple to figure out who was who.

As a resident of the Tampa area, Hercules had heard all about my fight at Robiconti's and thought it was a big deal. Most of the other wrestlers from Tampa were also very impressed by the tale. Brutus Beefcake, who claims to have been at Robiconti's that night, gave me a once over, and immediately launched into a description of the incident the first time he ever met me.

"I remember that *fight*, man!" Beefcake said. "You tore that guy's *eye* right out!"

To some of these guys, I was a hero for defended the honor of professional wrestling in a real fight against two local monsters at the same time.

I had no problem putting Jody and Hercules over at Starrcade, because Jody was a very unselfish worker in every way, including with his booking practices. If he thought Rufus and I should put his team over, there was bound to be some solid reasoning behind his thought process.

Wearing the trademark tophat

Starrcade was handled as if it was a very big deal. I think I dropped the pinfall and left the building shortly thereafter. We'd worked in the first match at the very first Starrcade, which is probably of some historical significance to somebody. Different people have been credited with booking Starrcade. With Gary Hart, Dory Funk Jr. and Jody Hamilton all around, they certainly had a lot of experienced booking talent to draw from.

If I recall correctly, everyone in the Mid-Atlantic territory was required to show up in the locker room the night of Starrcade, and everyone received a payoff even if they didn't work at the event. When you look at the lineup to the show, it was a true all-star event. Almost everyone involved had main-evented somewhere in the country.

Jimmy Valiant came out during one of the matches as "Charlie Brown" and beat Great Kabuki for the television championship. Since they wanted to feature Jimmy, that's how I wound up with Rufus as my partner. Otherwise, Jimmy would have been with me against The Assassins.

Given the huge roster we had, the amount of talent in the dressing room and how there were only eight matches on the Starrcade card, it was an honor to be included in the event.

The entire premise for Starrcade was developed around establishing Ric Flair as the NWA's flagship wrestler for the 1980s. While Flair had already captured the world title before, his first coronation wasn't handled properly. Dusty had been the champion prior to Flair, and he reportedly didn't want to lose the title to Flair in any cities where Dusty was a big star. So, instead of dropping the title to Flair in the Carolinas or Georgia, Dusty dropped the belt to Flair in Kansas City, which was really a Harley Race town.

Flair's first title reign had been fine, but not spectacular. Starrcade would remedy this by giving Flair a major event at which to win the championship, along with a huge audience watching via closed-circuit television throughout the South. The next time Flair toured as NWA World Heavyweight Champion, it would be in front of an entire region of fans who'd personally shared in his crowning moment.

The NWA championship wasn't a championship I *ever* thought about winning. Several wrestlers approached me over the course of my career, suggesting that I would make a good world champion for the NWA. It was never something I seriously considered for myself. The people who mentioned it thought I could draw money with the world championship if I was working as a heel. With my big-bumping style, they reasoned I could make the babyfaces in the different territories look very credible. I always dismissed it and said, "They'll never make me the world champion as long as they keep their current mindset of not having *gimmick* wrestlers as world champions. They wouldn't even consider it."

From Gene Kiniski to Dory Funk Jr., to Jack Brisco, to Terry Funk, to Harley Race, to Ric Flair... *none* of those guys were gimmicks. Terry Funk and Ric Flair were the closest to being gimmick wrestlers out of this group, but at their core, they were average sized ring technicians who could work long matches and keep the fans interested. That was the mold of the NWA champion.

Right after Starrcade, I made some shots in Atlanta for Georgia Championship Wrestling. I still didn't care for the state of Georgia at all, no matter how I was being treated in the ring. However, working in the Omni was the one nice thing about the territory. Stan Hansen and I worked a match there against the Road Warriors - Hawk and Animal. Ole told them, "Be aggressive!" which was the right thing for them to do. They were young, and not great workers, but their aggression saved their match quality. At least if you're aggressive, the action looks real, and nothing attracts fans to an arena quite like a vicious heel. The Road Warriors were so big and strong, that you really had to work hard to control them as you called the match.

After our match in the Omni, Joe "Animal" Laurinaitis came up to me in the dressing room and asked me, "Can you tell me what I did right and wrong during the match?"

Joe's attitude really impressed me, because the Warriors were being pushed to the moon, yet he still had the wherewithal to know he needed to improve his performance in some key areas.

"Just keep your aggression, but try to be a little *less* stiff," I laughed. "The fans will believe in everything you do because you're so big and strong. You don't have to *actually* kill anybody!"

Brute Power: The Autobiography of Buggsy McGraw

The Road Warriors were actually a lot like Stan Hansen in that respect. Stan was also a big aggressive guy, and he'd *maul* you. On top of that, he was practically blind. If he threw a big meathook punch at you, he had no idea where it was going to land. To get Stan to sell, you *had* to beat the crap out of him. With that attitude, he was tailor made for the Japanese market. He and I were kindred spirits inasmuch as we would both tell guys, "If you want me to sell your moves, you *have* to stay on top of me. Otherwise, I will *not* sell you." Plenty of guys would work you over, but then they would want to back off, work the crowd or do other things to showboat. I would tell them, "Forget that crap! Stay on me, and don't strut around like a peacock. If you *don't* stay on me, I'm getting up and coming after you!"

In one of the GCW spot show towns, I got to work with Terry Szopinksi, also known as "The Warlord." Before our first match in Macon, I met Terry for the first time, and he was *gigantic*. He stood 6'5", 330 pounds, and he had muscles everywhere without a hint of fat. I'd see him every so often around the gyms in Charlotte, and he could do barbell shrugs with 1,000 pounds on the bar for five or six reps, which takes *serious* strength.

When Terry and I got down to business in the ring, it became clear what my greatest challenge would be. He was so big, strong and green that he would be almost *impossible* to control. I was strong, but the Warlord was an entirely different animal. If I tried to physically guide him somewhere, as if to subtly say, "Let's do this," he could push me in an entirely different direction and say, "No… let's do *this*!"

Later on, the Warlord was packaged with the Barbarian, and they became a carbon copy of the Road Warriors known as "The Powers of Pain."

After I became a Christian, I drank a *whole* lot less than I had prior to my conversion, and there were quite a few wrestlers who didn't want to hear it and stopped hanging around me at all. Other guys were supportive of me. In my experience, many wrestlers have some sort of belief in God, but when you'd present them with various aspects of the gospel message, they didn't want to live the life. They didn't want to submit in any way, because there were so many aspects of living a wrestler's celebrity lifestyle that were appealing, and that don't comport with a Christian worldview. Drinking, drugs and promiscuity are extremely strong vices and addictions that a lot of wrestlers embrace. They'll actually put as much effort as possible into getting more money and more fame so that they can become even more successful at indulging in these vices. As a result, many guys think becoming a Christian means you won't be able to have any more fun. This is the furthest thing from the truth; they simply have an incomplete or inadequate definition of what fun is, from my perspective.

After leaving Georgia, I returned to Memphis for another brief run. At one time, there was a lot of heat between Jerry Jarrett and the Poffo family. Angelo Poffo owned International Championship Wrestling, which was an outlaw territory that ran against Jerry Jarrett's NWA-backed Continental Wrestling Association. More often than not, Angelo's sons, Randy Savage and Lanny Poffo, were the champions of the ICW company.

In order to build the legitimacy of his father's ICW promotion, Randy routinely did interviews on the ICW television program in which he verbally lambasted Jerry Lawler and the rest of Jarrett's crew. One of the key components to Randy's interviews was that he professed of being able to back up everything he was saying if there was ever a true altercation between the companies, with the implication that Lawler and his associates were all talk.

I don't know how much of a shooter Randy was, but he was *certainly* intense enough to be believable. By the time I returned to Memphis, the Poffos were working alongside Jarrett, with Angelo always next to Randy acting as a true manager.

"I don't know if I've heard of you before," Angelo said in the locker room as he shook hands with me.

I then went out and had one of the easiest matches of my life while putting over Randy, who was a *phenomenal* worker. When the match was finished, Randy walked up to me in the dressing room and said, "Oh, *man*! You're *really* good in the ring, brother!"

That was *high* praise, because Randy was a *true* worker who went *all out* every time he got in the ring. He just wanted to make the match work, make some money, and then go home. After I returned to Florida, the Poffos invited me over to eat at their house where it wound up being just myself, Angelo and his wife, and Randy and his wife, Elizabeth. They all treated me with extreme kindness.

By the time I was working in Memphis, I was walking in and out of the camera frame on interviews, spinning in circles and smacking my head. I'd also carry out props, like the snow shovel I used once to cover my face during an interview. I used the shovel to block my face, then I walked toward my opponent. Then I'd quickly lower the shovel so he could see my face, and then turn and leave, like a crazy person.

I borrowed a lot of Curly Howard's material from The Three Stooges. I'd do the Curly Shuffle a lot, which the fans loved. I'd also walk in a circle along the ground, just like Curly would. A lot of wrestlers thought it was inappropriate because I was being too cartoonish and making a mockery of the business.

"You're just a clown in the ring," they would say.

"I'm not trying to be funny," I'd respond. "I'm working off the *principle* of action and reaction."

The action-and-reaction principle I relied upon meant I would take things from my surroundings and use them within the psychology of my interviews and matches.

Stan Hansen arranged for me to briefly wrestle for All Japan in April of 1984, which wound up being the last time I ever performed there. By that point, Hansen was revered as a wrestling god, and he was in the midst of a 327-day-long reign as the PWF Heavyweight Champion. This was the championship that was practically the exclusive property of Giant Baba, and the longest that anyone other than Baba had ever held that championship up to that point was 128 days, and that distinction belonged to Billy Robinson.

While Baba might have passed the title of native "ace" to Jumbo Tsuruta, he was also in the process of anointing Hansen as the foreign "ace," and the PWF title belt around Stan's waist was symbolic of this. On the streets of Japan, Hansen's merchandise was available just about everywhere.

I returned to Florida and got back to work, but my heart wasn't quite into wrestling like it had once been. Dory called me up at home and asked me to come down to the office. When I got there, Dory told me, "Eddie says we need to make room for some other talent, so we're going to let you go. We want the talent to flow."

"If that's the way you feel, I guess that's it then," I told him.

I stood up, shook Dory's hand, and walked out. In all seriousness, I was extra perturbed because Dory could have told me this over the phone. Instead, he had me drive over to the studio so he could tell me to my face. Maybe he thought the respectful thing to do was to tell me face to face, but I honestly didn't understand why he needed me to get up and drive to the office on my day off just to be fired. I wanted to say something cruel to him, but I knew that as a Christian I needed to be cognizant of my behavior and the image I was presenting to the world. As far as the Bible is concerned, you need to pray for your enemies and treat them well. Also, Dory gave me the impression this decision was coming from Eddie Graham, who was nowhere to be found during that meeting.

My concluding thought on Dory Funk Jr. is he benefited greatly from an era when the NWA World Heavyweight Championship really meant something during the heyday of the NWA. Dory Funk Jr. made plenty of money as the world champion, but to me, he was the *wrong* man at the *right* time. There was *nothing* special about him, and nothing exciting about his style. However, the championship belt carried so much prestige with it that he was able to draw plenty of money simply on the basis of having the championship belt around his waist. By working with every territory's top babyface each night, he was guaranteed to make a killing at the box office and add money to his pockets. I *never ever once* heard a promoter talk about how excited they were about Dory coming to town to wrestle his top guy. You'd hear that about every other major NWA champion, but *never* Dory.

Brute Power: The Autobiography of Buggsy McGraw

Between September of 1984 and March of 1985, I wasn't doing much other than living at home in Florida. After accepting Jesus Christ to be my Lord and Savior, I began to change around a lot of things in my life, including the way I conducted myself in public and dealt with other people. In the process, I felt myself moving further and further away from wrestling, and I found myself spending far more time reading the Bible and learning about what God wanted me to be doing with my life. Getting closer to God became my top priority, and that's how I spent the majority of my free time.

If you read the scriptures and believe them, the more you come to realize how much of a reality God is and what He has accomplished through the death of His son Jesus Christ on the cross. When I wasn't working for a wrestling promotion, I attended several church services, and I participated in a series of one-week Christian seminars. Whenever renowned evangelists would come to town, I would make it a point to attend their lectures and learn from them.

Once you accept Christ, it is not a panacea. It's not like everything in your life suddenly corrects itself and all of your problems go away. You simply need to accept Christ on His terms and understand His way is the only way. My problems certainly didn't go away as soon as I became a Christian, and it took some time for me to work through everything with God's help.

Eventually, Dusty Rhodes returned to Florida briefly to do some booking. I called the office to try to speak with Dusty about coming back to work. As I clung to the receiver, I overheard Dusty in the background saying, "Tell Buggsy I'll call him back!"

Dusty never ever returned my call, which I took as a gross insult. I was really hurt by that for a couple of reasons. First of all, Dusty knew I could work, and he knew I could draw money in Florida if I was presented appropriately. Back when Dusty was at the peak of his popularity in Florida, I was the only person who could really compete with him as the top babyface. Second, it wasn't like Florida was in the midst of an incredible business stretch at the time. The territory was slumping, and it wasn't easy to get hot wrestling talent to come there. Also, it's not like *everybody* liked Dusty anyway.

When Angelo Mosca got the call from Florida and found out it was Dusty on the phone, he said, "What the hell do *you* want?!" Then he hung up. Eventually, he accepted Dusty's calls and his offer to work in Florida, and made decent money working for him.

Later on, I ran into Dusty and his wife Michelle at Robiconti's club. They were hanging out with "Magnum" Terry Allen and his wife. I was still reeling from the financial problems caused by my tax issue, my car issue, my knee surgery and my investment troubles. Dusty was *well* aware that I needed a place to work. I was living at home with my parents because of these difficulties and had no other options. Not haveing a place to work at that time left me feeling depressed about my situation. It was embarrassing.

Almost as if he was trying to twist the knife even further, Dusty bought a round of drinks for everybody around him *except* for me. After all of the drinks were distributed, Dusty then turned his back on me. After all this time that we'd worked together and drawn money together, he'd denied me an opportunity for employment while having full knowledge of my problems, and then he bought drinks for everyone except me as a final insult. As far as I was concerned, that was the *last* straw.

"You son of a bitch!" I thought.

Dusty *really* pissed me off. I'd been willing to do anything he wanted the entire time I was in Florida, and to have him treating me this way was completely unacceptable. Given the depressed mood I was in at that moment, I had every intention of resolving things with Dusty in a physical fashion.

"Hey, I'd like to talk to you in private… *outside*," I said to Dusty.

"Okay…" Dusty said, and he followed me out into the Robiconti's parking lot.

I walked over to a secluded area outside of Robiconti's with Dusty a few paces behind me, and then I spun around and got right in his face.

"After all this time, you treat me *this* way?!" I asked him. "I'm *not* gonna take your shit anymore!"

Before Dusty could respond, I hauled off and *slapped* him as hard as I could. Dusty's designer glasses flew from his face and landed on the pavement. I held up my fists, awaiting some form or retaliation from the Dream so I could take out years of frustration on him. Instead of fighting me, Dusty broke down and cried like a baby.

As huge tears began streaming down Dusty's face, I lowered my hands in shock and disgust.

"Man, I *can't* believe you," I said. "You're not worth the effort."

I have to believe Dusty knew everything I said about him was true, and he was feeling guilty.

It was during my time away from the ring that Eddie Graham committed suicide. Shortly before I left Florida in 1984, Eddie walked into the babyface dressing room while I was the only one in there, and he drew me into a discussion about the people he associated with and how he dealt with them.

"I've got friends here and there, but they're not *real* friends; I just *use* them," he said.

I don't know why Eddie felt like opening up to me like that, but it always stuck with me. Before he committed suicide - by shooting himself in the head *twice* - he'd had a girlfriend who he'd been with for a considerable length of time, and she left him right after he lost a lot of money in a failed business venture. Dusty once told me how the FBI came into the Tampa office and bugged it because they were attempting to catch Eddie in the midst of some shady dealings. Through some fancy maneuvering, Eddie was able to get someone else to take the fall, according to Dusty.

When I finally came back to work for the Florida office after nearly six months away from the business, Wahoo McDaniel was handling the booking duties. The two of us didn't get along at all, and he didn't treat me very kindly. During the three years I'd worked in Florida during the late '70s and very early '80s, I'd been treated like a superstar. Now it was time for me to get a taste of what it was like to be expendable. I walked into the dressing room during a show in Lakeland and came face to face with Wahoo, who was running the show, and Mike Graham.

Wahoo took one look at me and proclaimed, "I'm not gonna use you tonight. Go home."

"I can't go home; I've been advertised!" I responded.

"Don't worry; we'll change it," said Wahoo. "Go home."

Enraged, I stormed out of the dressing room, and Mike Graham chased after me.

"Hey, Buggsy… wait!" Mike yelled.

After catching up to me, he said, "Don't worry. You're working tonight. Forget about Wahoo."

I worked that evening, but I never forgot about the dismissive way Wahoo spoke to me .

Billy White Wolf was actually an Iraqi wrestler whose real name was Adnan Al-Kaissie, and he would later achieve his most notable success in the WWF as General Adnan. Billy called me at home and asked, "How do you feel about coming to the Middle East with me? I'm planning to run shows over there for three weeks."

"Sure!" I told him. "I just need to let the Florida office know I'll need that time off."

I informed the office about my need for time off, but Billy called me up ten days before we were set to go and said, "They cancelled the whole thing on us. There's no trip. I'm really sorry about this."

I let Wahoo know I was once again available to work, but Wahoo wasn't excited about using me, especially since he wanted me out anyway. It wasn't long afterward that I was sitting in Wahoo's office on the second floor of the studio building. Wahoo said something to me, and I can't remember precisely what he said, but it was so infuriating and insulting that I stood up, walked over to the door, and locked it. It was my way of signaling to Wahoo that I had every intention of kicking his ass, and I didn't want anyone coming in to save him from the beating I was planning to give him.

"*Now* let's talk, you son of a bitch!" I screamed at him.

Wahoo started to crawfish, which is to say that he started to back out of the altercation. It occurred to me that I wasn't exhibiting the most Christ-like behavior in that moment, so I turned around, unlocked the door, and walked out without saying another word.

Even though Wahoo and I were part of the same locker room in Charlotte, we *never* hung out. I considered him to be a loudmouth who was constantly bragging about how great he'd been during his prime, or how awesome he was as a professional football player. His boasts would have meant more to me if he wasn't constantly drunk or strung out on cocaine while the words were coming out of his mouth. He was probably somewhat depressed, having been married five different times to four different women, each of whom took their share of Wahoo's earnings from his long and lucrative wrestling career.

All of the boys had heard the story about one of Wahoo's wives who left him and fled to Mexico with another man. Anxious to get her back, Wahoo called her up and said, "If you come back, I'll buy you a mink coat."

"Nope... I don't believe you," she replied. "Send me the mink and we'll talk about it."

Wahoo actually bought a mink, boxed it up and shipped it to her. She *still* never came back to him.

EIGHTEEN – "You're still alive?"

In 1985, wrestling in Florida just didn't have the same energy or prestige it had in prior years. In the past, they had a booker like Dusty who wanted to be successful, who could think on his feet, and who had a cohesive idea of how wrestling should be handled. It was highly appealing to Florida's audience and demographics.

Without Dusty on the card, without Eddie Graham's oversight, and with a rotating crew of clueless bookers, the atmosphere at our shows just wasn't the same. When Dusty first took over the book, he was already over, and was a huge attraction who could work incredibly well in the ring. He featured himself, which was usally a wise thing to do, and he generally knew how to use the other talent on the roster well.

I got along with Dutch Mantel, but he didn't strike me as being on Dusty's level as a booker. Putting Wahoo in charge was a straight up mistake, because he didn't know what he was doing at all. As far as I'm concerned, if a booker is prepared to advertise talent and then send them home, he's disrespecting the fans and doing a disservice to his company.

No one can say for sure what would have happened if Dusty was booking Florida in 1985. My guess is, it would have been an improvement, but how much of an improvement would it have been? There's just no way to know for sure, and there's no way of knowing if it would have kept the company from going into its irreversible downward spiral.

By now, we couldn't ignore the fact that Vince McMahon Jr. and his World Wrestling Federation were beginning to *crush* every company in their path. I can't knock him for what he did, and the only professional gripe I ever had against him is from the time in New Haven when he took all the funds out of the house. Vince was an innovator. Even though Turner had cable television, no promoters realized how to capitalize on the exposure that came through cable television until Vince showed them how it was done. He went on USA cable, broadcast his show around the nation, and then physically followed his show into every major city in the country. Then he went in and handpicked all of the most talented wrestlers in the country for himself.

In the mindsets of the old promoters, they thought $2,000 a week was enough to give the top guys. When Vince came in and demonstrated his willingness to pay more money for the top talent, he blew up the whole system. If the WWF went to an old AWA town, Vince could headline the show with stars he'd lured away from the AWA with the promise of more money. If Vince went to Kansas City, he could repeat the process with the former main-event NWA talent who'd once worked in Kansas City and were now loyal to him.

As a case in point, when I was working in Florida in 1985, the CWF brought in Dewey Robinson - The Missing Link. When Dewey was in Kansas City as Dewey Robinson, he didn't make any money to speak of. Then he got in great shape, painted his face, shaved his head down to a bushy ponytail, and adopted a madman gimmick. He went down to Dallas to work for Fritz with the mindset that he was going to make a change and make some money. He was tired of making $300 a week, so he took his career into his own hands and made a change. As the crazy, muscular and charismatic "Missing Link," Dewey was able to make a *lot* more money than he had in prior years.

"I want you to work for me," Vince told him. "I want you under contract."

In addition to the highly competitive salary Vince promised him, Dewey said they offered him an additional $5,000 just to seal the deal, and it worked. *That's* how Vince did business.

The last major year of my wrestling career was 1987, when I was in Charlotte. By then, Dusty Rhodes was the booker for Crockett. He had two airplanes, one of which was a jet, and the other was a prop airplane. The jet could hold ten people at the most, and the larger plane could hold up to 22.

Everybody wanted to ride on the jet because it was the more prestigious and luxurious way to travel, and I used to be among those people until I actually rode on the jet and became annoyed by how I had to duck my head in order to walk around on it. The ceilings were so low!

"Hey, Dusty, I'm okay with just being on the regular plane from now on," I said after one of our uncomfortable jet flights.

Not being scheduled to fly on the jet meant it could take an extra hour or more before I got to our destinations, but I didn't care. To me, the prop plane was *far* more comfortable. There were *plenty* of people anxious to take my seat on the jet, and as far as I was concerned, they were welcome to it.

By this point, Crockett was holding shows just about everywhere. We went to Cleveland, Los Angeles and Toronto, and he even ran a show at the Nassau Coliseum in New York. We were still headquartered in Charlotte, though, and if I heard about a Christian conference or another special event that didn't conflict with my performance schedule, I would go. I was so on fire to learn, it was nothing for me to drive more than 100 miles to attend a church meeting or conference. In my attempts to get closer to God and learn about Him, I was willing to do whatever it took. I attended several churches while I was on the road, including a church in the Carolinas.

Starrcade 1987 was in Chicago. Rather than participating in the main show, Jimmy Valiant and I opened the New Orleans branch of the show in a tag match against "The Jive Tones" - Tiger Conway Jr. and Shaska Whatley. We wrestled at the Lakefront Arena, and our crowd was a paltry 1,600 people. I recall looking into the stands and knowing our payoff wasn't going to be substantial.

In the meantime, Vince McMahon Jr.'s WWF was a runaway freight train by 1987. In late March, they drew more than 93,000 fans to the Silverdome in Pontiac Michigan to watch Hulk Hogan pin Andre the Giant to retain his WWF Championship at Wrestlemania III. The event broke the world indoor attendance record, and it showed every other wrestling promoter in the world just how much of a gap existed between their promotions and Vince's. If Dusty Rhodes had been the hottest babyface wrestler in the United States at one point, he couldn't hold a candle to Hulk Hogan by the late '80s.

Brute Power: The Autobiography of Buggsy McGraw

Vince Jr. rehired Hogan after Vince Sr. had fired him, which was well after Hogan had a feature role in the film Rocky III as "Thunderlips," the wrestler who brutalizes Rocky Balboa during a charity wrestling event. The surge in national mainstream popularity Hogan received after the release of the film transferred over to his wrestling career. Seeing this, Vince promised Hogan the moon if he would jump to the WWF from the AWA and become his champion, and Hogan agreed. Pinning Andre the Giant cleanly in the middle of the ring in front of the largest crowd ever cemented him as the top box-office-draw in the business, and immortalized him in one night.

Crockett was running roughly four towns a night, and two of the top guys in the company were undoubtedly "The Rock and Roll Express" - Ricky Morton and Robert Gibson. Dusty had the Express relegated to the spot show towns, and the shows in the larger towns would usually get Dusty and Flair. The thing is, a lot of times we would go to a spot-show town and *outdraw* the shows in the big markets as long as the Rock and Roll Express were booked on our spot shows, and that pissed off a lot of people in the office.

I knew Dusty had talent and was a solid booker, but there was no accounting for the popularity of the Rock and Roll Express. Johnny and I used to ride with the Express a lot when we were driving in and out of the small towns. These kids certainly didn't have their heads up their asses, and they could plainly see how much money they were drawing for Crockett. However, it was equally as plain as day that Dusty Rhodes was suppressing the Rock and Roll Express and holding them back from realizing their full potential. If Dusty had turned them loose, the company could easily have made millions and millions of dollars on the backs of those two kids. They were *that* over with the fans… especially the women.

After the matches, there would be seven to ten carloads of women who would follow them away from the arenas, and in some cases, they would follow them all the way back to Charlotte. When I say carloads of women, I mean there were three or four women in *every* car. I was sitting right next to Ricky and Robert in those cars at the time, so I know what I'm talking about, and I *guarantee* you the girls sure weren't following the cars to try to get to me or Jimmy

Valiant. It didn't matter who was driving the cars, either; even if I was behind the wheel of the car, if the girls knew the Express was in there with me, it wasn't uncommon to have eight cars full of girls following us out of town.

People who tell stories about the popularity level of the Rock and Roll Express from that era usually don't do them justice. The only thing I ever saw that compared to their popularity was the way the girls reacted to "Wildfire" Tommy Rich in Georgia, and even that comparison doesn't adequately describe the passion Ricky and Robert evoked from their female fanbase.

Make no mistake about it; Dusty held the kids back because he wanted to be the top babyface in the territory. If he'd rebuilt the territory around Ricky and Robert, they would have been huge. However, Dusty kept them out of the shows in major cities even though we could outdraw them in the small towns and had larger gates. Dusty didn't want them anywhere near the shows he was on.

"How stupid can you get?!" I would say to Jimmy. "We should be running where the money is taking us!"

The thing I really didn't understand is why Jim Crockett didn't intervene and do something to remedy the situation. After all, it was *his* company, and he was investing big money in reserving venues all over the country and the transportation to get us there. Meanwhile, Dusty was killing the geese that were laying the golden eggs. If he'd played his cards right, Crockett might *still* be counting the money the Rock and Roll Express would have earned. They were a potential goldmine and should have been promoted to the fullest extent imaginable.

I can only hypothesize they were worried about the success going to the heads of Ricky and Robert, and resulting in them do stupid things, like overindulging in drugs and alcohol. To counter that, Crockett could simply have smartened the kids up and advised them about how to avoid those sorts of pitfalls; it would have been worth the effort given the potential benefits of launching an act that hot into the stratosphere.

Not to belabor the point, but an act like the Rock and Roll Express could have successfully sold all sorts of additional merchandise like shirts, posters and headscarves. The Road Warriors were also getting over huge as a tag team, but they were primarily working as heels, and Dusty didn't see any need to sabotage the top heels.

In the long run, I think Dusty's mismanagement of the Crockett talent roster played a major role in why they eventually lost the war to the World Wrestling Federation. Dusty wanted to be the one who drew all the money, but the Rock and Roll Express exposed him when they outdrew him head-to-head at smaller venues. To me, it was a more extreme version of how Dusty tried to kill my momentum years prior in Florida. The difference was, the Express was even more over than I'd been in Florida, Dusty was even older and fatter than he'd been eight years prior, and this was playing out *nationally.*

We would film our shows at Ted Turner's complex in Atlanta, which comprised several office buildings. The ring was set up in an large open space, and all of the wrestlers had to dress on the second floor in the middle of an office. I was getting dressed before one set of tapings, and this smartly-dressed man walked in wearing a well-tailored suit, flanked by two small children.

For roughly 20 years at that point, I'd lived by the code that no one was allowed to simply waltz into the wrestlers' changing area, whether it was a locker room, a dressing room, a broom closet, or the makeshift dressing room set up in an office area that I was standing in at that very moment. Whatever space was established for wrestlers was exclusively for use by the wrestlers, bookers and owners. Besides, I was standing there wearing only my briefs and was feeling somewhat more exposed than usual.

"What the hell do you think you're *doing*?!" I yelled, rising to my feet. "This is *our* dressing room. You don't belong in here!"

As soon as the last word escaped my lips, the realization hit me that I'd just screamed at Ted Turner – the billionaire owner of CNN, TBS, TNT, the Atlanta Braves, and almost everything else of value in Atlanta. It certainly didn't make matters any better that he was with his *children.* I could see rage dancing in Ted's eyes, and for the briefest of moments I began to mull over my career options outside of Jim Crockett Promotions.

"This is the guy who *owns* it all!" I thought.

Rather than incinerating me on the spot, Turner gently said, "Yeah… but my kids *really* want to meet the wrestlers!"

"Okay, great!" I said, in a mixture of forced enthusiasm and very real relief. "Come on *in!*"

That was my only interaction with Ted Turner ever, and it caused what remained of my wrestling career to flash before my eyes.

During 1987, tragedies began to strike several of the wrestlers I'd worked with over the years. My good friend Mal Kirk died while wrestling Shirley "Big Daddy" Crabtree in England. Big Daddy was a mammoth wrestler who might be the greatest box-office attraction in the history of English wrestling. His signature match consisted of him squashing the guys he was working with in just a couple of minutes with his big body splash. Well, Mal took the famous Big Daddy splash and *died* as a result of it. I'm guessing Mal didn't know how to take the move properly, held his breath, and had his lungs blown out when Big Daddy crashed down on top of him.

That same year, my buddy, "The Viking" Scott Irwin, died of a brain tumor. I heard about his death from his brother, Bill Irwin. We were always in competition for the title of the top bumping heel in Florida when we were partnered together. When Scott and his wife got divorced, I felt like it had a massive affect on his mental state. We didn't talk a whole lot once we were no longer working together, but his death left me stunned and hurt me a great deal.

By this time, the unfolding tragedy of the Von Erich wrestling family was well underway. David Von Erich had already died in Japan in 1984. He was on one of the All Japan tours right after the one I'd been on. One of the WCCW referees told me he was the one who had to go over to the house and tell Fritz about David's death.

"That was *really* hard for me," the referee admitted.

In 1987, the second major Von Erich tragedy occurred when Fritz's second youngest son Michael committed suicide. Michael had been going through a ton of health issues, and he decided to resolve them by going out to the desert, taking more pills than his body could handle, and sealing himself up in a sleeping bag. He was only 23 years old.

In the 1987 Wrestling Observer Newsletter, Dave Meltzer ranked Jimmy Valiant and I as the *worst* tag team in all of wrestling. We were two gimmick babyface wrestlers who were packaged together by Jim Crockett. I know Meltzer cares a great deal about the quality of a wrestler's work inside the ring, and as far as working is concerned, I considered myself to be right at the top. I wasn't afraid to sell at all, I knew what I was working toward within the context of my matches, and I knew how to effectively lead other guys through a match.

On the flipside, Jimmy had a set style, he was not a great seller, and he was only over with the audience because of his theatrics before and after the matches. When we teamed together, seventy percent of the selling was done by me out of necessity, because Jimmy flat out refused to sell convincingly or meaningfully. After I'd absorbed the beating and sold for the heels, Jimmy would get the hot tag, hop in the ring, make the save, and usually get the victory.

Jimmy would hardly ever leave his feet for any reason. Not only did he despise taking bumps, but he rarely ever left his feet to deliver any offensive maneuvers either. Most of Jimmy's offense consisted of punches and kicks, pokes to the throat, or pulls of the hair. In many matches, he wouldn't even put forth the effort it took to lift someone for a bodyslam.

On the rare occasions when Jimmy *would* take a bump, he would lazily fall to the mat. If he was struck by an opponent, he would do his best to land in the corner or fall into the ropes, and from there he would casually roll onto the mat. In fact, Jimmy selling was so irregular that he would barely even sell getting whipped into the ring post!

Don't get me wrong; Jimmy was over… as a *gimmick*. I wanted to get over as a *worker* who had a gimmick. To Jimmy, selling for the heels meant selling a move for only a second, then jerking and moving around, followed by jiving and dancing, and culminating in a comeback. Rather than making himself a good wrestler, he was solely a good gimmick. I actually had a strong desire to be a good wrestler in addition to being a good gimmick. *That* was the difference between us.

In my opinion, there wasn't a single person in the profession I couldn't work a good match with, and there were only a few guys who were as unselfish as I was during my heyday. If the guys I worked with were willing to listen to me, I could make them look very good, and I could make sure both of us were memorable to the audience once the night reached its conclusion.

As most people who follow wrestling are aware, Bruiser Brody was famously stabbed to death in Puerto Rico in 1988. The man who stabbed Bruiser Brody was Invader 1, Jose Gonzalez, who I'd first met in Oregon when he was a young kid. I liked Jose, and I even saw him a few additional times when he and Carlos Colon came to Florida to talk with Eddie Graham. I *didn't* like Bruiser. The way he treated people was consistently reprehensible. He was rude and belligerent, and he was constantly putting people down. During one of Bruiser's tours through Miami, I remember deciding to be nice to him in spite of the rude treatment he'd given me in the past. I walked into the dressing room when we were the only two in there, and I greeted him by saying, "Hey, Bruiser! How are you?"

Bruiser glanced over at me only long enough to say, "You're still alive?" before turning back to whatever he'd been doing before I'd arrived. When Bruiser died, a lot of wrestlers immediately denigrated Jose without stopping to consider things from any other perspective. Even Harley Race said Bruiser Brody was a bully, and he's 100 percent correct. When I heard Bruiser had been murdered, my initial thought was, "I can see why."

I don't know what the situation was between Bruiser and Jose, but I don't condone murder. Jose is *unquestionably* wrong for killing Bruiser no matter how it went down, and he should have gone to prison for it. However, I find it telling that the first thought that entered my mind when I heard Bruiser was stabbed to death by a fellow wrestler was, "I wonder what Bruiser said or did to Jose to make him want to kill him." Given the way he bullied and treated people, it wasn't shocking to me that Bruiser met a violent end. Also, just because Brody was a popular main-event wrestler who worked in several territories and countries, that doesn't magically, retroactively make him a nice person just because he got murdered by someone that he'd probably bullied to begin with.

By 1988, Vince McMahon truly ran the entire country, took the WWF wherever he pleased, and was the only person who knew how to run a national promotion effectively. Anyone he couldn't buy out, he would compete with and defeat because the talent on his roster was usually better, and if it wasn't, his production values were undeniably superior. When Verne Gagne refused to accept his buyout offer for the American Wrestling Association, Vince simply beat Verne, outdrew Verne in his own towns, and watched as the AWA crumbled.

To Vince's great credit, he was also willing to pay wrestlers what they were worth. In general, wrestling promoters would put a hard cap on the amount they thought a wrestler should make, and they would disregard how much money that wrestler was drawing for him. Vince seemed to be the only promoter willing to pay wrestlers their full market value, and then he would maximize each wrestler's earning potential by creating new forms of merchandise around him. With so much more money at his disposal, Vince could easily drain all of the other territories of their top talent.

As an illustration, Ernie Ladd was known to be a big complainer about payoffs. Once, he complained to Eddie Graham because he only made $2,500 in a week, and Ernie thought he deserved more money. The gist of the conversation was, Eddie said to him, "You made $2,500 this week, so what are you complaining about?!"

That was the mentality of the old wrestling promoters. They didn't argue on the principle of what a wrestler was worth; they argued on the principle that the wrestler *should* be happy as long as he made a certain amount of money, no matter what sort of a profit the wrestler actually generated for the company. These older promoters were always very reluctant to pay more, whereas Vince Jr. wasn't.

That was one of the reasons I wanted to work for Vince in the first place, but part of it was out of sheer necessity. The writing was on the wall for the regional territories; if you didn't work for Vince, you were going to have a very difficult time earning a living as a professional wrestler. Working for any company other than the WWF soon became a waste of time. In the eyes of the public, it soon seemed like if you didn't work for Vince, you weren't really a pro wrestler.

The most memorable thing I did in the ring in 1988 was also one of my most embarrassing wrestling assignments. Dusty had this idea to have me wrestle as "The Green Machine." For that gimmick, I wore a green mask, along with a head-to-toe green bodysuit. It didn't matter; the fans saw right through it. Nearly every time I entered an arena dressed as The Green Machine, I'd hear loud cries of, "Buggsyyyyy!!!" After about one month, the gimmick was scrapped completely. I ended my run with Jim Crockett Promotions by wrestling Larry Zbyszko, who by this point had come into his own as a multi-time AWA World Heavyweight Champion. Ironically, my second-to-last match for Crockett took place in Detroit's Cobo Arena.

Toward the end of 1988, I'd been working out, and I got into outstanding shape. I wanted to go to work for the WWF, so I went to the matches they were holding at the Sun Dome. I knew Pat Patterson from years ago when we both worked for Shire in San Francisco, and he now had a high-ranking position within the WWF hierarchy. I decided to pay him a visit in the hopes that he could convince Vince to add me to the WWF roster.

When I got to the Sun Dome, I asked to speak to Pat. I was escorted into the hallway outside of the dressing room, and that's when Pat came out and shook my hand.

"Buggsy! It's so good to see you!" Pat said. "What brings you by?"

"I'd like to go to work for you guys," I replied. "I've been working out hard, and I think I'd fit in well with what you have going on here."

Pat looked really excited when I pitched the idea to him.

"Yeah! You'd fit in *real* well!" Pat said. "Next week, I want you to call me at my office in Connecticut. We *need* to get this set up. You'll fit in well!"

I left the Sun Dome confident that I would soon be working matches as a heel against guys like Randy Savage, Tito Santana, Brutus Beefcake, Koko B. Ware and Hulk Hogan.

The next week, I called Pat's office at the appointed time. His assistant said, "Pat's not available right now." I left my number, but Pat never called me back. I called again the next day, and I was told, "He's not in the office today." I called the office for three additional days, and each day, I was given an identical response.

When it became crystal clear I was *never* going to get a phone call from Pat, I said to myself, "Okay. That's it. Your wrestling career is over with."

I had to face the facts. My wrestling career was functionally over at that point because if I wasn't working for Vince, I wasn't going to make any money worth mentioning. At best, I might have been able to find roster spot with a much smaller promoter and bring home $400 every week, but that really wasn't a lot of money at all considering the lifestyle difficulties professional wrestlers deal with, including the travel expenses, and the strain of being away from family members.

"I'm going to change my life," I told myself, and I immediately dropped any dreams of pursuing another full-time wrestling position.

NINETEEN – "Is this as bad as it gets?"

When I weighed my options for making a full-fledged career change, I thought about my two main interests, which were medicine and psychology. I visited Purdue University's extension campus in Indianapolis and conversed with a professor of psychology to weigh my odds of becoming a psychologist.

Ultimately, I decided it would take far less time for me to become a nurse. In retrospect, I made a *huge* mistake. It wouldn't have taken me more than a few years to earn a master's degree in psychology since I already had a four-year degree, and I'd minored in psychology at Purdue. Still, we can't rewrite history. I applied to the nursing school at the Plant City campus of Hillsborough Community College, and got accepted.

Right away, I was a little unsure of myself when nursing school began. I knew I could handle the educational component. The sole subject I wasn't very fond of was chemistry, and I had to work my butt off to get through that course. I cut myself off from the world, barricaded myself in my bedroom, and just plugged away at my studies and homework. When I wasn't in class, homework and reading consumed all of my time. Failure was not an option for me in my quest to change my life, get away from wrestling, and forge a new path for myself. If wrestling didn't need me, I wanted to prove I didn't need wrestling either… at least not in order to survive.

There was a period of time when Mick Graham and Steve Keirn were attempting to run shows in Florida with their brand new "Pro Wrestling Federation." Steve Keirn called me up and said, "Hey, do you want to work again?"

"I do," I told him. "There's just one thing, though."

"What's that?" Steve said.

"I'm in nursing school right now," I said.

"Nursing school? Steve repeated in disbelief. "*Really?*"

"Yeah… and I can't afford to sacrifice it for wrestling at this point," I said. "As long as working for you doesn't interfere with school, I'll do it."

There actually was one night in particular when they asked me to work and it conflicted with a scheduled nursing school exam, so I had to tell them, "No."

The PWF didn't last very long anyway. Dusty Rhodes eventually got involved with the company after he was let go from Ted Turner's World Championship Wrestling company. While working with Steve and Mike, Dusty ran up *huge* bills on their behalf, and then he bolted to work for Vince and the WWF as soon as they made him an offer. By 1991, the PWF was finished for good, along with any serious attempts to ever again run a major Florida-based wrestling territory.

At nursing school, it was suggested that all of the student nurses should get part-time jobs as nursing aides. I went to the James A. Haley Veterans' Hospital in Tampa and got a job working on the spinal cord floor. The only patients on that floor were paraplegics and quadriplegics. I wound up holding onto that job right up until I graduated from nursing school. Whatever tasks it took to learn a new craft apart from wrestling that I could use to support myself, I gladly performed them. The full-time nurses used to load me up with all kinds of work, and I did it happily. I refused to complain about anything.

I had to work on Christmas, which was nothing new for an ex-wrestler, and there were four full-time nurses on the floor with me to oversee eight patients. Most of the work on the spinal cord floor involved washing the patients, dressing them and feeding them. They assigned me four patients, and each of the other nurses took only one. I didn't say a word about the disparity; I just did as I was told. I wanted to learn to do my job properly and to be accepted by my coworkers.

Before I finished nursing school, I was already working for "Golden Boy" Jerry Grey. The former CWF wrestler was now running independent wrestling shows in Florida under two different names, World Pro Wrestling and the Southern Wrestling Federation. Later on, he would start running shows throughout the country. He presented wrestling using a sold-show format that wasn't reliant on fan attendance to make money. Between 1988 and 2000, I worked for Jerry an average of one to three times every month.

Jerry's shows could vary greatly in quality from one show to the next. Some of them were outstanding and well attended, but others were substandard. Regardless, Jerry always treated me as a top guy, and the work was easy since I was still very over with the fans in Florida, and reactions from the crowd were easy to come by. Most of the wrestlers on the shows consisted of young guys who weren't used to working snug. After the matches, some of these kids would says things like, "Damn, Buggsy! Why are you working so *stiff*?!"

"What are you talking about?" I'd ask in response. "You've got to lay 'em in, kid!"

During this time, I also worked at one show for Blackjack Mulligan at the Poinciana Arena in Nassau, Bahamas. It was an unmitigated disaster. At most, there were 20 people present, which might make it the most sparsely attended show I ever wrestled in. I still got paid my full rate, though, and it was all given to me in the form of $20 bills. A year later, Mulligan went to prison for counterfeiting $20 bills, so I don't think the fact he paid me with $20 bills was coincidental.

As soon as I graduated from nursing school, the VA hospital immediately offered me a permanent job. I'd established myself as a hard worker, and I considered the job offer to be the reward for my strenuous efforts. They wanted me to work on the vent floor, which was for spinal cord patients who were also on vents. The thing is, I *didn't* want to work there anymore. First of all, I knew I needed to learn far more in order to be at my best. Second, I didn't want to be taken advantage of, and the nurses who were working there had already established how willing they were to take advantage of my work ethic. I'm sure they were hoping I would continue to do the lion's share of the work once I was brought aboard full time as a regular nurse. I refused to extend that luxury to them.

Instead, I applied at Tampa General Hospital, and was offered a job on the trauma floor after interviewing with the head nurse. Tampa General is a Level 1 trauma center, which is the highest ranking a trauma center can receive. Sadly, that ranking isn't a measure of quality; it means they get all of the worst trauma cases. At one time, Tampa General was ranked as the number one trauma center in all of Florida, so you can only imagine how *horrific* the trauma cases were that we dealt with considering we were competing with hospitals in Jacksonville, Orlando and Miami.

During my interview, it was obvious that I had a speech impediment, and nurses are required to be effective communicators. The head nurse asked me, "How much does your speech problem affect you?"

"It isn't too bad," I told her.

"Is *this* as bad as it gets?" she pressed.

"About 75 percent of the time, this is as bad as it gets," I assured her.

After I was hired, they put me to work on the night shift, which is always the shift marred by low levels of medical resources and staff assistance. Tampa General was already notorious for trying to cut costs and save money, so during the night shift, we were often starved for help.

I was based on the 8C1 floor, which had four members of the nursing staff - two registered nurses, one licensed practical nurse, and also one tech - to handle a full load of 25 patients. *That* is a tall order. The RN's have to cover the LPN's. If you have a full house of 25 patients, one LPN is expected to cover nine patients, and the two RN's would get eight patients between them. Legally, the RN's *has* to cover the LPN if the LPN had trouble with any patients because the RN is considered to be the top nurse in the hierarchy.

It was unadulterated *chaos* on that floor. If only one of your patients was having a serious problem on the trauma floor, that alone could ruin your night. If *two* of your patients were having problems, your night was *completely* destroyed because the other six patients who were allocated to you would have been incapable of getting any aid. Helping them would be a borderline impossibility.

When I first started working at Tampa General, I was as green as grass. On one of my first days on the job, there was a code - which meant the patient stopped breathing. The patient in question wasn't my responsibility, though. I was *really* new, and I was shadowing other nurses who I had to follow around during the day and train with in an understudy role. This patient who coded was the responsibility of the nurse I was following. When a patient codes, the room can fill up with 20 people in a hurry. I walked into the room, and the resident - or student doctor - who had ultimate authority over the patient's care came walking in, casually sipping a can of Coca Cola. He was Mr. Cool.

The resident calmly started doling out orders and suggesting medications and procedures. It was one of the *coolest* things I'd ever seen. Without raising his voice, he took total control of an emergency situation, including managing the patient's compressions and giving orders for medicines, all while taking small sips from his Coke between his sentences. I went and stood right next to him, because I identified him as someone I needed to be learning from.

In the midst of the resident's command performance, the head nurse of 8C2, a flamboyantly homosexual man, walked into the room and stood beside the defibrillator.

"Stop compressions," the resident ordered. "I want him shocked."

No one moved. The resident calmly looked at the head nurse and said, "Take the paddles, and shock the patient."

The head nurse didn't move a muscle.

"Take the paddles and shock the patient," the resident repeated to the head nurse.

The head nurse *still* didn't budge.

"Take the *goddamn* paddles and shock the patient!" the resident yelled.

The head nurse snapped out of his daze and dutifully reached for the paddles.

"But you didn't *have* to yell, *did you?*" the head nurse said, with plenty of attitude.

I noticed the head nurse was struggling to remove the paddles from the defibrillator, so I walked over to the other side of the room, gently shoved the head nurse out of the way, ripped the paddles right off the machine and handed them to him.

"Here!" I yelled. *"Shock* the patient!"

After the startled head nurse took the paddles from me, I walked back and regained my spot next to the resident. Most of the other nurses were enamored with the head nurse and thought he was impressive. Contrary to the popular opinion, I wasn't impressed with him at all. For him to stand there in a daze while orders were given to him three times, and then for him to need so much help getting the defibrillator paddles ready, I thought his "head nurse" title was a *joke.* The resident, on the other hand, was *awesome.*

"That's the kind of demeanor I need to develop if I'm going to work here," I thought to myself.

The first three months I was there, I wanted to quit *so* badly. I was trying to learn from all the other nurses I was working with, but I was getting conflicting instructions from each of them and not really learning anything despite all of my questions. Upon returning home each night, I would sit in a chair for hours and just stare at the wall, trying to convince myself not to quit. The stress was like nothing I'd ever experienced before in my life. The lives of these patients were in my hands on a daily basis, and I felt *every* bit of the pressure. If something bad happened to a patient, I would be held fully liable.

None of this takes into consideration the individual working relationships between nurses and the additional stress that can add if those relationships aren't based on a foundation of teamwork. Some of the nurses I worked with weren't very good, didn't take their jobs very seriously, or didn't fully grasp the responsibility of having to keep people alive. Also, it became glaringly obvious there were racial issues that manifested themselves amongst the nursing staff.

From my experience working in a hospital, I can testify the racism I saw from black and hispanic nurses was some of the worst racism I'd ever seen. If I was having a problem with one of my patients and I asked a black or hispanic nurse for assistance, more often than not, they would seem to look for any excuse not to help me, but they would bend over backwards to help someone of their same race.

I had to comfort myself and say, "Michael… look at all these other nurses here. They know how to handle their jobs. You know full well you're smarter than all the other people on this floor. You don't need to listen to these other nurses at all. It's time to start acting entirely on your own."

Once I began to think for myself, handling situations in the hospital became a much simpler task for me. Setting my priorities and managing my patients also became much easier. From then on, I became the person the other nurses listened to because I had the answers. If someone needed help getting intravenous therapy going for a patient, they came to me for help with the IV. It may sound like I'm blowing my own horn, but it's the truth.

At Tampa General, they had the student doctors - also known as "residents" - who were on call from 24 to 40 hours. Things got to the point where one of the main attending physicians who supervised the residents approached me when he came to the trauma floor and said, "Oh, wow! I'm really glad they have the A-team working here tonight!"

Considering where I'd started from, I took it as a huge compliment.

TWENTY – "Michael... you look sick"

When you're working as a nurse, the nature of the work you perform is all dictated by the department you're assigned to: trauma, cardiac, GI or respiratory. When I was at Tampa General, all of these departments were on separate floors. Later on, we even had an AIDS floor.

On the trauma floor, we saw every type of patient, and we were also the recipients of the patient overflow from every other floor. Our reputation was phenomenal; doctors told me they considered our floor to be very efficient and professional, and one of the residents told me he thought of our floor as being like the intensive care unit. We had to know what we were doing, or otherwise we would have been killing patients left, right and center.

Patients needed to be cared for efficiently, quickly and rationally. If my patient had a serious problem, and that problem persisted, I would put a code on them. Half of all patients that are coded die, and we had to be aggressive when dealing with whatever problems our patients were experiencing before we lost them.

There were times when my patients had problems, and I would have to write my own orders rather than talking to the resident. I'd write the order for the respiratory therapist, or for the x-ray department, or for the EKG department. Once I'd finally get ahold of a resident and he would start to tell me what he needed done with a patient, he was usually very relieved to discover I'd already submitted the orders for him and solved the problem.

My goal was always to get patients into the ICU before they coded. If they coded, everyone assumed they probably wouldn't make it. Problems like that were always easier to manage in the ICU where they had monitors. On the trauma floor, we might have had seven patients or more at any given time, whereas the ICU normally only had one or two patients, so the patients could receive far more individualized care there.

Most of the doctors I interacted with had a ton of unjustified ego. From my vantage point, 75 percent of doctors have their heads completely up their asses. When they would approach a situation and begin to assess it, many doctors automatically assumed they knew everything simply because they were doctors, and I was just a lowly nurse. The other 25 percent of doctors were professional and congenial, and they seemed eager to listen to my perceptions of the patients' conditions. To make sure my patients received proper care, sometimes I had to be willing to confront the most aloof and oblivious doctors on our staff.

On one such occasion, a doctor who I halfway liked wrote an order on one of my patients who was having heart problems. To counter these problems, the doctor ordered *10 milligrams* of nitroglycerine. If you've ever seen the container nitroglycerine comes in, you know it arrives in a tiny, one-inch-tall bottle. Ten milligrams amounts to *the entire bottle*. If I'd fulfilled that order the way it was written and given the requested dose of nitroglycerine to that patient, he would have been dead within 30 seconds, without question.

When I saw the order, I assumed the resident was tired when he wrote it. I tracked him down on the floor and said, "Hey... are you *sure* you want this order?"

"Yeah, I do," he replied.

I was trying to give the resident an opportunity to realize he'd written the order incorrectly. There was *no way* I was letting the patient have all of that nitroglycerine.

After some time passed, I went back to the resident a second time and asked him, "Are you *absolutely certain* you want the patient to have this order?"

"Yeah, I'm sure," he said.

After waiting a few more agonizing minutes, I finally went back a third time and asked, "I don't know, Doctor. Are you *really* sure you want me to fill this order?"

"I wrote the order, didn't I?!" the doctor snapped, angrily. "*Yes!* I want the order!"

So, I went back and procured the bottle of nitroglycerine. Then, I walked the bottle over to the doctor and held it in front of his face.

"If you give the patient this much nitroglycerine, you're going to *kill* the fucking patient!" I screamed. "Do *you* understand me?!"

"Oh, oh, oh… you're *right!*" the doctor conceded, apologetically. "I *don't* want to do that! I'll change the order!"

Within the resident system, we had the residents, the chief resident, and the attendings. The attendings are at the top of the pecking order, and we were ordered *never* to call them. During my shifts, which were at night, the attending physicians were usually at home, and not on call.

On one particular night, I called *four* different residents to try to get a problem solved, and none of the four could give me a straight answer about what needed to be done. Finally, I got the number for the attending physician and called him at 3:00 a.m. His wife answered the phone and snarled, "*How* did you get this number?!"

"I had to look around for it, ma'am," I said. "I'm sorry to bug you, but I really need to speak to your husband. It's an emergency."

The woman put her husband on the phone, and he wasn't too happy with me either.

"What are *you* doing calling here?!" the attending physician asked me.

"I had a problem, and I took it to four different residents," I explained. "None of them are willing to handle the problem!"

"Okay! No problem!" he said. "I'll take care of this. Bye."

Within five minutes of getting off the phone with the doctor, I received phone calls from four startled residents who were practically bending over backwards to help me.

"You bastards!" I thought. "You're only doing this because you got your asses chewed out by the attending physician!"

Another time, the patient I was working with was an elderly lady. The resident covering her that day was one of the stereotypical residents with his head up his ass who thought he was the most intelligent guy in the medical profession. He wasn't interested in hearing any input whatsoever from the nurses.

Brute Power: The Autobiography of Buggsy McGraw

On that day, the resident who was full of himself came to visit my patient, and he proceeded to write two full pages of orders. As the nurse, I was the person required to execute these orders, so I began examining what he was asking me to do. I quickly realized he'd handed me two pages of total *crap*. My patient didn't even need *half* of what he'd ordered for her.

Instead of talking to the resident, I went over his head and phoned his boss, the chief resident. His name was Tom, and he liked my work. He also seemed to operate under the general impression that I could handle myself if a problem arose. For the most part, if I had a suggestion, he listened to me.

"Tom!" I said into the phone. "Your resident wrote two full pages of orders for my patient here; they're *completely* unnecessary!"

"So *cancel* them!" Tom said.

"Thank you, Tom!" I replied, relieved. "Bye!"

Gleefully, I crossed out the resident's orders and then did what I knew needed to be done. The resident was pissed at me, but I didn't care. If I hadn't stepped in, he might have *killed* that poor woman, and if I'd spoken with the resident beforehand, it would've resulted in an unnecessary argument.

When you become a psychiatrist, you have to go to medical school, and then go to *another* school after med school. Well, I had to work with a resident whose department was psychiatric. This guy came in to see a patient who I'd established a room for directly across from my nurse's station. Immediately after the resident came in, the patient coded. I bolted into the room, and the two of us performed compressions and administered whatever procedures we could to save the patient.

The two of us walked out when we were finished, and the resident turned to me and said, "Wow, man... that's my first code. How did I do?"

That question stopped me in my tracks. Very seldom have I encountered a resident who'd deign to ask a nurse to evaluate his performance.

"You did fine, man," I reassured him. "You were good."

"Thanks, Mike," he told me. "I really appreciate that."

Frankly, I appreciated him for asking me for my opinion. His is an example of an ideal resident who is open to constructive feedback from any source.

On the other hand, my very worst incident involving a resident at Tampa General occurred one Thanksgiving Eve. I was called from the ER to receive a 19-year-old patient. This kid had been riding in a car with his girlfriend when an argument ensued, and he asked her to stop the car and allow him to get out.

When she wouldn't stop, he opened the door and leapt from the car, dashing his head on the pavement in the process. When I got the report on him, they told me he was fine and had been medically cleared. Curiously, they took the IV out of him before they sent him to me, which is virtually unheard of.

Once the young man was in my care, he was relatively unresponsive, and only communicated by making guttural noises. Concerned about my patient's well being, I called the resident on duty and said, "This kid is acting really funny. He's not talking. All I'm getting out of him are grunting sounds."

The doctor said, "Forget it. The kid is a butthead."

It became clear to me this resident was writing the kid off and judging him because of the actions taken by the kid that had landed him on the trauma floor. Granted, the kid might not have been particularly bright, but he was *still* our patient! The next time I checked on the kid, his fever had increased to 103 degrees. Panicked, I called the resident again, only to hear him say, "I told you *not* to worry about it!"

Soon, the kid began spewing red foam from his mouth and fell unconscious. We couldn't revive him. Within three hours of leaving the ER and arriving on my floor, the kid died.

When a 19-year-old young man dies in your care, everyone wants answers, and the resident decided to point his finger at me as having been the person responsible for the kid's death. I had to speak with the risk management department at our hospital, and then I was interviewed by the Florida Board of Medicine. After I explained my side of the story, the director of the FBM looked me directly in the eyes and said, "We believe *you*. We *don't* believe the doctor."

As you might expect, the resident who'd been blaming me got into some serious trouble over this episode. His wife was also a resident at the same hospital, and she began to do everything she could to try to get me fired. Fortunately, nothing ever came of her repeated attempts to ruin me.

My father was very ill with COPD for a long while. I used to try to get him to do assorted exercises to maintain his functionality. He wasn't very active in his old age, but every so often he would peak, get out of bed, and exercise vigorously for 20 to 30 minutes at a time. These flourishes of activity would only happen once every two weeks, though. Dad was on a walker, and I'd encourage him to practice getting up and sitting down repeatedly, and I'd also try to get him to use his legs to walk around as much as possible.

"Michael, I'm tired," he'd say.

"I *know* you're tired, Dad, but you need to keep going!" I'd reply.

On April 27th, 1999, I was on the other side of town in Clearwater and my parents were in Brandon. A supernatural dread came over me, and I knew it concerned my father. Fearing the worst, I got in my car and drove over to my parents' house; the sheriff and some of the neighbors were already there. That's when I learned my father had passed away. He'd lived to be 84 years old.

My friend Jos Leduc passed away only a few days later on May 1st. He and I were part of the same locker room in Calgary, Japan, Florida and Memphis at different points of our careers, and he was always there for me and had my back. I miss him greatly.

By then, three additional members of the Von Erich family had also passed away. Chris, the youngest of the brothers, shot himself in the head in 1991. He'd been unable to come anywhere near the success of any of his taller and more athletic brothers, and it seemed to have eaten away at him. The results of the psychological trauma inflicted by experiencing the loss of two of his brothers also has to be factored in.

Brute Power: The Autobiography of Buggsy McGraw

Kerry, the most professionally successful of the boys, shot himself in the heart with his father's own gun in 1993 while paying a visit to his parents' property. He'd been experiencing some legal difficulties of his own, and I have to think the deaths of his brothers also weighed on him, like a problem that compounds with each death, and with the survivors feeling an even greater strain as the issues and casualties mounted.

Finally, Fritz passed away from brain and lung cancer in 1997. I can only imagine the sense of loss he dealt with after seeing five of his six sons pass away from *highly preventable* causes, and then to have his wife divorce him after 42 years of marriage.

During my nursing career, I was publicly recognized as Buggsy McGraw the wrestler on a few different occasions. My wrestling persona was never something I advertised to any of the patients I treated. Ten or fifteen years after I'd retired from mainstream wrestling, some of the people who recognized me could still quote my interviews verbatim. I guess I came across as erudite during my interview time, because a few of my patients said they'd envisioned me as a college professor, a lawyer or a judge… *not* as a nurse.

It goes without saying that nursing is not considered a very masculine profession. When I got involved in it, I thought it would be a way to fast track a career in the medical field, and I wasn't worried about the stigma attached to being a male nurse. No matter how my career change might have been received by others, I couldn't be concerned with their opinions. I wanted to make sure I had a career that could sustain me long after my body was incapable of absorbing bumps inside of a wrestling ring.

Back then, nursing was advertised as a career where you could always find a job, and today, that *still* holds true. I've seen far too many old wrestlers who've held on to their wrestling careers for far too long, hoping against all reasonable probability for one more big-money run. Many of them lost everything and wound up destitute because they didn't pivot in another direction or acquire another valuable, marketable skill while they still could. I couldn't afford to fall into that category.

Brute Power: The Autobiography of Buggsy McGraw

In 2001, I met a lady who owned her own veterinary practice. The two of us hit it off instantly and became romantically involved. We spent all of our free time with each other. The entire situation with her was *100 percent* built on my own stupidity. Everything appeared to be perfect on the surface since we liked most of the same things and got along very well. I remember praying to the Lord about how I wanted to marry this woman, and I began to pray out loud, "Lord, even if you *don't* want this, *I'm going to do it.*" That was one of the *dumbest* things I could have ever said, and I wound up paying a huge price for my hubris later on.

The two of us got married in Las Vegas. When we arrived back in Florida after our nuptials, everything went on a straight slide downhill practically overnight. Every little thing in the relationship began to go wrong, but I decided to try to make it work.

There were several times I considered going back to school and becoming a psychologist, and one of those times was in 2001. I also considered going to a school for physicians assistants in Gainesville, or to a different school for advanced registered nurse professionals. When you walk into a room and you say you're a physician's assistant, it means much more to the family than when you say, "I'm an ARNP." Physician's assistants get far more respect, and a lot more money.

Truth be told, I would have made more money if I'd followed through with *any* of these actions, but I also would have been away from my family. At the time, you would be allowed to enroll in the program if you only had a four-year degree, which I did. Now, you're required to have a masters degree before they'll even consider allowing you into most of these programs.

Around Christmas, my mother, my wife, my six-year-old stepson and I were all enjoying dinner over at my mother's house in Brandon. When my wife went outside to take her son for a walk, my mother looked at me and said, "Michael... you look *sick!*"

"Mother, I *am!*" I replied, weakly.

When your near-90-year-old mother is telling you that you look sick, and it's all stress related, you *know* you have a problem on your hands. I was in so much turmoil as a result of the unhappiness

294

in my marriage. I knew I was paying for going against God and His word. My wife and I ultimately got divorced, and it was all finalized in 2003. When it was over with, I had zero desire to go outside or see anyone. I shut myself indoors for quite a while, refusing to interact with people. In particular, I didn't want to see or talk to any women. Being freed from the shackles of that toxic marriage was a major relief, but it left me feeling shell shocked, which took quite some time to overcome.

As a nurse, you're engaged in a constant struggle against human nature. Although most people like to think they can endure pain and discomfort, the reality is, most people are complainers. In my nursing career, I might have had only *four* patients who didn't complain about anything. One of them was a man who had major abdominal surgery at Tampa General. I asked him, "Do you want anything for your pain?"

"No!" he replied. "I don't want *anything* for pain. I'm *not* going to take anything for pain. I won't be here that long anyway!"

"Praise God!" I thought to myself. *That* guy had the right attitude!

Most patients whine constantly about discomfort, and they beg for medication. In general, I'm not a fan of medicine. Antibiotics only work for between 24 and 48 hours. Beyond that, they're a waste of time. Another patient had a fever of 103 degrees and the doctor on our floor refused to treat the fever. The doctor knew sometimes the best course of action is to let the fever run since a fever is often the body's defense mechanism for ridding itself of infection. That was an exception, though. Most doctors would simply have treated the fever without letting the body do what it's supposed to.

In the midst of all of this medical drama, you might have thought I'd have been itching to try to sneak back into the mainstream wrestling business, especially during the era of the Monday Night Wars on cable television between the WWF and WCW. However, working three nights a month for Jerry Grey and World Pro Wrestling kept me active enough to leave me satisfied. It was local, which meant I didn't have to drive that far, and most of the fans who went to the shows remembered me.

Jerry always had me in the main events when I worked for him, so I always felt respected. Over the course of my time working for Jerry, he had me win his company's American Championship and Florida Championship, and he made me one half of his World Tag Team Championship team. Jerry's promotion was small, but the trips were short, and they provided me with some extra spending money.

I also took some bookings for other wrestling companies in Florida, but they often didn't go as smoothly as Jerry's events. I worked a show for Mario Savoldi when he was attempting to expand his International World Class Championship Wrestling promotion from the New England area all the way down to Florida. The Savoldi family purchased the World Class Championship Wrestling name from the Von Erichs after the Dallas-based promotion went out of business, and they merged its name with that of their existing International Championship Wrestling company to create the illusion that the two promotions shared the same lineage.

Mario's show was in Bradenton, and Nick Bockwinkel was handling the booking for him. I wound up getting paid only *half* of the money I'd been promised, which wasn't all that much to begin with. Bockwinkel called me into the dressing room and started giving me a host of excuses for why he couldn't pay me my negotiated rate.

"You can either wait to receive a check for $150, or you can take the $75 in cash right now," Nick offered.

Given those options, I took the $75 in cash. I had no guarantees the Savoldis would ever bring IWCCW back to Florida, and it would be hard to squeeze any money out of them if they retreated back to New England and never returned. If anyone talks to a member of the Savoldi clan, tell them they owe me my other $75, with interest.

TWENTY-ONE – "I know who the *hell* you are"

I moved into my mother's house in Brandon in 2004 after she turned 94 years old. She was having some health issues and needed someone to help take care of her.

In 2005, I bought and sold two condos in Daytona Beach. I made some money on that investment, so I pursued real estate investment more aggressively in 2006. That was also around the time I started attending a new church called "The River," which had a total membership of around 2,500 people. One of the members of The River's ministry team had gone to the three-year Bible college there. He had once been the leader of a motorcycle gang, and had done a whole host of unruly things. After he got saved, the church paid for him to go to college.

A year after he graduated, he felt directed to go over to a former homeless shelter in Tampa which was filled with a lot of trash. He went in there and removed the trash by the truckload, and then he converted the building into a church called "The God Center," with the intent of tailoring the gospel message to the local homeless population. I went over to The God Center with him, and helped out with donations. Once the new church was completely up and running, the pastor permitted me to start a Bible study there, and I consistently led it every Friday for four years.

By the end of 2007, my real estate ventures had gone bust, and I lost a *ton* of money when that happened. After that awful experience, I got a sour taste in my mouth for the real estate market and decided it was no longer worth the trouble. Aside from that financial setback, I also had a lingering physical issue. The average nurse walks between three to seven miles during every shift. As a result of that constant foot pounding, and after years of working in the wrestling ring, I was having problems with my hips and my feet. I was in *constant* pain, yet I still had to suck it up when I was taking care of my patients *and* my mother.

At times, it would take me up to two minutes just to be able to sit down thanks to the pain I was feeling. I'd begin to sit down, but then I'd have to straighten all the way up, and I'd gradually work my way down over the course of two minutes. People who would catch me in the act would sarcastically blurt out questions like, "Why don't you just sit down?" They had *no idea* what I was feeling. People at work would see me walking on my toes and ask, "Is there something wrong with your feet?"

While caring for my mom, I assumed the responsibility of handling all of her finances, and also doing whatever shopping she required. After a three-week hiatus from grocery shopping, I went to Walmart for her because we were completely out of everything. I'd been putting off the trip to Walmart for a while because I knew how much pain the shopping trip was going to cause me, and also because I was in enough agony from my shifts as a nurse and didn't need the discomfort to extend outside of the hospital.

I sat in the car outside of Walmart for a full 35 minutes trying to convince myself I *didn't* need to go in because the pain was excruciating. Ultimately, our need for sustenance won out, and I went inside. During a subsequent trip to Walmart, I concluded my shopping venture and went outside to my vehicle, and it took me *over 17 minutes* to sit down in the car because of the pain. Sitting down and getting my right leg in may have taken only five seconds, but sliding my left leg into the vehicle took all of 17 agonizing minutes. By the time I was fully within the vehicle and ready to go, I was sweating so much that I'd soaked *clean through* the shirt I had on!

In April of 2006, I hadn't been able to work out for what seemed like forever because my body felt like it was dying every time I tried. I was trying to stretch on my bedroom floor, and the futility of it all was making me progressively more miserable. All of a sudden, I said, "Lord… I'm at the end of my rope. I can't go any further. I'm done. I'm going to quit my job, get a wheelchair and live out the rest of my days in that wheelchair. I can't take anymore. If you don't do something right now, I'm getting up, going to Tampa General, and I'm going to tell them 'I quit!'"

At that moment, I got up, and all the pain was gone from my feet. That was a huge blessing. I still had the pain in my hip, but the pain in my feet was gone, so I no longer had to walk on the tips of my toes. I still wound up quitting at Tampa General, though. After 16 and a half years of working in trauma, I got a job working in the rehab department at University Community Hospital in Tampa. Because of the way I was scheduled, which gave me one week on duty followed by one week off duty, I would work for hospice during my off weeks. It was a welcome change of pace from trauma. When you worked hospice, you only had one patient at a time. When you worked in trauma, you had to contend with hundreds of things.

In 2007, I visited the restaurant of Joe Gomez, a local Florida wrestler. I had no clue John Laurinaitis was there, along with his family and friends. By now, John was the WWE's Senior Vice President of Talent Relations, and the company was in the process of touring through Florida. I'd met John years ago in Florida, when he'd been wrestling under the name "Johnny Ace."

"Buggsy!" John exclaimed when he saw me. "I haven't seen you in so long!"

John invited me over to the table, ordered me a drink, and then had me entertain his entourage by demonstrating the Curly Shuffle for them. I obliged and gave them a performance of my signature dance move right in the middle of the restaurant.

I conversed with John for a good while, and then I tried to dismiss myself since I had no desire to overstay my welcome. Before I could leave, John stopped me and asked, "Wait a minute... Why don't you come to Lakeland tomorrow night?"

"No thanks," I replied quickly. "None of the young guys who work there know who I am."

"Sure they do!" he said.

I didn't want to be known as one of the old guys hanging out backstage, and going to the matches wasn't something I typically did. However, John continued to prompt me to the point where it would have been truly rude if I'd turned him down. Reluctantly, I agreed to attend the WWE show in Lakeland.

Flanked by John, I met with a few guys backstage, and Vince McMahon eventually emerged and swaggered his way through the hallway.

"Hey, it's the Donald Trump of professional wrestling!" I called out as Vince strolled past.

Vince turned and looked at me with a puzzled expression on his face. I'm sure I looked quite different to him; we hadn't seen one another in more than 20 years.

"You don't know who I am, do you?" I challenged him.

"To be honest with you, I'm having a brain fart at the moment," Vince replied.

"I'm Buggsy McGraw," I informed him.

Vince just stared at me for a few moments before bursting into uproarious laughter.

"*You*!" Vince said. "*You* were the most entertaining wrestler I ever saw!"

Vince moved on and went about overseeing the production of his show. It was a huge compliment to receive from him, but it raises a legitimate question: If I'm *truly* the most entertaining wrestler Vince McMahon ever saw, let alone the most entertaining wrestler of my era, *why* am I not in the WWE Hall of Fame?

The next year, I was backstage at the WWE Raw show after Wrestlemania 28, which was in Orlando. I was sitting around in the catering area at the Amway Arena, generally keeping to myself. John Laurinaitis walked by me, and I called out to him, "Hey, John!"

John looked up and said, "Hey, Buggsy. I'm going to have to talk to you later."

I nodded and stayed put. Obviously, John had a lot of work to do, and he walked back and forth near the buffet and talked to various members of his staff. Part of me figured he was just blowing me off because he was so busy that night.

Instead, John wrapped up his business, then came over and started talking with me. As the evening stretched on, more and more members of the WWE roster approached John to ask him questions, and he dismissed them all one by one in favor of sitting to talk with me. Even Ric Flair - the night after his WWE retirement match against Shawn Michaels - tried to snatch John's attention away for a moment.

"John, I need to talk to you," said Ric.

"Not now, Ric!" replied John. "I'm busy!"

I'm sure that the only time I ever took precedence over Ric Flair!

Eventually, I told John I needed to go, and he said, "Well, let me walk you out, Buggsy."

It was a *long* walk from one end of Amway Arena to the other. All the way down the hall, we passed by Diva after Diva from the WWE's roster, and John dismissed them all just to make sure I found my way safely out of the building. I have great respect for John Laurinaitis and the way he treated me that evening.

Parents' grave marker

In 2009, my mother's doctor told me she was very sick and on the verge of death, and then she was transferred to hospice. When I walked into my mom's room, there was a ARNP there. I noticed my mom looked really bad and unresponsive.

"Your mother will be *dead* in three days," the ARNP informed me.

"That *may* be true," I told the ARNP, "but right *now*, she needs *respiratory treatments!*"

"Hmmm… I agree," the ARNP said.

I *really* shouldn't have had to tell the ARNP what to do.

As soon as my mother received respiratory treatments, she began to improve rapidly. Before long the manager of the hospice center came to me and said, "You need to move your mother."

"Why?" I asked.

"She's going to live, so we can't have her here!" she smiled.

So, I moved my mother into a nursing home with a rehab center. From that point, she lived another seven months. The moral of the story is, you can't take the word of all of your medical professionals at face value.

When my mother passed away, I sold her house and moved to the Towers of the Channelside, which is probably the finest condominium complex in Downtown Tampa. There were two, 29-floor towers there, and I wanted the direct view of the downtown area. I stayed there for five years.

I had a couple friends who were working for Total Nonstop Action Wrestling, which filmed all of its shows in Florida. They'd been wrestling locally for Jerry Grey when they managed to secure their positions with TNA. One of the guys was Bruno Sassi, who was about 5'10" and 240 lbs, and he wrestled as "Sally Boy." The other guy, James Tilquist, was around 6'0" and 400 lbs, and he wrestled as "Big Tilly." TNA was taping shows at Universal Studios every three weeks, and also running some house shows there. When they taped there, it was usually an all-day event.

Bruno and James were working as production assistants for TNA. When we wrestled, they would tell me how stiff I was in the ring. I had no intention of lightening up on them. I thought I was educating them on what it was really like to be a wrestler.

I got myself into really good shape again, having decided that I had one more run in me. The old Tampa Bay Buccaneers stadium hosted monster truck events. Myself and several other wrestlers would routinely sit in the luxury boxes at the top. Sometimes Randy Savage or The Nasty Boys would also show up. I also saw John Laurinaitis there.

Since the pain from my injuries had subsided, I'd been consistently working out at LA Fitness, and even the personal trainers would come up to me and tell me they were impressed by how strong I was.

This monster truck event was for charity, and I had zero interest whatsoever in the action going on in the arena. When John and I saw each other, he said, "Oh my god! It's *Buggsy McGraw*! How are you?"

We made small talk and caught up with one another for a while, and then I said, "I've been working out, and I've gotten into pretty good shape. I'd like to work in the WWE as a manager if that's possible. What are the chances you can bring me in?"

"Well, we can try it," John said. "There's nothing wrong with *that*. What I need you to do is to make a video of your recent work, and send it to me in Connecticut. Remember, I get roughly *700* videos every month. You need to label it clearly so I know it's from you. Otherwise, it will never make it past my secretaries."

After that, I phoned a few video editors about putting something together, and they all wanted to charge me an exorbitant rate to get a simple video shot and edited. While trying to get things ironed out on the video production end of things, I also asked James and Bruno who the top man was at TNA Wrestling.

"It's Vince Russo," they told me. "He runs everything there."

"Can you get me a meeting with him?" I asked.

"No problem," they said. "We can set that up easily."

At their behest, I went to the TNA tapings with my scrapbook in hand. After shaking hands with me, Russo pointed at the scrapbook in my hands.

"What's this?" asked Russo.

"My career scrapbook," I replied.

"I *know* who the hell you are!" laughed Russo.

"That's a relief!" I said.

I then told him a story about how George Scott once brought Johnny Valentine into Crockett's territory for a period of six months. When Johnny wasn't drawing, Crockett asked Scott to fire him. Scott refused, and Valentine gradually got more and more over until he was one of the top draws in the territory. Then I transitioned from that to talking about what I felt I could do for TNA.

Clearly impressed with my presentation and knowledge, Russo said, "I wish my wrestlers had the same enthusiasm you do."

"Well, then, you need to hire me!" I responded.

"Yeah... I *do*," Russo said.

And that's when he hired me, right on the spot, and I forgot all about sending a tape to John Laurinaitis and Vince McMahon.

One of the TNA ownership partners was Jeff Jarrett - Jerry Jarrett's son - and we got along very well. The other major partner at the time was Dixie Carter, the daughter of the owners of Panda Energy International who had purchased a majority stake in TNA.

Vince Russo was creative, and he seemed to know what he was doing, at least as far as I could tell. When he described to me what he wanted me to do during my TNA appearances, he explained it down to the most minute detail, and then I would try to execute his vision.

"Exactly what you want is exactly what you'll get," I'd tell him.

One time, Vince stopped me as we were walking down the hallway and simply said, "You know... I really like everything you're doing. It's really good."

All I could do was say, "Thanks!"

Vince made me a manager for Bruno and James, who he packaged as a tag team. James was supposed to lose weight before we all made our debut as a team, but he never got around to it. In the meantime, they put me together with Mick Foley as part of a storyline that was intended to lead to me managing my own tag team.

One of the things Vince Russo told me while we were backstage was, "The wrestler here with the most heat is Awesome Kong."

"No way!" I said.

I couldn't believe it. Back in the day, there would have been *no way* a woman would have had more heat than any of the men on the roster.

"Go out there and watch her," Russo said.

Sure enough, when Awesome Kong came out, she had instant heat with the crowd, over and above everyone else on the TNA roster. Wrestling had come a long way for that sort of response to be possible.

I was with TNA for a little more than three months, after which the company let go of around 40 people in a single bloodletting. Even though Vince told me everything was going well, I wasn't in a position to draw the company any money, and I was one of the newest employees. Bruno and James also saw their production-department pay slashed in half.

I don't know if it's a coincidence, but the group I was part of that got let go from TNA was released right around the time they hired Hulk Hogan and Eric Bischoff in an effort to compete head to head with Vince McMahon and WWE. Hogan received $35,000 per appearance from TNA, or around two million dollars that year, which is probably why they had to shed so many performers. From what I've heard, that proved to be a disastrous decision for them in the long run.

While I was on the verge of finishing out my tenure at University Community Hospital in 2010, I got a call from Gerald Brisco. It turns out his brother, former NWA champion Jack Brisco, was a patient at UCH, and Gerald wanted me to check on him.

Jack had chronic obstructive pulmonary disease, just like my father did. I don't know where he was being treated before, but Jack was sent to a nursing home that also had a rehab center. Jerry told me about the lack of quality treatment Jack received in the nursing home, including how the nursing staff wouldn't answer Jack's call lights, and how they would drop Jack's food off outside the door without bringing it to Jack personally. Because of his COPD condition, Jack could barely walk, which meant there were days he didn't even have the strength to climb out of bed, struggle his way over to the door, open it, and get his food.

In the nursing profession, there are all sorts of personality types, and many nurses are frankly not that professional when it comes to their job performance. This is the exact reason that I would check on my mother day and night when she was at a nursing home, and I would interact with the staff regularly and scrutinize them to make sure she was receiving the proper care.

After Jerry explained the full situation to me, he asked me if I would be willing to check on Jack. Without hesitation, I said, "Okay! I'll take care of it, Jerry. It's no problem at all."

The Briscos and I certainly weren't best friends, but I *never* had any problems with them. They were regulars at the legends luncheons in Tampa, which meant I saw them semi regularly. I couldn't recall every receiving a phone call from Jerry before, so I was surprised to hear from him, but he was rightly concerned about the well being of his older brother.

Before I began my regular night-shift duties, I would check on Jack, and then I'd check on him a second time after my shift was over. That included checking on his machines, his IV fluids, and also personally consulting with his nurses to make sure he was receiving the highest level of care. Jack was having *horrible* respiratory problems. The simple act of drawing air into his lungs was causing Jack to experience immeasurable pain.

Every day, I'd walk in and say, "Hey, Jack… How are you doin'?"

"Not great," was Jack's typical, pained response. "I can barely sleep because I can't *breathe.*"

That made sense; if you can't breathe well, there's no way you're going to sleep well. Adding to the concern was how Jack was barely consuming any solid foods. I grabbed Jack's chart, which is a record of all procedures performed on a patient, and I rifled through it. When I saw something that concerned me, I reached out to Jack's respiratory therapist. She told me Jack was going to be assigned to an outpatient rehab nursing home, which I was *very* concerned about. As far as Jerry was concerned, Jack's treatment in a nursing home is what exacerbated his medical condition in the first place.

"When they're ready to send him to rehab, just have him sent upstairs to us instead," I told her.

Jack wasn't on my floor, so I was doing everything I could to get him reassigned to my floor in rehab. The way I saw it, if Jack was in rehab on the sixth floor, it would be far easier for me to monitor his progress and help him recover. On my floor, I could simply request that Jack be one of my regular patients, and then I would always be responsible for his care. You have to force patients to do things when they go to rehab, because none of them *really* want to engage in any exercise. In many rehab centers, if a patient won't do as they're instructed, the staff members will just give up and let the patients deteriorate.

The attending physician denied my request, and said "Our rehab center is too aggressive. Jack won't be able to handle it up there."

Against my strenuous objections, Jack was sent to a rehab center at another nursing home. Sure enough, within a few days of being assigned to that center, Jack passed away. If Jack had been assigned to me, I'm sure I could have challenged him to do more, and I could have forced the other staff members on my floor to challenge him in the same fashion. I'm not saying I could have saved Jack's life, but I'm pretty certain I could have prolonged it by at least a little while.

At Jack's memorial service, there was a huge crowd, and plenty of wrestlers were in attendance. During the post-service lunch, Jerry Brisco approached me.

"Hey, Mike, thank you for everything you did for Jack while he was at the hospital," Jerry said. "Jack said you were always there for him. It meant a lot to all of us."

"You don't have to thank me," I replied. "I was just doing my job."

"You know, Mike... you were the real deal," Jerry continued. "Most people are bullshit."

In February of 2010, the month Jack Brisco died, I retired from the nursing profession. My next mission would be to find productive things to occupy my time in the next stage of my life. In 2011, I started to teach a Bible study at a homeless shelter in Tampa, and I taught there every Friday night for the next four years.

This was all volunteer duty; I wasn't paid a dime for any of it. The people at the homeless shelter had a hard time seeing the light at the end of the tunnel. I had to work hard to get them to realize all things are possible. I've really been blessed in the name of Jesus Christ, because I've been through all kinds of things and survived them. One of my joys is to share that story and the source of my hope with people who desperately need hope in their lives.

My parents left me some money when they passed away, which was a huge blessing and made my retirement decision much easier. Honestly, I would never want to be a nurse again.

While living in the Towers of Channelside, I suffered through a wide assortment of health problems with my hip injury, which I'd fought through for seven years. I think if I would have been a little more focused on the Lord, I could have overcome it, but I went ahead and had surgery performed on my hip in 2012, which went very well and greatly alleviated my discomfort level.

The suicide of Mike Graham in 2012 was devastating to deal with. I liked Mike Graham a lot, and I'd been legitimately concerned about him given that his father and son had both committed suicide using a firearm. I can imagine the grief of coping with those tragic deaths weighed heavily on Mike and drew him into making a perilous decision of his own. I would see Mike every so often at the luncheons, and I would talk with Mike about God because I was so concerned about his mental state. On at least four occasions, I invited Mike over to my Bible study, but he never came.

Even after the suicide of his son, Steven, Mike seemed to be okay the few times I saw him. He was also doing a weekly radio show with Ted Webb, a local personality in Tampa, who is also a regular at the wrestling legends luncheons. I met Mike's wife Diane once when I was a guest on the show, and we all went out to eat afterward.

Overall, I thought everything was working out for Mike, but I was obviously wrong. He committed suicide while he and his wife were in Daytona Beach for Biketoberfest. Diane said she was outside when she heard the gunshot, and then she raced inside and upstairs to find Mike lying next to the gun. Once Mike shot himself, Diane told me no one helped her to clean up after her husband's body was removed from the scene.

"Seriously, nobody helped you?" I asked her.

"Nope," she said, tearing up. "*No one* helped me."

"That's it," I told her. "Don't tell me anything else."

Hearing that a woman had to wipe up the blood and residue from her own husband's suicide was more than I could handle. I can't even imagine what a distressing experience that was for her.

I eased my way into living in Daytona Beach in 2013. The process started when I rented a condo there for six months to see if I really wanted to live over there on a permanent basis. In the later stages of life, you have to be very careful where you choose to spend your time, because you don't know just how much life you've got left.

Two weeks before I began my six-month rental of the Daytona Beach condo, I got the idea in my head to put together an outline of the Bible. Once I arrived in Daytona Beach, I began piecing together outlines of every book and chapter of the Bible. I'd read a chapter, then outline it, and then I'd move on to the next one. It took many hours of diligent work, but I really enjoyed the process and learned a lot about God's Word. That project consumed a massive amount of my time at the condo, and I finally completed it during the fifth month of my stay.

At the same time this was going on, I was still directing the Bible study at the homeless shelter. I knew, just because I wanted to take a vacation from the Tampa area, that didn't mean I could take a vacation from the Bible study. Since I'd committed to hosting the

Bible study, I knew I needed to keep my word, so every Friday night, I made a 300-mile round trip to do the Bible study and return to Daytona Beach. Yes, I had people who covered for me on six occasions, but I still made that trip 20 times. Ron Bass even participated in my Bible study once. It was clear to see he had a true heart for God in the years before he passed away.

Although I prided myself on my commitment to teaching my Bible study, please remember you don't need to be in a specific location, or for it to be a specific time for you to talk *to* God, talk *about* God, or to *learn* about Him. If you're gathered with others who have accepted Christ, you *are* the church! You're a true ambassador for Christ, and your true teacher is the Holy Spirit.

In 2015, I attended Dusty Rhodes memorial service, which was held in the same venue as the memorial service for Jack Brisco. Dusty passed away from stomach cancer on June 10th, 2015. I'd tried to talk to Dusty about God a few times, but he always seemed neutral with regard to spiritual topics. The last time I saw him alive was in 2010 when I stopped in at the WWE's NXT training facility to talk with Dusty and Steve Keirn, both of whom were helping out with the training of the next generation of WWE stars. I tried to take Dusty out to eat, but he refused to come with me.

"God is waiting on you, Dusty, and he *won't* wait forever," I admonished him.

During the memorial service, the priest announced that Dusty had been in contact with him, and he said Dusty was able to get closer to God during the final years of his life. For the sake of Dusty's eternal soul, I hope what the priest said about him is true.

The death of Tommy Rogers of "The Fantastics" is another wrestling death that negatively affected me. The two of us spoke on the phone at least once a month for a long while, right up until he passed away. He was living in Honolulu at the time of his death, and Kevin Von Erich was one of his neighbors. Tommy informed me that Kevin had become a solid Christian, which was some *very* welcome news. If true, that's a conversion that further illustrates the redemptive power of Christ and His message.

If anyone had told me back in the early 1980s that four of the Von Erichs would have died early, and three of those deaths would be confirmed as suicides, I would have bet any amount of money that Kevin would have been the first to go based on his behavior during that time.

After visiting Kevin at his ranch, Tommy also informed me that Kevin was having a number of health problems and was having trouble walking. I can certainly relate to what he was going through. Wrestling extracts a toll from all of us, including Tommy, who was one of countless wrestlers to have hip-replacement surgery. I didn't even know Tommy had died until I was informed about it at one of the legends luncheons in Tampa. I'm not sure what he died from, but I know he lived in constant physical pain. He was only 54 years old when he passed away.

In 2016, I put my condo up for sale in the Towers of Channelside. When that sold, I rented a home in Daytona Beach, and then finally I bought the home I'm in now, which is on the ocean. I believe it had been a model home before I purchased it. When I moved in, it was already fully furnished, with everything you could ever imagine needing in a home. In fact, I actually had to throw away some of the unnecessary items that were already in the house when I purchased it.

Being on the ocean is practically a necessity for me at this point of my life. When I hear people say they like walking on the beach, I laugh. I couldn't care any less about the beach. I like walking *in* the ocean, *with weights*. Then I work out in the water while holding the weights as the waves are trying to knock me over. When I perform this fitness routine regularly, it keeps me in excellent shape.

Having the option to do things like this is one of the main reasons I wanted to be close to the ocean. Otherwise, there isn't a whole lot happening in Daytona Beach. It's nice and quiet out here compared to Tampa. The only time things really pick up here is during Biketoberfest, when there are motorcyclists all over town. Fortunately, that doesn't last very long, and things quickly go back to normal.

In 2018, the wrestling world lost two individuals who played valuable roles in my career: Bruno Sammartino and Nikolai Volkoff.

In my experience with him, Bruno was a quiet man unless you did something to make him angry, and he was never afraid to stand up for what he thought was right. His strong character, values and integrity all impressed me. We never really hung out together, but I really liked him, and his conduct was exemplary, both in and out of the ring.

In terms of professional attributes, Bruno was in excellent shape and was a strong ring performer. His passing was very sad and caught me completely by surprise. When I worked in New York, Bruno went out of his way to help me even though I never once asked him for any assistance. I consider it a very high compliment that the *best* world champion of all time looked out for me to that extent and made my life better.

Nikolai Volkoff was someone I truly liked. Like Bruno, he was both physically strong and strong in terms of the caliber of his character. Before my babyface turn in Florida, Nikolai was my constant travel companion, and my in-ring interaction with him helped to launch my very successful run as a fan favorite. He took tremendous care of his family, and when his wife wanted to go to nursing school, Nikolai went off the road to stay home and take care of their children. In every way, he was a good man.

As far as modern wrestling is concerned, I seldom watch any of it. The only time I usually catch it is when I'm flipping the channels. If I see it, I'll watch for a little while to see if the wrestlers can keep my interest. Invariably, they fail. When Florida was a cohesive territory, we were running spot shows every week. Today, Vince McMahon visits Tampa twice a year at the most. I'm sure he draws a crowd for those two shows, but if he tried to run five towns in Florida every week, his crowds would dwindle down to nothing very quickly if he presented them with the modern wrestling product. In my era, we were able to keep that level of attendance high every week, because most of the people believed what we were doing was real.

Brute Power: The Autobiography of Buggsy McGraw

On Christmas Day or New Year's Eve, we would sometimes have two shows on the same day, because our events would be part of the traditional holiday celebration for many local families. In some instances, we might have had one show on Christmas afternoon in Orlando, and then another show on Christmas night in Jacksonville. If Vince tried something like that now, he wouldn't last very long. I don't think you'll ever see an era in wrestling like the one I participated in ever again, where a wrestling territory could run the same five towns every week, all year long, year after year, and still keep selling out shows with ease.

I had a police officer friend who was a big wrestling fan, and when Vince would come to town, he would call me up and ask if I could take him there, which of course meant he wanted me to walk him in the back door with the rest of the wrestlers. Every time I went to a WWE show, they were filming for television, so the crowds always looked good. In the territory days, we made people *pay* to see the best matches in person. Since fans can watch every conceivable matchup on free cable television now, there's virtually no reason for them to buy a ticket to watch wrestling in person... especially without the added attraction of getting to appear on television.

I never had children, but there are times I thought it might have been nice to have a child, and then raise and direct that child in the right way. As a Christian man and a child of God, I see how children are truly precious possessions. When you're around them, you have to strive to do the right thing at all times, and that responsibility was a little too much for me to undertake when I was younger.

After long careers in both wrestling and nursing, and after traveling around the world several times, there is some important advice I want to impart to you, just in case you need it. First, remember that your life on this earth is only composed of four things: Your thoughts, your attitudes, your words, and your actions. Once you think about something, you develop an attitude, which you put into words, and then once you speak about your attitudes, you convert them into action. So, you need to be extremely careful about your thoughts, because they will ultimately manifest themselves in your actions and produce your destiny in life.

Second, and far more importantly, if you haven't already done so, you need to accept Jesus Christ as your Lord and Savior. Jesus *is* God, and He is the Creator of all things. Christ is the true Life, and He died on the cross as a holy sacrifice to save you from your sins so that you can have eternal life with Him.

In Mark 11:22-25, it says, "And Jesus answering said unto them, Have faith in God. For verily I say unto you that whosoever shall say unto this mountain, Be you removed, and be you cast into the sea; and shall not doubt in his heart, but shall believe that those things which he says shall come to pass; he shall have whatsoever he says. Therefore I say unto you, what things soever you desire, when you pray believe that you receive them, and you shall have them. And when you stand praying, forgive if you have ought against any: that your Father also which is in heaven may forgive you your trespasses."

For many years, I was not willing to face my number-one fear, which was my speech problem. *You* need to face your fears, and you need to be willing to stand up and speak boldly against them, in faith. That is what Jesus asks us to do: Speak boldly and confidently, and pray while believing in Him.

Always remember, Christianity is a process, and I'm learning all the time.

"When negative voices leave you few choices, and confusions and illusions beset your mind, I know the wisdom of man will not stand the test of time. The battle is yours, Lord. The battle is yours."

Afterword

You've just finished reading *Brute Power*, the story of Mike Davis, a man who did what it took to turn his dreams into reality. As you've learned, Mike was known at various times during his wrestling career as "The Big O," "Beautiful Brutus," and "The Brute," but his character that I loved the most is "Buggsy McGraw."

When I first saw Buggsy on television on WTOG Channel 44 in Tampa, Florida, I was instantly awed and impressed beyond my 16-year-old mind! Buggsy was larger than life in the Florida territory, and my friends and I never missed an opportunity to listen to his interviews and watch his matches on Saturday mornings, which culminated in our attendance at must-see house shows in the Tampa Fort Homer Hesterly Armory on Tuesday nights.

Buggsy's feuds with The Great Malenko, Hans Mortier, Blackjack Mulligan, Outlaw Ron Bass, and a host of others were amazing to watch. Watching him team up with "The American Dream" Dusty Rhodes was a sight to behold as they always had a match that brought down the house.

Buggsy has been such a friend to me and so many others in the wrestling industry that he has become our unofficial uncle. Uncle Bugsy! That has a nice, fitting ring to it. Buggsy is also a Christian man who not only talks the talk, but walks the walk. He is a man of faith, integrity, and a person that anyone would be excited to know.

Now that you've finished this book, you've heard about some of the most interesting tales of professional wrestling you could ever read, and I trust that you are not disappointed. In his long career, one thing Buggsy McGraw never managed to do was to disappoint me.

B. Brian Blair
President – The Cauliflower Alley Club
October 22nd, 2018

Author's Acknowledgements

My book would not have been written without the help of three men: John Crowther, a lawyer from Deland, Florida, who started the ball rolling; Kenny Cassanova of WOHW Publishing; and Ian Douglass, my ghost writer who spent over three months, week in and week out, listening to me tell my tales for hours at a time. Ian's knowledge of professional wrestling and ability to make my story come alive in words is nothing short of amazing. It was a pleasure and a blessing to work with him.

Additional thanks is owed to all of the fans who contributed large sums of money toward the creation of my autobiography. These fans include Anastasia D.C. Davis, Don Depaulis, Andrew Sparkman, Harold Strassler, Mark Beaudry, Ian Ross, Jeff Freer, Greg Goode, MANGO, Jason Presley, Prof.Ouch, Phil Thompson, Jason Freeman, David D. Kaminester, and Mark and Betsy Trexler.

I grew up in Indianapolis, Indiana when professional wrestling was first put on TV in our city. In 1958, wrestling was undeniably the hottest program on television. WWA wrestling stars like Dick the Bruiser, Cowboy Bob Ellis, The Sheik, Yukon Eric, the Shire Brothers, Angelo Poffo and others were truly exciting and inspirational to me. I also owe a debt of gratitude to WWA referee Lou Thomas, my neighbor, for bringing me to several wrestling events when I was just 14 years old.

I will always be grateful to Tom Jones for training me, and to the Sheik for giving me my first in-ring experience as a professional wrestler. Also, Killer Karl Kox was a tremendous help to me in Australia. He was a true master in the ring and I learned a great deal from him.

Thanks is also deserved by Vince McMahon Sr. who brought me to the New York territory where I was blessed to sell out Madison Square Garden with Bruno Sammartino. As a great world champion both in and out of the ring, Bruno went out of his way to make sure I made good money.

Kevin Sullivan was a top performer and a good man . I traveled and worked with him in New York, the Carolinas, and Florida and I always appreciated his insight.

I was the only child of Hubert and Remine Davis who always provided me with a safe and secure home and went out of their way to make sure I had a good education and a good start in life. I was truly blessed to have the parents I had. They both worked hard to make sure we had a good home, and always supported me in my endeavors.

Life has many ups and downs, but I know without a doubt that I would not be alive today without my Savior and Lord JESUS CHRIST. He has kept me from trouble, kept me from death, kept me from prison, and kept me from poverty countless times. I HAVE TRULY BEEN BLESSED IN THE NAME OF JESUS CHRIST.

Michael "Buggsy McGraw" Davis
October 5th, 2018

Cowriter's Acknowledgements

Thank you to Michael for allowing me to be involved in the telling of his incredible life story, and thank you to Kenny Cassanova for all of the help he lent me in putting everything together.

Also, thank you to my wife, Teisha, for permitting me to work on this project throughout 2018.

Finally, thank you to Jesus Christ for permitting me to be associated with a wrestling autobiography that has a redemptive overall message which hopefully honors both His deity and His name.

Ian C. Douglass
December 14th, 2018